Curriculum and Reality in African Primary Schools

Hugh Hawes

with Audrey Aarons, John Croft, Colette Hawes

LONGMAN

. . . Go, said the bird, for the leaves were full of children,
Hidden excitedly, containing laughter.
Go, go, go said the bird: human kind
Cannot bear very much reality.

T. S. Eliot (*Burnt Norton*)

Longman Group Ltd

Associated companies, branches and representatives throughout the world

© Longman Group Ltd 1979

First published 1979

ISBN 0 582 60769 8

Printed in Great Britain by
Western Printing Services Ltd, Bristol

Contents

Foreword

In 1954 I went to Uganda to teach in a junior secondary school. In 1978 I teach courses concerned with curriculum development in developing countries in the London Institute of Education. In between these dates I have spent a good deal of time trying to think of what schools in Africa should teach and how they should do it.

In 1975–76 I took time out from my teaching and tried to reflect in a little more depth about the primary curriculum in ten English-speaking African countries: Botswana, Ghana, Kenya, Lesotho, Nigeria, Sierra Leone, Swaziland, Tanzania, Uganda and Zambia.

Seven of these countries were visited and brief country profiles produced as a result. Audrey Aarons, who now teaches Curriculum Studies at the University of Papua New Guinea, worked with me on these. This book, therefore, comes out of both my working experience and our survey.

So many people have helped me towards writing this book that it would be impossible to list them. They include professional colleagues in curriculum development centres, universities and ministries in all countries visited and others whom I have bothered by letter or on their travels through London, together with teachers, inspectors, parents and children in schools, students and staff in our institute here in London; friends at the British Council and in UNESCO agencies in Paris, Geneva and Hamburg; library staff in our Institute Library, UNESCO, the Ministry of Overseas Development; my own friends and family who have had to suffer having bits read to them; R. C. Honeybone and C. E. Beeby who were patient enough to read through the completed manuscript and comment on it, and finally my typists Sue Rintoul, Alice Henfield and most especially Joyce Maxwell who have transcribed it all so patiently and efficiently.

I have included three names in the authorship of this book: Audrey Aarons, who helped so greatly in the country surveys, in collecting materials and in the preparatory work for the bibliography; John Croft who undertook much of the collection, synthesis and presentation of information in the tables; Colette Hawes, my wife, who has worked with me during the whole period of writing. If you find the style readable, thank her. If you disagree with the opinions, blame me.

H.H.

Chapter *1*   A story worth telling

A curriculum – our most important concern

No society can escape the responsibility for trying to plan the education of the children who grow up in it, but the more complicated a society is, the more difficult it is to make such plans and the more tempting it is to see them as somebody else's concern. In less complex societies the shared responsibilities, an inescapable part of the provision of education, were apparent and were accepted: the family, religious agencies and community institutions all played a part in helping a child to live with the past and to prepare for what was to come. The means of education: the home, religious or tribal initiation, apprenticeship and, at a later stage, the local school and its teacher were easy to recognise and often far more closely related than they are today, yet the choice of what children should learn, what selection should be made from the culture[1] – in short the curriculum – was never and will never be simple. Is education to prepare for the life now or the after-life to come? Does it preserve tradition or encourage change? Do we teach our youth to question or conform? It was over a question of curriculum that Socrates drank hemlock.

Today the same issues remain, but both our societies and our cultures have become bewilderingly complex and there is a tendency to employ professional educators, you and me, to make the selection. And often we too are bewildered and have tended to seek security – a false security – in those elements we can most easily comprehend. We have concentrated on the formal school because this institution is most manageable and amenable to planning and the society has often been content and relieved to let us do so. We have also tended to endow the actual process of going to school with a quite unreal importance. Thus we commonly confuse education with schooling and attendance at school with its results. We will speak quite cheerfully of a child having received six or seven years education when what we mean is that he has sat more or less regularly in a school building for that length of time, sheltered at the same time from the rain and from other educational influences within his community.

Lately poor countries and those who give them aid have become preoccupied with the arithmetic of equity and the phrase 'Universal Primary Education' is used (by which is meant school attendance). It is accounted a blessing for a forty per cent nation to become a sixty per cent and eventually a ninety per cent nation, such statistical calculations being made with considerable panache on the basis of insufficient and often politically influenced census figures for age groups which seldom correspond with the actual realities in schools.

In this book I examine the process of 'selecting from the culture' from the viewpoint of the formal school system, which is logical if we consider the primacy with which we currently invest school in the educational process, yet only rational if we accept that parallel selections are also being made by a number of other educational agencies: the family, nuclear and extended; religious agencies; the local and wider community; the state through its information services; the Coca-Cola Company and its many friends and relations and numerous others. The strengths and limitations of the school curriculum have thus to be seen within this context.

Those of us who are involved in trying to effect this selection for schools and in the even more difficult task of attempting to transform intention into reality are a very numerous band. For curricular decisions are made, often unwittingly, at various levels and by all manner of people: the politician and the party who pronounce policy, the planner and the administrator who apportion money to build and equip schools, the syllabus makers who issue the curriculum plan and divide it into different sized subject packages, the writers, the teacher trainers, the inspectors and above all the headmasters and the teachers themselves in schools. It is with all these in mind that this book is written.

It concentrates on the problems of poor countries, poor because they lack money or manpower or (usually) both, and uses as examples information gained from a study in 1975 and 1976 of ten English speaking African countries, though many of the issues raised have application to similar conditions elsewhere in Africa, in Asia and in Latin America, for the problem of trying to do more with less is hardly uncommon.

It may be profitable to look back over the years at the same time as looking across different countries, and the early 1960's are as good a place as any to start. For most of the countries surveyed, this was the time of transition from colonialism to nationhood, with all the challenges and aspirations that this entailed, but for all of us in the education game this period will be remembered, perhaps a little wryly, as the time we 'discovered' curriculum development and set about applying the new principles with such passion and conviction and with considerable confidence that the transformations we all agreed to be necessary could be swiftly achieved.

Now, fifteen years on, the impact of our ideas on children in schools is far less than we expected. The curriculum is neither as appropriate nor as efficient as we had hoped and gaps between plans and realities are very, very great. The processes of selection from the culture and of transmission of such a selection to the learners now stand revealed as progressively more complex and complicated and our attempts to prescribe solutions as naive in both method and assumptions. Hence our disappointment. I have suffered my share and so have many others.

But out of these disappointments has grown experience, for in those fifteen years, which is a short, short time in the scale of educational change, we have received many knocks and learnt many lessons. In this book we relive that experience and invite discussion on it, identify common problems, review apparent growth points and successes and open a debate upon the issue of priorities – for if there is one master lesson we have learnt from experience it is that when you have big problems and little time and money to solve them, something has to be done first and done properly.

We examine these processes in the light of certain principles of curriculum development (most of which are somewhat uncomfortable to live with) which have become clearer as we have gained our experience and suffered our disappointments.

Uncomfortable truisms

There is a state of mind with which we are all familiar where consciously or unconsciously we avoid examining the full implications of a concept because we are frightened of what we shall find. This has happened and is happening with our ideas of curriculum and curriculum development.

It would be comfortable if we could satisfactorily describe the school curriculum in a country at any one time, if we could lay down an easily recognisable and easily operable model of curriculum development. Yet though we attempt (and have to attempt) both these, it would be dishonest to believe that we can ever accomplish the task with any degree of precision, for the following good reasons:

(i) *A school curriculum is very difficult to define.*
In our first instinctive bolt towards the security of categories we may tend to equate a country's curriculum with the official national syllabus, but this security evaporates even as we begin to consider the meaning of the word curriculum. We could fill pages with definitions, some of which conflict quite sharply: for, as Stenhouse observes:

> 'We appear to be confronted by two different views of curriculum. On the one hand the curriculum is seen as an intention, plan or prescription, an idea about what one would like to happen in schools. On the other it is seen as the existing state of affairs in schools, what does, in fact, happen.'[2]

But whatever definition we take[3] it is certain that our main concern should be with what is planned, provided, selected from the culture for *the individual learners* in schools and here, alas, we begin to realise how slippery and varied is the concept we are dealing with, for these selections are being made by a variety of different people in different contexts. They involve activities, generated by the school or by a higher authority for the school, which take place in class and out of it, as well as activities like health habits, home farming projects and community service planned in the school and taking place out of school hours in the communities. They involve the generation of attitudes and skills as well as the inculcation of knowledge. They are spread by teachers, by materials, by older children and peers, through direct teaching, individual learning, informal contact and example. Thus as people and places are different and interests, values, enthusiasm and motivation are different, so the school curricula also differ.

(ii) *The process of curriculum development is a curiously complicated one.*
Decisions take place at various stages and are made by various people, from poli-

3

Education or shelter? (November 1976, Lesotho)

The teacher has insisted that I sit on her chair – the only one in the room. There are eighty-three children of varying ages sitting on the floor. Thirteen of them have a copy of an English reader, bought by their parents. The teacher has a copy. Seventy children have no book.

The teacher, untrained, has written three sentences containing two English mistakes on the board. Very few children in the room can read them or the text in the book. Yet these children attend school six hours a day, 190 days a year in similar conditions.

Can these children be said to be receiving education or are they merely statistics fodder?

Where are the most important curricular decisions taken?

Two small rural schools exist in, let us say, Sierra Leone. Both have the same syllabus, time allocation and financial provision. In the former the headmaster is a community leader, a conscientious, skilful and imaginative professional. In the latter he is drunken and disillusioned. Taking curriculum in its fullest sense (the only acceptable sense) as the transmission of values, skills and knowledge selected from the culture, the differing impacts of these two educational situations on the learners who participate in them is most striking.

tician to parent and teacher, in respect of *aims and objectives* at various levels; the production of *curriculum plans* (syllabuses for schools and colleges, schemes of work, timetables); the selection and emphasis of *learning materials* (including not only written and audio-visual materials but also learning resources derived from the school environment); the selection of an appropriate *methodology* for learning and teaching and the *evaluation* of both the process and the product.

Complex though this process may be, its efficiency may be measured at one point and one point only – its ultimate effect on the learner and what he learns. Learners are individuals just as teachers, headmasters, inspectors, planners and ministers are individuals, so that the whole process is one of changing people rather than paper, dependent on the qualities of trust, understanding and flexibility which are so unevenly distributed among us. Consequently it can be accomplished with neither the tidiness nor the speed with which it is possible to write a plan or distribute money or erect buildings.

(iii) *Both 'curriculum' and 'curriculum development' are, therefore, dynamic rather than static concepts, necessarily untidy and unfinished* ...

... since schools, contexts, acceptability and possibility for change vary in time and place. To accept such untidiness appears exceptionally difficult. The politician almost by definition expects large demonstrable nationwide change. He may even be, by training, a military man, whose troops attack when they are told. Now faced with teachers, parents and children perversely disposed 'to reason why', he may attempt to cover up obvious discrepancies between the orderliness of a government's intention and the disorder of its implementation.

For the educationist, too, the acceptance of untidiness is hard to bear, for so many of the conventional instruments by which change has been effected – the plan, the syllabus, the examination, the textbook – are solidly rooted on a postulate of uniform development. Admittedly, the prospect of 'rolling reform',[4] the idea of continual and gradual evolution in a country's curriculum is one which many of us contemplate with unease; yet I see no logical alternative to it and further suggest that the rolling must take place unevenly. We must learn to live with the untidiness, the humanness of change, control our exasperation and be thankful that we are dealing with individuals who can laugh and can change, rather than what one aid proposal (in a particularly sinister piece of educational gibberish) described as 'learning stations'.

(iv) *The process of curriculum development cannot be separated from the machinery for its implementation.*

There can be no artificial distinction between professional and administrative matters, nor can we ignore the fact that to plan and implement change costs money. Once we plan, provide or limit teacher training or retraining, appoint and train inspectors, allocate money for equipment, consider ages of entry, discuss promotion or examination policy, design a classroom or divide a school year, we are making a decision which affects our school curriculum. It may be convenient and it is certainly usual, to keep separate the 'administrative' and 'professional' duties of those who plan and execute educational policy but it is hardly profitable to the process of curriculum development; the very wide gaps which exist between policy and practice in many countries are to a considerable degree a result of misunderstanding compounded by not a little arrogance (a legacy among the most unlovely of those bequeathed by the British to their successors in office).

(v) *The process of curriculum development must always be subsidiary to the purpose for which a curriculum is selected.*

What is being selected from the culture and transmitted to learners remains our most important concern. Yet it becomes easy, and often less disturbing, to concentrate on whether a curriculum is working rather than whether it is appropriate. The more we have invested in a new curriculum, the more painful it is for us to consider its value. Among the most disturbing experiences in my own recent visits to African countries was to find men and women implementing with uncritical passion and devotion, curricula whose value and importance to the culture had never been seriously or deeply debated.

(vi) *The importance of the school as an instrument of development must not be overestimated and the school curriculum should take into account the school's role.*

Education is only one of many related factors contributing to development. The school, as already indicated, is only one instrument in a process of lifelong education. We educationists are often incorrigibly big-headed when modesty would befit us better, for the school curriculum and its development must be seen as a part and partner with other agents in the developmental process. It must relate horizontally with all those other contemporary influences on a child's growth and, vertically, with that which has been and is to come. Looked at in this perspective it becomes obvious to us that there are certain aspects in the educational process in which the school as an agency can take a lead, certain others where it can merely act as a support.

(vii) *We are all participants in choosing, developing and evaluating the school curriculum ...*

... for the process is far too important to be left to experts. Of recent years curriculum development has become a field for much theorising, often supported by weird cabalistic models and has acquired a specialised and technical vocabulary. In the exportation of this theory to Africa, a dangerous and imperfectly understood mystique has grown up, some of it centred around the two Taxonomies of Educational Objectives by Bloom,[5] Krathwohl[6] and their associates in Chicago. These excellent works have been taken in senses for which they were never intended, as bibles in a creed of systematic centralised curriculum development. There is a widespread belief, and it is growing, that curriculum development and curriculum evaluation are to be accomplished by experts who have had a substantial period of initiation into a highly technical field. There is an earnest and somewhat bewildered questing for the 'right way' of stating plans, arranging materials and evaluating them and while this is being sought, common sense is obscured.

The 'selection from the culture' and the evaluation of our success in transmitting it to our youth has to concern every responsible educator within a community. Throughout the history of good teaching we have set goals and formed judgments which, however imprecise, were always worth making. We wanted our learners:

to learn 'more'
to understand 'better'

to acquire learning skills (like reading 'better')
to think 'more clearly and logically'
to be 'better citizens'
to be 'better people'

and we evaluated our children's success towards these goals and judged our curricula according to how well it matched them. The fact that we are now more concerned as to the precision of the terms we use and are in process of refining instruments to clarify our thinking in no way absolves us from the responsibility of setting goals and making judgments. The acquiring of means to do both these more efficiently is an activity which concerns us all.

Recurring themes

One of the difficulties in writing this book has been that of maintaining a balance between seeing the wood and pausing to examine the very interesting and different varieties of trees which make it up.[7] In all but the last two chapters it has been necessary to generalise more than I would have wished and to select, often arbitrarily from a number of very compelling local examples. But provided you, as readers, can accept the shortcomings of this method of treatment as well as those of my own knowledge and experience, the building up of an overall comparative picture may prove both interesting and worthwhile.

Certain themes recur throughout this book, questions which can never be answered with dogmatic certainty but which must continue to be asked in each different context of time and place:

What is important for children to learn and what is less important?
There is no escaping the implications of the second half of this question, which is that in order to ensure that priorities are attained certain non-priorities will inevitably have to receive less attention and support or be omitted altogether.
What do we need to know before we can take decisions relevant to each area of curriculum planning and development?
A cynic examining the record of precipitate action over the last couple of decades might reply 'nothing'; in fact a growing awareness can be traced of the need to understand who wants what kind of change, what current conditions are and what resources are actually available before setting forth on journeys into the dark.
How fast and how evenly can we expect change to proceed?
Inevitable tensions exist between the aspirations of educational and political leaders towards rapid uniform progress on the one hand, forces of educational conservatism and the uneven means and motivations for change on the other. Nobody suggests that these can or should be reconciled. Without tensions there would be little progress. It is the degree of tension which is at issue.
What is the balance between central direction and local initiatives?
I have postulated a degree of involvement by all educationists as a prerequisite of dynamic curriculum change. The nature of this 'degree', how it is determined and

A thought from Chairman Mao (June 1943, China)

'In any given place, there cannot be a number of central tasks at the same time
. . . [the planner] should not act upon each instruction as it comes from the
higher organisation without any planning of his own, and thereby create a
multitude of 'central tasks' and a state of confusion and disorder. Nor should
a higher organisation simultaneously assign many tasks to a lower organisation
without indicating their relative importance and urgency. . . .'

Mao Tse-Tung, 'Some Questions Concerning Methods of Leadership', *Selected Works*, Vol III
p 117.

What kind of an argument? (Nigeria 1976)

Kano State, a Moslem community, deeply Islamic, mostly rural, and with less
than 20 per cent enrolment, faces a national announcement of UPE. The following conversation is reported to me:

Kano official: Should we not modify our primary curriculum to suit our needs?
Federal adviser: Would you want your own children to receive a sub-standard
   curriculum?

by whom, how local autonomy and initiative can be channelled within a national framework and a sense of national purpose, is one of the most important recurring themes of this book.

What machinery is necessary to link plans with their implementation?
The growing realisation of all of us concerned with curriculum development that our efforts to devise and present our product are wasted unless we make a sale, are a necessary beginning to a continuing debate. How can the 'designers' and 'salesmen' learn to work together harmoniously and efficiently?

Who are the agents most instrumental in promoting these links between design and implementation . . .
. . . and hence reducing the sad gap which still exists between intention and reality? Experience has revealed that these comprise various sorts and conditions of men and women: headmasters, tutors, mobile teacher trainers, education officers, inspectors and that they, like teachers, are human beings who are basically sensible, moderately honest and conscientious and who, provided demands made on them are reasonable and can be understood, will respond to trust and accept responsibility.

It is, perhaps appropriate for this introductory chapter to end on a note, stressed and restressed, I hope, throughout the study, of what R. S. Peters calls 'respect for persons'. Much education policy, much curriculum policy has failed precisely because it lacks the appreciation of the humanity of humans – either because it has undervalued education workers by giving them no independent responsibility and therefore by implication treating them as potential shirkers and embezzlers (which in these conditions they frequently become), or because it appears to expect them to be a sort of amalgam of Robinson Crusoe and St Francis of Assisi, rather than individuals who are prepared to do a reasonable day's work for a reasonable wage, but thereafter crave the opportunity to watch football, visit friends, dance the high life, make love and drink beer.

Notes

1 The definition is Dennis Lawton's. See *Social Change, Educational Theory and Curriculum Planning*, ULP, 1973
2 Stenhouse, L., *An Introduction to Curriculum Research and Development*, Heinemann 1975, p 2
3 At an International Seminar held in 1974 at the UNESCO Institute of Education in Hamburg we accepted as a working definition R. H. Dave's 'all goal-directed activities that are generated by the school whether they take place in the institution or outside it'.
4 The concept of 'rolling reform' is a Swedish one first used in relation to the last stages of their own comprehensive school reorganisation.
5 Bloom B. S. et al., *Taxonomy of Educational Objectives I*, David McKay 1956
6 Krathwohl, D. R. et al., *Taxonomy of Educational Objectives II*, David McKay 1964
7 . . . and nothing varies more strikingly than the national differences between countries and peoples. It would be hard to argue that Yoruba and Basotho were closely linked by the affinity of being 'Africans' any more than Swedes and Sicilians reflected a 'European' personality. There are certain common experiences, colonialism being the most obvious, but as colonialism recedes, national differences are intensified.

Chapter 2   Curriculum in context

Planning a school curriculum has something in common with planning a journey. Unless the traveller has some idea of where he is starting from and the conditions he may meet along the way, he is unlikely to be able to decide upon a satisfactory route. In this chapter I discuss what we need to know before we start on our travels, which I call examing the *context* of the curriculum and Malcolm Skilbeck refers to as 'situational analysis'.[1] Clearly, it is important to consider who undertakes this analysis, how, and where it is likely to lead us. These issues I touch on in the latter part of the chapter.

What do we mean by context?

Schools are part of a wider education system. An education system is part of a political, social, and economic framework.

Schools are also composed of individuals (children and teachers) and are responsible to other individuals (parents) within the framework of a community. This gives each school situation a life and an entity of its own. Schools also have an existence in time and place. Their development and their curriculum are often conditioned by practical and administrative problems.

This chapter reflects these aspects of context and the interrelations between them, and further emphasises the diversities, the inequalities and the conflicts within systems that a curriculum planner has to deal with.

Politics and economics

The two most important decision areas in educational planning are to decide how many children should be provided for in the school system at what ages and levels, and to decide the purpose for which they are sent there. These decisions and many more are usually politically motivated. Elsewhere[2] I have argued that the whole fabric of a primary school curriculum in a socialist state like Tanzania will differ from that in a capitalist state like Kenya, for the different philosophies will affect not only selection of syllabus content but also languages of instruction, policy towards competition and examinations, links between school and community and above all the attitudes which teachers foster in the learners. It is no surprise that Tanzania is the first country in Africa to introduce a less centralised and examination-oriented system of selection for secondary schools and that Zambia intends soon to follow suit, nor that Kenya and Ghana are much concerned with giving primary leavers the skill and the incentive to set themselves up as entrepreneurs when they leave school.

Political decisions may also be taken suddenly and drastically to increase school enrolments. In recent years political leaders in three of the countries considered in this book, Kenya, Nigeria and Tanzania have very suddenly announced fee-free, and in the last two cases, 'universal' primary education. Such a policy adds an entirely new dimension to the primary school curriculum and its planning. In the first place, if education is for all, it is for all conditions and all abilities. In the second, if educational opportunities are suddenly opened for all, it invariably involves a spreading of financial, material, and human resources more thinly than previously.

Frequently one senses a certain unwillingness on the part of professional educators to accept these decisions and work with them. There is a fear that 'standards' may suffer, and a certain civil servant's distrust for 'politicians', bred of British traditions. It may also be asked whether national political and economic policies are always debated and discussed with the seriousness they should be in curriculum committees or teachers' colleges. Kenya's 'Harambee', Ghana's 'Operation Feed Yourself', Botswana's concern over water resources and the concept 'One Nigeria' are far more than political slogans. They are instruments for national survival and should be woven into the whole fabric of the primary school curriculum.[3] Yet because they are politically motivated they may be, in some degree, distrusted.

Of course I have vastly simplified the situation and the arguments. Often political and economic policies are unclear to educationists, sometimes they may be in the hands of tyrants, not infrequently they conflict, but they can never be ignored. There is no such thing as non-political education. Education is for citizens; citizens form a state.

The social context

The typical primary school in Africa is in every physical sense a neighbourhood school, small, local, reached on foot – the teachers well-known and despite their protestations to the contrary, usually well respected. In the school, children are expected to receive the education of the book.

Parallel to this education and close round the school, the life of the community goes on – the child plays and is expected to play a very full part in it; fetching water and firewood, minding little brothers and sisters, running errands, buying and often selling in the market, performing religious duties at Koranic schools, catechist classes or in traditional preparation for circumcision and other initiation

A world apart

A fascinating and hitherto unpublished study exists of a day in the life of two northern Nigerian school age children (R. Tabatchik's *Two Children, Two Days*). The contrast painted between the intense, vibrant, imaginative life of the child outside school (where at the end of the day the eight-year-old collapses into deep sleep a few seconds after rushing round 'being a lorry') and the drab, pointless monotony of his classes is as striking as it is disturbing.

Evidence from a headmaster (Kenya 1976)

'Usually I need to ask the school committee if I have to replace any equipment, but if I need something really essential like a new clock I can buy it straight away.'

A reminiscence from Uganda

An education officer friend of mine had occasion to visit a primary school on the outskirts of a small town. The register page for Class I had forty-five spaces and there were forty-five children in the class. Further investigation revealed another fifty Class I children cowering behind sacks in a food-store. The following conversation is recorded:

Education Officer: Headmaster – who are these?
Headmaster: These, sir, are the etceteras.

ceremonies, alongside all the watching, the imitation, the play, the chit-chat and the 'mucking about' which is part of growing up everywhere.

Besides the relationships which a child has with his extended family are those maintained with the spirit world and the living dead. For, particularly in rural areas, this other world is still very close to the villager. As Castle writes:

'For centuries he has lived close to calamity: drought and flood threaten his crops and beasts; diseases, infertility and death afflict his wife and children; ghosts disturb his peace. All evils have to be dealt with; nothing happens by accident; every occurrence that threatens his existence has to be explained. And the explanation, according to his interpretation of his experience of his world lies in the extra-human agencies that surround him. He is not concerned like Western man with mechanistic explanations of how things happen; he is concerned with *why* afflictions befall him, how to forestall them and remove their menace. . . . Magic thus represents a view of causation utterly at variance with the concepts of the Christian scientific West, which are now as much a part of the African's world as is ancient tradition.'[4]

No valid consideration of the school curriculum can be made without consideration of a child's view of causal relationships and no analysis of causal relationships in African children can be made without consideration of the nature of these spiritual beliefs.

To attempt any close analysis of the social contexts in which African primary schools operate is obviously to court unacceptable generalisations but two points may, nevertheless, be worth making. The first is that these contexts offer an inequality of educational opportunity even more striking than that evident (and so commonly deplored) between the primary schools themselves. A child in a materially and culturally rich area has a casual and continuous fund of experiences, in the market, at festivals, in the lorry park, by the roadside. A child in a deep rural community preoccupied with seeking survival has far fewer. Wide variations predictably exist not only in what children know but in their perceptual and cognitive development.[5]

A second generalisation concerns the overall relationship between school and the community it serves. To a great degree they are places apart and the separateness is often maintained by a sort of mutual consent between school and community, despite exhortations to integrate from curriculum makers and earnest protestations from headmasters and teachers that the process is underway. ('There's an old man who comes in sometimes to show them how to make musical instruments.' 'Last term we had the dispenser in to talk to them.' 'The village football team uses our field.') In fact the average teacher values the security and the formality of the classroom and the book, the sense or order and status which it accords him. The particular characteristics of a school – time and timetables, fact and figures, books and writing, tests and class orders – belong to a category of ideas which are separate from those in the village and which both the teacher and the parent accept as school business.

How much the language of instruction used helps to set the school apart from the community is a matter of some controversy. Yet by any measurement it is an important factor. Certainly a visitor to rural schools in Kenya, Swaziland, Sierra Leone or parts of Nigeria notes with some amazement a community, homogeneous linguistically and culturally, which supports, often proudly, a school where the medium is English. In it young children, with the great enthusiasm children always show for a colourful ritual which they do not fully understand, recite with actions an English nursery rhyme for his benefit.

The formal school, in short, remains separate from the community it serves very largely because the people in that community wish it to be so. Mere exhortations in syllabus documents will not change this situation. But where the political and social values of a country redefine the function of a school, as they have done in Tanzania, or, as with the growth of universal primary education, it becomes more obvious that the school is not mainly an escape route out of the village and on to secondary and higher education, so the separateness may become less pronounced and the desire for integration more genuine.

At various points in this book, we may be able to discern how changes in attitudes of curriculum planners to the purpose of the primary school manifest themselves in new ideas about languages of instruction, a new urgency in finding out about community needs, an increased commitment to the concept of basic education. This change of attitude is significant, but there is a long road still to travel between the discussion of these ideas in high places and their transmission into action at the level of the village school.

CHILDREN IN SCHOOL

The pattern of enrolments in school exercises so much potential effect on the selection and ordering of material that it is surprising that it causes so little apparent concern to curriculum planners. Because of the odd separations we make between qualitative and quantitative aspects of planning, enrolments tend to be regarded as the purview of the educational administrator. Yet consider the potential effect upon curriculum planning of the following:

early or later age of entry
mixed or homogeneous age groups
high or low – drop-outs
– repeating
– transfers in from other schools
homogeneous or mixed language or ethnic groups
sex equality or sex imbalance
high or low numbers in class
high, low, regular or irregular attendance at school

A cruel generalisation, but probably justified, would be to suggest that the large majority of curricula in Africa are designed for an ideal situation – namely a uniform six-year-old entry, relatively homogeneous in age and culture, equal in sex and of average size (say 30–45 in a class) who attend regularly, repeat seldom and complete their primary course. Yet such a situation seldom exists. Even official statistics record wide variations, particularly in class sizes, sex distribution and drop-out rates. The actual situation is a great deal more complicated for two reasons. In the first place the conditions in schools hardly tally with what is entered on forms submitted to the Ministry's Planning Division. Ages tend to be entered initially as six, seven or eight mainly with a view to achieving an acceptable age of completion for secondary entry. In fact in recent visits to schools I have been struck increasingly, not only by the 'over-age' children but by the considerable number of very young ones, conveniently parked in classrooms so that mothers could take employment, trade or visit.

Two other factors often at variance with official statistics are attendance and repeating. Registers tend to be filled in, often to a pattern, sometimes in advance, whereas actual attendance, particularly in rural areas may be far more sporadic than indicated, while in certain communities (as with nomads such as the Kenya Turkana or Moslem communities suspicious of the corrupting influence of western schools on their children) it is not uncommon to find considerable numbers of pupils who are on the roll, but attend sporadically and unwillingly. For such, (and I have very clear pictures of them sitting illiterate and uncomprehending in the back of classes), school attendance is merely a sort of 'protection money' to pacify inquisitive authorities. At the other end of the scale one finds the hard pressed teacher or headmaster, besieged by parents, yet limited to a certain class size by government regulation (or even by the number of spaces in his register page). Frequently he admits pupils without declaring them and very large classes result.

False figures for repeating exist, almost invariably, when governments attempt to insist on an automatic promotion rule or attempt to limit numbers of repeaters in upper classes. Secondary entry is important enough for parents, especially of a particular social class, to encourage their children to repeat again and again, sometimes under assumed names, until they achieve their goals.

A second reason why official statistics give an imperfect picture of the real situation in primary classes is that they average out differences. This applies particularly to class sizes which tend to vary dramatically between urban (high) and deep rural (low and uneven). In the latter it is common to find small classes sharing a classroom, sometimes with a single teacher, sometimes with more than one but nearly always seated as a separate group with their own 'territory' and blackboard, for there exists a strange orthodoxy that a teacher with modest education and training 'cannot be taught to handle more than one class at the same time'.

I have tried to give an indication of the very varied actual pattern of enrolment in schools. To this we may add the variations in cognitive, linguistic and perceptual growth between children of different backgrounds indicated in my last section. The picture I am trying to convey, and it is one which is borne on me with passionate intensity almost every time I enter a primary school class, is of rigid and often unsuitable instruments (the centralised curriculum plan, textbooks, methods of assessment) imposed in situations where they do not apply or where they apply only to a small number of individuals within a group. The faces of the many others remain with me, the bored and the bewildered; those who lost the battle at Book 2 but who are confronting Book 4 'because it is there'; those who can mouth Book 4 to the teacher's satisfaction but do not understand the concepts in it; those who know Book 4 by heart already. These situations point to two needs: firstly for a greater awareness and concern for a variety in learning groups together with a greater knowledge of what an individual learner can and cannot understand, and secondly, for a degree of controlled flexibility in design and application of plans and materials for learning. Both these concepts will be examined later in the book.

National and local variations in education, training and experience between the teachers employed to implement school curricula are almost as great as between children themselves. An obviously desirable situation is for a country to have a sufficiency of well educated and trained teachers working for reasonable lengths of time in areas where they are familiar with the people and their culture.

This ideal, as everyone knows, is far from being satisfied. There are large numbers of untrained or lowly trained teachers and in certain situations, as in Nigeria and Kenya, percentages of untrained teachers have increased in the face of rapid rises in primary enrolments. There are many teachers working out of their cultural contexts, and very frequent movement and transfer. There is also a wide, wide disparity in the paper qualifications of teachers between different parts of the same country or between urban and rural areas. Tables 1 and 2 show differences in the composition of the teacher force between seven African countries and the internal variations within two – Nigeria and Zambia.

Table 1 Teachers in primary school: training and education levels (i)
        (a) Eastern and Southern Africa: variations between four countries
        (b) Zambia: variations between five regions

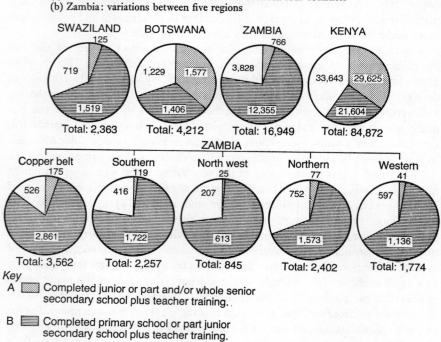

Key
A ▨ Completed junior or part and/or whole senior secondary school plus teacher training.

B ▤ Completed primary school or part junior secondary school plus teacher training.

C ☐ Untrained

Statistics from Ministries of Education 1975

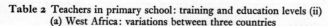

Table 2 Teachers in primary school: training and education levels (ii)
    (a) West Africa: variations between three countries
    (b) Nigeria: variations between five states (pre–1977 borders)

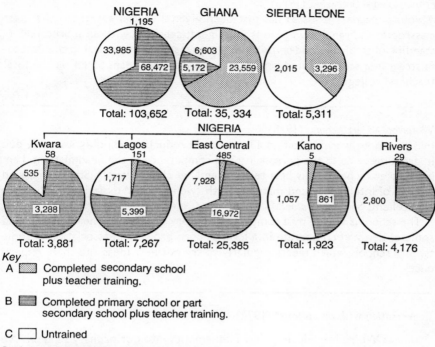

Key
A ▨ Completed secondary school
plus teacher training.

B ▦ Completed primary school or part
secondary school plus teacher training.

C ☐ Untrained

Statistics from Ministries of Education 1975

Note
All Grade 2 teachers in Nigeria have been clasified in B. In
recent years however, a number of entrants, particularly in
southern states, have completed secondary school.
Ghanaian teachers who are shown in official statistics as
uncertified, but awaiting results from examinations, have been
included in B.
All statistics: 1975

But to base comparisons on statistics of teacher education and training would be
extremely unwise. The fact that a teacher has a secondary education and a framed
certificate tells us a little about his potential, but practically nothing about his
actual value in the classroom situation. If he is drunken and disillusioned, owns a
taxi or spends most of his time chasing higher academic qualifications with the
express view of escaping from the job he is doing (and all this happens very
frequently in practice), he will be of considerably less value to the children under
his care than a man or woman with humbler qualifications but greater maturity,
integrity and interest in children.

Thus if the potential competence of teachers is an important determinant of the
actual curriculum in schools, their morale is an even greater one. In his influential

The right person – The right support

Francistown – Botswana (1975)
A young teacher (Class 3) has just been given a special award for the 'best classroom' in Francistown. He is intelligent, sensitive with an inbred understanding of children – *and untrained*. He enjoys support from an excellent headmistress in a school visited regularly by an inservice team based on the local teachers' college.

Waterloo – Sierra Leone (1975)
I visit without warning to find a happy and productive school – obviously due in great measure to the personality and competence of the headmistress. I am introduced by her to 'my best teacher' and her class (Class 1). She is a married woman of intelligence and maturity with twenty years' experience. The class is excellent. *She is untrained*.

The school is visited by a competent advisory service. The headmistress and some of her staff co-operate in a local Science project, an association of some twenty schools which meets regularly to try out new ideas and share experiences.

Conversation with an optimist (1972)

Optimist: We're introducing New Mathematics into our primary schools. We hope to develop a spirit of active enquiry in children and to replace rote memorisation.
Hugh Hawes: What are your average enrolments?
Optimist: Very high. Many classes have eighty children to a single teacher. Classrooms are often packed full.
Hugh Hawes: What is your equipment position?
Optimist: Very sad. We lack furniture and essential books. There is no apparatus and little material to make it out of.
Hugh Hawes: In these conditions are activity methods possible?
Optimist: Hardly possible.

book *The Quality of Education in Developing Countries*, C. E. Beeby advances a 'hypothesis of the stages'[6] in which he argues that teachers' competence, flexibility and ability to innovate, depend largely on their level of education and training. My own experience, backed up by that of field workers I have talked with and beginning to be supported by some research evidence[7] suggests that other factors such as personal maturity and the will and opportunity to keep up to date are even more important. Certainly no impression from visits to primary schools in Africa has been borne more strongly on me than the importance of providing opportunities for the professional growth and survival of teachers in schools. For no-one would deny that before any growth and development of curriculum in schools is possible, it is necessary first for teachers to be physically present in the school they are employed in and second for them to be sufficiently interested at least to contemplate change. While there are countless instances of cheerful competence in schools, there are many others where morale has dropped so low that even these two minimum conditions cannot be met. At this level of crisis, details of content in the syllabus document – if ever anyone in the school could find it – are irrelevant.

In addition to the teachers themselves, many other people make up the human context in which the curriculum operates: supervisors, inspectors, administrators, managers and many more. All are linked, in their own special way, with the business of selection and implementation and, in an ideal world, should have a common interest towards maintaining quality in schools. Since, however, we are as we are, there are conflicts to resolve, lack of understanding, preoccupation with irrelevancies (mostly administrative ones) and at worst, disinterest and corruption.

But this in no way negates the importance of understanding the role which all these people play in the context of curriculum change, for while the picture of an obscurantist inspector or manager eager to discourage the innovative teacher is one which is often conjured up by teachers themselves as an excuse for inaction, it can be all too true. In contrast one frequently meets cases where a local field worker through his initiative and enthusiasm has transformed the curriculum in schools in a local area. Indeed it will be argued later in this book that it is at this level – the level of field support – that the greatest single power to achieve innovation may lie.

The material context

At its most obvious this refers to the placement of the school in the natural or man-made environment and I have already commented on the vast variations which exist, from town to country; seashore to savannah, forest or mountain. In two senses the rural environment currently puts children at a disadvantage. In the first place it is notably less rich not only in human resources (for isn't education very much about people) but even in things like straight lines, angles or congruent objects. Moreover country children often discover their syllabuses, materials, examinations, all tend to be framed by and for people from more prosperous environments. Occasionally this is a result of lack of knowledge or lack of sensitivity on the part of urban, middle class curriculum workers, as in Kenya where an early version of the New Primary Approach for African Schools contained four 'centres of interest': the Post Office, the railway station; the game park and the coast.[8] Yet in its essence the problem is inescapable. A social studies programme must suggest the use of resources such as the market, the shop, the dispensary or the roadside, even though its makers may be aware that a very large number of deep rural schools have none of these resources at hand. Mathematics or Language or Science programmes for young children must be accompanied by suggestions for the use of 'waste' materials such as cartons, empty milk tins, bottles and bottle tops even in the knowledge that in many areas these are impossible to come by or that articles such as tins or bottles when in very short supply acquire a cash value in communities.

But while dilution of a national curriculum to the lowest common denominator of the poor, isolated rural school is clearly ludicrous, the reality must be faced that poor rural schools exist in large numbers and that a curriculum policy needs to be framed with them in mind – which it very rarely is.

The material context of education also includes the buildings and furniture provided for children and teachers and the scale of books and equipment available to them. At their poorest, buildings and furniture can be exceptionally restrictive. 1975 statistics from Lesotho reveal the following figures:

Primary classrooms	2,840	
Primary classes	4,683	
Type of seating	*Numbers*	*Percentage*
At desks	71,422	32·5
On chairs	1,604	0·7
On benches	56,778	25·9
On the floor	89,888	40·9

Schools in Cameroon and in rural areas in Sierra Leone and Ethiopia are unlikely to fare better, while there is no country in Africa without substantial numbers of schools where physical conditions inhibit any but the most basic instruction.

At the other end of the scale there are those schools, and they are numerous, where children enjoy the benefit of an adequate weatherproof classroom, something to sit and something to write on. In certain areas – Botswana, Lagos State and Ashanti come to mind – such conditions will be available for most children. Elsewhere one may expect to find a variety, from the very adequate to the very bleak.

There is a similar wide variety in the scale of teaching and learning equipment provided, which can be explained by a number of factors: the financial provision made to schools by central or local authorities, the type and efficiency of supply and distribution mechanism (bureaucratic centralised distribution systems seem universally inefficient), differences in attitudes and capabilities of communities to help in the provision of services or equipment to schools or individual children, the initiative and morale of teachers, the richness or poverty of the school environment.

My own recollection of school visits amply bear out these differences. I have found full cupboards and empty ones, children with books and children without; schools and classrooms where the resources of the community have been mobilised, where well stocked classroom shops have been organised using packets, wrappers and tins collected by children, where great varieties of natural and man-made objects have been collected for children's use in science and mathematics – and schools with none of these things. I have seen schools where children drew and made clay models, gathered and displayed local crafts collected, made and used local musical instruments – and schools as bare and empty as any prison cell. I have seen schools with their own livestock – chickens, goats and rabbits; and schools where the only livestock in evidence were the bats in the roof and the cockroaches in the latrine. With such a wide variety – and the variations exist within as well as between countries, it is difficult, again, to make useful generalisations about the material context. Certain issues, however, seem general enough and important enough to warrant discussion.

The first regards the priority accorded to providing an adequate minimum scale of equipment to schools. This issue becomes most significant in countries which are very poor or where school enrolments have increased very suddenly. In these instances it is not uncommon to find a government's revenue (as in Lesotho) almost totally committed to paying its teacher force – hence nothing left over to equip the schools; in which case it is worth asking whether the whole costly mechanism of providing school education has not come to an unprofitable full-stop just before the only point where it can be productive – enabling children to learn. For a child without reading books cannot learn to read adequately, and I have met many children without reading books and many who could not read.

One common solution to this problem, which avoids the politically undesirable alternative of imposing or reimposing fees, is to rely on parents to provide equipment, just as they are very widely expected to help in the construction and sometimes the furnishing of schools. This principle of self-help, of 'harambee' when applied at school level, may emphasise local differences, may lead to some difficulties over matters of replacement and repair, but, because it emphasises the community's participation in the education of its children, must be accounted a social as well as a financial good. Yet it is very much less easy to defend the policy of expecting parents to buy their children's books. Not only does this increase costs[9] and emphasise differences between richer and poorer children but it also contributes to a very inflexible and inefficient distribution of learning materials, since under this system 'shared' material is never bought – only class texts – and it is by no means uncommon to find that as a result a class may end up with only two or three books at its disposal, all in multiple copies. For allocation of resources is an area where conservatism of approach ('each child must have a textbook') tends to combine with administrative convenience and often with the commercial interests of publishers and suppliers to ensure that limited financial resources available to schools are *not* used to their best advantage. Frequently, moreover, there appears to be little concern that advice should be available to the teacher or headmaster, to ensure that he uses what few resources he has to best effect.

This lack of expertise sometimes seems to apply also to the maintenance and storage of equipment, a very essential part of the material context for curriculum development. It is all too common to find schools without stores, classrooms without cupboards, books without covers and a quite alarming rate of materials loss in schools often bearing little relationship to the official 'life expectancy' of materials on which the cost of replacements are calculated. This is not for want of official

Conversation piece (Uganda 1969)

Hugh Hawes: Why is your school so well equipped – when your neighbours have so little?
Headmaster: Some headmasters have Voices in the Education Office.
Hugh Hawes: Have you a Voice?
Headmaster: Of course.

Books or uniform (Kenya)

In theory, Peter Osogo's Class 3 schooling is free. In practice his father is faced with a formidable list of charges, a building fund, a sports fund, a book fee and a uniform fee. Now the headmaster is insisting that every child should possess a pair of lace-up shoes. Reluctantly the shoes are bought, for who would wish their son to attract comment for not wearing what others wear. But no such social constraints exist over possession of books, and the new reading book Peter had asked to buy – that had to be sacrificed. Peter has to be content with the single class reader provided by the school, which he already knows by heart. He attempts reading it upside down, which temporarily relieves the boredom.

How long does it last?

Official policies, in their delusion, often calculate a three year book life. Consider the realities.

Alice Kamara (9) attends a rural school in Western Sierra Leone. Apart from her exercise books Alice possesses just two textbooks, an English and a Mathematics reader. These she carries to and from school daily in a distressed plastic bag and uses continually. The books are paper covered and not very well bound. Both at home and at school they usually have to remain on the floor and Alice (9) doesn't always remember to put them back in the bag. The floor isn't clean and neither, often, are Alice's fingers. Miraculously, however, the books hold together, with the loss of only a few pages, until the end of the year.

concern by education commissions, curriculum projects[10] and national ministries. It appears to stem rather from a lack of awareness and concern at a more local level – a very basic question of attitudes.

The administrative context

Schools must also be seen within a system of administration (usually centralised) conforming to certain patterns and practices of control and within a hierarchical structure often difficult to change. Certain instruments like terms and timetables are familiar and institutionalised. In particular, transition from primary to secondary school is usually governed by a highly organised examination system understood and accepted by administration, teachers and parents alike. The effect of this system on both the official and actual curriculum in schools is examined in later chapters.

The historical context

Whatever new curricula are introduced into a school the influence of educational traditions remain as much a source of continuity and stability as they are of unacceptable 'educational conservatism'.[11] The strength and nature of these traditions has been brilliantly analysed elsewhere[12] and we need only remind ourselves here of their importance and their diversity. For in English-speaking African countries there can be found many strands and many contradictions. In each case we may trace from them important effects on learning in schools today on the curriculum plans, on policy and programmes for teacher training and, most significant, on the attitudes of teachers themselves and of those who train them. In the briefest analysis the following may be identified as particularly significant.

INFLUENCES OF INDIGENEOUS EDUCATION

These are evident in attitudes to authority and in learning styles used or preferred. Oral explanations and discussion may convey a meaning and a depth lacking in written explanation which may tend to be accepted at an uncritical and somewhat superficial level. There is some evidence[13] that the desire to find one rather than alternative answers to a problem may have its origins in patterns of indigeneous education.

RELIGIOUS AND MISSION INFLUENCES

The styles of learning in Koranic schools and catechist classes have predictable effects on the way children learn in school, but the missionary tradition in education is responsible for so much else besides, (over a long period of the history of formal education the great majority of schools *were* missionary schools). On the

'Not cricket'

'It is notable that Native ministers are often the most emphatic in their opposition to Native amusements. . . . Their convictions are sometimes the result of their intimate knowledge of the degenerating influences of Native amusements, but often have their source in a narrow conception of recreation imported to them by the missionaries.'

Phelps Stokes Reports on Education in Africa (1922 and 24), edited and abridged L. J. Lewis – Phelps Stokes Fund 1962.

Two points of view

'If more intelligent natives were taught to read, write and speak English, and to acquire a sufficient knowledge of Arithmetic in English they would be able to occupy many of the minor posts in the service of the Administration.'

Report by His Majesty's Special Commissioner on the Protectorate of Uganda, Cmd. 671, 1901.

'There is a very proper feeling abroad against mere book-learning as a complete course of school education. This is felt to be an inadequate preparation for the work of life, because it tends to produce a super-abundant supply of an indifferent clerkly class and to create and foster a distaste for agriculture and the handicrafts, which are more indispensable to the country and are better calculated to promote independence of character.'

Henry Carr, 1902. Quoted in Taiwo, C. O., 'The Purpose of Secondary Education' in *Report of National Curriculum Conference*, Lagos 1969.

credit side there must be recorded the conscious emphasis on the school as a transmitter of moral values and as an instrument in building up the attitudes necessary for an active citizen: co-operation, integrity, industry and many more. On its debit side there is sometimes observable a certain strange ordering of priorities in moral codes and very often the systematic and conscious neglect of many aspects of African culture, particularly that great cultural legacy, music and the dance. It is exceptionally ironic still to find children in a culture which has fathered half the popular music in the modern world, condemned to drone away in their music lessons over nineteenth-century hymn tunes, with dancing relegated to a few minutes at the conclusion of the physical education lessons.

INFLUENCES FROM PATTERNS OF COLONIAL EDUCATION

It has been frequently noted[14] that two separate streams run through the history of the development of African primary school curricula in the last fifty years of the colonial period. On the one hand we may trace the influence of the theories of 'adaptation to environment', a natural extension of the policy of indirect rule, argued in the influential reports of the Phelps Stokes Commissions in the early nineteen-twenties and brilliantly summarised in the memorandum of the Colonial Office's Advisory Committee on Native Education, *Educational Policy in British Tropical Africa*,[15] 1925 – hence the school gardens (or the remains of them), the handwork, the needlework, the local History and Geography programmes and the 'vernacular' syllabuses. On the other hand there was the demand, often locally generated, usually far more enthusiastically supported by parents and teachers, for an education which would produce a competent and reasonably docile junior civil servant, a clerk, storekeeper, interpreter or later an assistant this or junior that to work under a white colonial officer. Hence the emphasis on English, on Arithmetic, on the very desirable virtues of neatness and punctuality, on examinations and class order. Hence the moulding of that most deplorable product the 'humble boy' and the strengthening of what I had always referred to as 'the civil service mentality' until I encountered Michael Manley's much more telling phrase the 'psychology of dependence'.[16]

BORROWING FROM BRITAIN

Linked with colonial traditions we may trace the conscious borrowing of contents, practices and methods from metropolitan education systems (in this case Britain). Two contrasting reasons exist for these importations. On the one hand there were those introduced by British or British trained educationists because they appeared at the time to represent the 'best' education (though naturally criteria for judging quality varied widely). On other occasions specific contents or practices were introduced following demands by nationals themselves because they represented a type of education practised in Britain or in 'European' schools in a segregated education system like Kenya. Thus they assumed all the glamour and promise that forbidden fruit always holds. But in either case there was a tendency for such borrowings, whether they were syllabuses, textbooks or examinations to become fossilised and consequently to represent a historical rather than a current picture of British educational practice.

To a certain degree such borrowings have continued,[17] often prompted by the same underlying sense of insecurity which seeks the new or the modern uncritically rather than as a result of any conscious selection of educational objectives or examination of alternatives.

SURVIVAL TEACHING

A final set of influences come from that oral tradition, I call it 'survival teaching', handed down by one hard pressed disillusioned teacher to another in the face of long hours, poor conditions and low recognition. These traditions, and they are very strong, all contribute towards maintaining authority, reducing pressures, saving time, achieving passable examination results. They lead to a formal, didactic, teacher-centred approach, they operate with devastating force upon teachers newly trained in 'activity methods', but in the tough, bleak conditions which obtain in some schools they may well represent the only possible alternative for a struggling teacher to adopt.

Issues relating to curriculum context

This brief discussion of the nature and importance of educational context in curriculum change would appear to lead up towards discussion of two major issues. First, what do we need to find out, who may be involved in the process and how? Second, after we have got all this information what are we going to do with it?

INVESTMENT IN RESEARCH AND SURVEY

Two separate 'orders' of information may be required, though we should guard against closing our categories. The first is the more sophisticated 'university research type' evidence, much of it psychological and sociological, involving not only what Tyler called 'studies of the learners'[18] (their social background, cognitive, perceptual and linguistic development, attitudes and aspirations, health and nutrition) but similarly studies of the teachers who teach them and the communities which support the schools. The more evidence becomes available, the closer we lie to answering those key questions: what content may profitably be introduced in what manner and at what speed?

Second and equally important, for there is no 'first' and 'second' class research, is that body of information about schools – you might call it a 'professional inventory', which is as important to a curriculum planner as statistics are to a ministry planning officer. I refer to information regarding school buildings and equipment, to relevant financial information, to details of the type, number, education and training of teachers in an area, to languages understood and spoken, to the availability or scarcity of local resources.

26

It would be wrong to conceive of these two 'orders' as being respectively University and Ministry based, for both types of information may be collected at a number of levels including school and teacher's centre level.[19] Nothing is more important than teachers finding out more about their own educational contexts.[20]

Recognition of the need to invest in both types of research has been slow to materialise possibly because other pressures tended to shut it out, but also because of the remarkably esoteric image which University research workers have given themselves. Nevertheless in recent years considerably more interest has been aroused and in at least some cases governments and international agencies are showing themselves willing to put real money into research.

AN INSTITUTE FOR APPLIED RESEARCH – CAMEROON

In one country at least – the Cameroon – a research institute, The Institute for the Reform of Primary Education at Buea, was set up in 1974 with reasonable resources in terms of personnel (a team of twelve to fifteen nationals and experts has been employed), adequate funding jointly from Government and UNESCO/UNDP, and in its initial stages a sensible time scale to work to.[21]

The initial aim of the Institute at Buea has been to assemble reliable information on the most appropriate way of preparing pupils and school leavers for integration into the life and work of communities. Such information is seen as a preliminary to the trial of materials and the subsequent, final design and implementation of new curricula. There has been a familiar aura of UNESCO optimism about the plans of the project and it remains to be seen how far the recommendations of its *Report on the Reform of Primary Education* issued in 1977 will be accepted by the Government.[22] But the work so far attempted is fascinating.

There are four teams working closely together: two in environmental studies concerned respectively with village technology and agricultural and social aspects, a third on Mathematics and the fourth on Language.

The team concerned with *Environmental Studies, agricultural and social aspects* (I refer to it somewhat unwillingly by its official title) made a random sample of visits throughout the two English speaking provinces of Cameroon. They interviewed teachers, headmasters, parents, chiefs and their counsellors, local farmers and final year pupils in schools in an attempt to bring out a picture of the local and school environment and of needs and aspirations of young people and adults. The wealth of information collected and most ably synthesised in the project's report was used as evidence on which to base suggestions for possible key topics round which teaching could be based. Since different communities with different needs were identified – from remote, isolated environments to well-served rural and semi-urban ones, separate community-orientated activities were suggested to suit each of these. Figure A reproduces the suggestions offered for 'poorly served rural communities'.

The *village technology* team initially used teachers' training college students to gain preliminary information on crafts and skills available in the two provinces. It visited chiefs, and worked through them to find out about local resources, tools, apprenticeship patterns and market locations. This provided background informa-

27

Crafts and techniques identified in Northwest and Southwest Provinces of Cameroon, 1975/6

Aluminium casting
Bamboo work
Beadwork
Brasswork
Broom and brush work
Butter and cheese making
Calabash decoration
Cane work
Carpentry
Carving
Coconut crafts
Embroidery
Hides and skin curing
Iron smelting
Ivory work
Knitting, needlework
Leatherwork
Masonry
Mattress making

Mechanics
Milking
Palm oil extraction
Polythene bag making
Pottery
Rattle work
Repairs
Smithing
Sponge making
Spinning
Shoe making and mending
Thatchwork
Tinkering
Tie and die
Tree bark cloth
Weaving
Salt extraction
Tailoring
Wine distillation

The project then examined each of the crafts identified to show how they could be correlated with teaching in other school subjects, in particular, Language, Mathematics and Science. Not surprisingly the analysis revealed a large number of ways in which such correlations could be made.

Information contained in *Report on the Reform of Primary Education*, Buea, 1977.

Fig. A Activities appropriate to poorly served rural communities.

ACTIVITY	DEVELOPMENT NEEDS		
	Agriculture	Infrastructure	Community growth
Classroom teaching	Methods of food crop and oil palm growing not relying on bought inputs; maintaining soil fertility; erosion control, improvement of tools, crop minimum labour input, crop sequence.	Different types of bridges (hammocks, bamboo bridges); making paths safe during rainy season; suitable materials; hygiene and drinking water.	Hygiene, first aid, simple local drugs for first aid; nutrition; disposal of faeces; administrative structures and procedures.
Practical work	Gardening, variety trials (maize, yams, oil palms), demonstrating crop sequences, storage, transporting surpluses to nearest market.	Participating in the maintenance of roads and bridges; trying out dams, rails, ropes; participating in communal road water projects, putting up a water filter.	Building a good latrine; collecting and documenting medical herbs, leaves, barks, etc.
'Animation' (out of school) by teacher	Bringing in new varieties (high yielding or disease resistant), noting occurrences of pests and diseases; discussing with agricultural field staff, proposing remedies.	Helping establish and maintain relations with bodies responsible for road and water projects, acting as secretary on project committees, using a water filter in his home.	Operating a first aid kit and drug supply financed by community; co-operating with local healer(s) to list and classify local drugs; participating in local societies; helping with administrative procedures.

From IPAR, Buea, *Report on the reform of primary education*, p 40

tion which was extended through visits. Visits were made to fifty villages throughout the two provinces and included interviews with school teachers, village heads and local craftsmen together with personnel at craft stores and co-operatives, and a very large number of other individuals and groups such as parents, prospective employers and education personnel.

From discussion and interviews with these people, the team collected information on the skills and crafts of the people, the tools used (local and foreign), the work procedure used, market demands, training obtained by craftsmen and the training offered, conditions of training and apprenticeship, the cost of the article produced, the time taken and the profit made from the sale. From all this information the team drew up a matrix of crafts, materials and local resources, analysed technologies applied locally and attempted to order skills development in level of difficulty and in relation to social custom as a preliminary to curriculum design.

Teams in *Mathematics and English* were concerned with finding out what knowledge and what concepts children and teachers have and can master at different levels and of assessing the strengths and limitations of the environment and the cultural traditions within that environment for teaching and materials production in these two areas.

Whatever action is taken on the final report of the Buea project (and I have fears that the heavy reliance on expatriate experts in the project and in drawing up the report may not contribute to its being widely read and followed in Cameroon) there can be no question that the project marks an important landmark in curriculum planning in Africa. The importance of situational analysis as a preliminary to curriculum design *has* been recognised, investment *has* been made and important questions *are* being asked. In the sister institute in the French-speaking Cameroon[23] set up somewhat earlier at Yaounde, workers embarked more conventionally straight into a programme of materials production and were able to announce confidently that by March 1973, 'about 47 tons of textbooks and 33 tons of documents have been produced',[24] but you cannot profitably assess the success of a curriculum by weight; many megatons of unprofitable material have been produced (and will still be produced) all over Africa just because no preliminary study had been made to ascertain whether children and parents wanted them, could afford them, read them or understand them.

Elsewhere in Africa, national and international concern towards establishing a basis of research information for curriculum decision grows slowly and fitfully, but noticeably, nevertheless. Within ministries there is an increasing disposition to mount surveys into actual conditions in schools and opinions of parents and community leaders. In Lesotho a four man primary curriculum research unit has been set up and has undertaken a sample survey of primary schools under four headings (i) The physical environment; (ii) the curriculum; (iii) methods of learning and teaching leading to (iv) recommendations. The report presents the truth about conditions in what is, probably the poorest (financially) of all the countries I have visited and makes compelling reading (if you like horror stories).[25] Research sections have been set up at the Institutes of Education in Kenya and Sierra Leone and there have been important regional conferences on educational evaluation (at Dar es Salaam in April 1975) and on the growth of scientific and mathematical concepts in East African children (Nairobi, September 1974). A small international centre for educational evaluation at Ibadan has been set up (and will be described further in my next chapter) and another on child development is being planned in Nairobi.

But for all these little awakenings and small scale investments, it is impossible to pretend that the volume of interest or commitment is anything like what, on sober reflection, we realise it should be, nor that any proper partnership has been achieved between universities who should have the expertise and interest to conduct and co-ordinate research, and ministries of education who should be increasingly aware of what they don't know and need to know.

One apparent stumbling block to mounting more research is that we lack qualified people to do it or the resources to employ or deploy them, but as so often, a wider and less conventional look at the problem reveals one possible solution. For rapid changes are taking place in the structure and content of teacher education and, with it, a massive increase in part-time school-based schemes for initial and further training together with a more extensive use of 'sandwich' type training especially for higher grades of teachers.

Currently there is considerable discussion about the possibility of harnessing the resources provided by mature students who attend full or part-time diploma, associateship and master's courses and who write 'long studies' in part fulfilment of these courses. What if such studies could be written on subjects and to designs jointly devised by ministries, colleges and universities? The possibilities opened up are exceptionally exciting and realisable provided certain strange notions of academic freedom (in this case often amounting to a student fishing desperately around for an 'original' and totally useless subject like the history of his old school), can be avoided.

In fact the channeling of reports and dissertations towards educationally productive goals is merely part of a wider and far more important issue, that of establishing a new climate of opinion among teachers and those who train them which regards enquiry about the learners and the environment in which they learn as an important part of a teacher's professional life, which seeks to develop interests and provide skills for them to do so as part of their training and retraining and which rewards initiatives undertaken in college and subsequently.

AFTER RESEARCH WHAT?

Hitherto such emphasis and recognition have not been current, nor, I believe, has there been sufficiently widespread recognition of the need to spread the information we have to those who should use it – it may therefore be appropriate to end this chapter with a few rude questions.

1 How often are relevant descriptions of educational context made available and studied by curriculum workers as a basis for their decision making?
2 How often are staff seminars on these issues held in university departments, teachers' colleges or curriculum centres (or are all the workers always too 'busy' to attend them)?
3 Do syllabuses and textbooks used in colleges or universities adequately reflect our considerable current knowledge about the educational context in Africa – particularly our knowledge about children? Or are we still largely dependent on British and American models?

When I look back over my own experience, I find these questions embarrassing. I wonder whether this feeling is shared by any of my readers?

Notes

1 Skilbeck, M., 'School Based Curriculum Development and Teacher Education', in the Open University's course *Curriculum Design and Development* 1976, Unit 7
2 Hawes, H. W. R., *Planning the Primary School Curriculum in Developing Countries*, UNESCO/IIEP 1972, pp 28–32
3 I am surprised to find that certain key political documents, e.g. the Kenya Government's *African Socialism and its Application to Planning in Kenya*, do not figure prominently on teachers' college reading lists.
4 Castle, E. B., *Growing up in East Africa*, OUP 1966, p 35
5 A considerable body of evidence now exists and Jerome Bruner's essay on Culture and Cognitive Growth in *The Relevance of Education* (Allen and Unwin 1971), provides a brilliant introduction to the field. A 1974 international seminar in Nairobi on the development of science and mathematics concepts in young children in African countries is both welcome and significant. (Report published 1974, UNESCO-UNICEF, Nairobi). It is a source of considerable concern that so little of this research finds its way into African college or undergraduate publications or programmes.
6 Beeby, C. E., *op. cit.*
7 E.g. Thias, H. H. and Carnoy, M., *Cost Benefit Analysis in Education: A Case Study on Kenya*, John Hopkins Press 1973
8 A situation soon remedied in later drafts of the same material.
9 Traders in the Onitsha market commonly create artificial famines of recommended texts and then release them at double the normal price.
10 See, for example, Education Commission reports Kenya (1964), Uganda (1963),

Sierra Leone Education Review final report (1976), and Education for Kagisano (Botswana, 1977). Large scale curriculum projects e.g. the Primary Education Improvement Project, Nigeria, have even designed and distributed lockable cupboards.

11 The phrase is Beeby's (*Quality of Education in Developing Countries*). I am sometimes concerned at the perjorative way in which words such as 'conservative' and 'traditional' are used and contrasted with 'hurrah' words such as 'modern', 'new', and 'progressive'.

12 See Foster, P., *Education and Social Change in Ghana*, Routledge & Kegan Paul 1965

13 E.g. Gay, J. and Cole, M., *New Mathenatics in an Old Culture*, Holt, Rinehart and Winston 1967

14 E.g. Foster, P., *op. cit.* Wilson, J., *Education and Changing West African Culture*, OUP 1966. Cameron, J. C. and Dodd, W. A., *Society, Schools and Progress in Tanzania*, Pergamon 1970

15 Cmd. 2374. Reproduced in Scanlon, *Traditions of African Education*, Bureau of Publications, Columbia University, New York 1964

16 Manley, M., *The Politics of Change – A Jamaican Testament*, Andre Deutsch 1974

17 Attempts to introduce the Initial Teaching Alphabet into Western Nigeria (now mercifully abandoned) are just one of a number of such examples.

18 See Tyler, R., *Basic Principles of Curriculum and Instruction*, Chicago 1949, p 5

19 A recent workshop of staff and postgraduate students in our department in the London University Institute has provided a useful listing of possible teacher based research projects: see Hawes, H. W. R. (ed.) *Locally based educational research and curriculum development in developing countries – the teacher's role*, IIEP Occasional Paper, Paris 1976

20 The possibility of recognition (in terms of promotion) for research and curriculum development by teachers in the field is being taken seriously by at least one government (Kenya).

21 Since 1977 political pressures have emerged to force the Institute towards a very rapid programme of curriculum implementation.

22 IPAR, *Report on the Reform of Primary Education*, Buea, April 1977

23 Institut de Pédagogie Appliquée a Vocation Rurale, Yaoundé. Its activities are described in Lallez, R. *The Case of the Cameroon*, UNESCO/IBE 1974

24 United Republic of Cameroon Seminar Report, 'The Reform of Primary Education Cameroon', Yaoundé, April 1973, p 52. Among the aid supplied to Cameroon for her education reform was a large gift of newsprint from Canada.

25 For more literature in the same realistic vein try a recent commission report from Jamaica. *The Report in Depth of Primary Education in Jamaica*, Prof. R. N. Murray (Chairman).

Chapter 3 Strategies for curriculum planning and development

Pressures towards change

THE PROCESSES INVOLVED

Curriculum changes and the planning necessary to achieve them originate at a number of points: in the cabinet, in the ministry of education, in the curriculum project or in the school; yet in every instance six similar processes are involved:

1 Gathering *basic information* about the context in which the changes are to take place and about their feasibility. For unless we know where we are we cannot plan a course of action.
2 Deciding *aims and objectives*. For, as the old Jewish proverb has it, 'if you don't know where you are going, any road will take you there'.
3 Planning a *strategy for change*. For resources in manpower, materials and time must be correctly deployed.
4 The process of *curriculum development* which involves devising the material and trying it out.
5 Its final *implementation* in schools with learners.
6 At every stage a process of *evaluation* takes place. Do we have sufficient information on which to base change? Are our aims and objectives sensible and realistic? Is the strategy sensible and workable; can it be afforded? Is the process of curriculum development efficient; is it working? How well and how consistently is the implementation of curricular plans being achieved? There are many such questions to be asked and answered.

In some degree, all these processes take place wherever a curriculum changes. What varies, and varies dramatically, is the conscious effort with which they are identified and undertaken. The strength and potential of the modern concern for curriculum development lies in the fact that we now realise how important it is to undertake these processes, and in a logical sequence.

In this chapter I look back over responses to the challenges of curriculum planning and development in Africa in the 'sixties and 'seventies. With the benefit of fifteen years' experience and from the security of a university in Britain, it is possible to pronounce with considerable confidence upon what should have happened; to comment owlishly on how untidy and illogical were the processes employed, how more information should have been spelt out with more precision, how more evaluation should have been undertaken sooner, how unreal were our expectations in terms of how quickly and how evenly changes can effectively take place. In making such judgments one is in much the same position as a journalist describing a battle after it had taken place from the bar of a hotel, for the pressures in the 'sixties were very great and very immediate and those of us in the Ministries[1] of Education responded to them as best we knew how.

INTERNAL PRESSURES IN THE 'FIFTIES AND 'SIXTIES

Self-government and independence came to the British colonial territories in Africa in the late 'fifties and early 'sixties[2] – with them all the internal pressures towards reshaping a school system and its curriculum towards new national goals and aspirations.

Foremost of these was the maintenance and strengthening of a sense of national unity with its implications for language and the content of history and geography syllabuses. Certain countries, Ghana first and Tanzania considerably later, developed their own particular political creeds and naturally saw the primary school as an important instrument to lay the basis of particular attitudes and values.

But other internal pressures were most strong, on the one hand towards providing a type of education both in quantity and quality which 'we had been denied', on the other towards meeting a need for high level manpower which the authority of the international planners then recognised as paramount. The effect of the former set of pressures can be seen first in the 'fifties and especially in West Africa[3] in a series of attempts, all politically inspired and none of them entirely successful, to introduce universal primary education – with all the over-extension of resources consequent on such a decision – and second in the popular pressures felt everywhere towards adopting a curricular content similar to that in 'European schools'. I can recall the phrase 'being left behind' (whatever it meant) being used far more frequently than it is at present.

Pressures towards manpower production meant in effect, that demands from higher levels of the education system fed down towards the primary curriculum and there was a certain rather questionable pyramid philosophy built on the premise that 'many are called but few are chosen'. Hence dropouts were to be accepted as a fact of life and the curriculum designed particularly with the needs of higher levels in mind. In some ill-explained way, manpower needs were held also to be closely linked with a shortage of mathematics and science graduates so that emphasis on strengthening and 'modernising' mathematics and science curricula at all levels was strong.

EXTERNAL PRESSURES

Such were the internal pressures for curriculum change in the 'sixties and they were very important. They were further reinforced by two sets of external pressures of almost equal strength. The first of these was the intense interest in, and massive support for, subject-based curriculum change particularly in Mathematics and Science which originated in the late nineteen-fifties in the United States, largely as a result of a realisation of the enormous gaps which were opening between what

34

university research workers were examining and what schools taught, between the demands of a computer based technology and the realities of a curriculum designed in the nineteenth century to serve a nation of shopkeepers. From these programmes which were largely for secondary schools, activities multiplied and interest spread quickly from America to Britain, from secondary down to primary, from subject initiatives towards the wider theory of curriculum development. What has been described as the curriculum revolution was well under way.

Now, like all revolutionaries, its earliest protagonists possessed a certain prophetic fervour and the time when this fervour was at its height coincided with a time when, following independence, aid to Africa had been vastly increased, with the usual mixed motives. Hence there were a considerable number of able and committed prophets around at a time when the gospel they were spreading – a gospel of modernity – was one which their auditors were anxious to hear.

These pressures I have described, both internal and external, invited change in almost every aspect of the curriculum, but in many respects they were also conflicting. The demands of higher level science and mathematics were often irrelevant to the needs of mass education. The 'curriculum denied us' was often a European-centred curriculum. Potential conflicts in language policies were already apparent. There was an underlying tension between curricular objectives which derived from traditions and conditions in capitalist and highly individualist societies and the goals of governments intent on imposing the discipline they considered necessary for nation building. The 'four cornerstones' of the Malawi Congress Party: unity, loyalty, obedience and discipline, match ill with the 'scientific spirit of enquiry' which the country's 1966 syllabus announces as the guiding principle for primary education syllabus change.

Syllabus change

In the period just before or just after their independence many countries embarked, quite naturally, on primary school syllabus changes. The Uganda syllabus, typical of many, will serve as a profitable example.

Uganda became independent in October 1962 and an education commission report followed in 1963. Primary subject syllabuses were reviewed and recast during 1963 by subject panels largely composed of experienced teacher trainers and inspectors, moderated and in some degree co-ordinated by an advisory committee, edited in the Inspectorate and issued in 1965. The syllabus reflected the good sense and experience of panel members but its shortcomings were typical of its time. Aims of subject syllabuses were very generalised, no attempt having been made to isolate any specific terminal or intermediate objectives in respect of knowledge, skills or attitudes to be developed. Co-ordination between subjects was lacking and the whole overloaded and exceptionally ambitious in scope requiring, moreover, a scale of expenditure well in excess of schools' ability to pay for it.[4] There was virtually no trial or possibility of modification of any of the subject syllabuses. They were sent to schools and teachers were expected to teach them.

New content and emphasis is to be found in all subjects of the syllabus but

35

radical changes (most of them very typical of other syllabuses of the time) included: earlier and more intensive teaching of English, the teaching of more Mathematics earlier (and less computational arithmetic), the localisation of History and Civics syllabuses (but with world affairs added in the upper classes), the introduction of a Science syllabus, with considerable time weighting, based on an 'experimental approach' and intended to integrate contents and approaches originally taught separately as Nature Study, Rural Science, General Science, Health Education and Gardening, and a revised, expanded, and considerably more africanised Music syllabus.

International projects for curriculum change (subject based)

During the years that the Uganda syllabus panels were meeting, the Lake Victoria Hotel, Entebbe was chosen as the venue for the first in a series of international workshops which heralded a new approach to curriculum development, a new dimension for pan-African co-operation and whose eventual product, the Entebbe Mathematics, proved to be possibly the most influential curriculum project yet to be launched in English-speaking Africa.

The 'Entebbe Maths' is the popular name for the African Mathematics Programme which in turn is part of the African Education Programme (AEP) of the American Education Development Center (EDC) formerly Educational Services Incorporated.

Educational Services Incorporated had emerged in the 1950's as a leading agent for curricular reform in the United States, and its development owed much to the concern and dynamism of some of the country's foremost scientists and mathematicians. It was the personal initiative of one of these, Jerrold Zacharias, Professor of Physics at the Massachusetts Institute of Technology, which was directly responsible for the inception of the AEP.

He had attended an International Conference on Science and the Advancement of New States at Rehovot in Israel and there met the Rev. Solomon Caulker, then Vice-Principal of Fourah Bay College. Caulker had been deeply concerned (and I am convinced rightly so) that the conference concentrated its time and discussion on the provision of sophisticated and expensive technology for developing countries, ignoring the need to lay foundations in schools for fundamental growth of knowledge, skills and attitudes to understand them. Discussions between the two men led to the organisation of an important and influential summer study in African Education at the Massachusetts Institute of Technology in 1961 (fifty-two participants attended, including fourteen from African states, a larger number of American academics and a few British). The conference split up into working parties including groups for mathematics, science, language, social studies with the humanities, and teacher training. From the discussions of the conference and its working parties and with considerable United States Government and Ford Foundation aid, the AEP and its various curriculum projects were born.

I have included this somewhat lengthy account of the inception of the AEP since it does a good deal to explain some of the subsequent strengths and weaknesses of these highly influential programmes. They were motivated by real, sensible and human concern by academics of the highest standing and reputation – Americans like Bruner, Zacharias, Morrison; Africans like Porter, Abubakkar, Dyasi, Kajubi. At the same time, however, discussion tended to be dominated by certain sets of people; by academics, by Americans, by mathematicians and scientists, by people with little experience of younger children or of the teachers who normally guide them, by scholars whose passionate concern for their own disciplines and the elegance of thought within them may have outweighed their concern for the school curriculum and the balanced development of school children.

The exceptional quality of the participants certainly enabled the curriculum workers (or most of them anyway) to adapt to their environment as programmes developed – but their heredity kept showing through.

Three curriculum projects originating from the African Education Programme are briefly considered in this chapter, the African Mathematics Programme, The African Primary Science Programme (APSP) and the African Social Studies Programme (ASSP). In the short term, at any rate, the first has proved the most influential.

THE AFRICAN MATHEMATICS PROGRAMME

The stated aim of the programme was 'to improve the quality of mathematics teaching and to develop in each participating country a nucleus of people knowledgeable in Mathematics and capable of undertaking improvement of Mathematics curriculum'. This has been attempted in two distinct phases, the first from 1962–69 with the initial development of the 'Entebbe' materials and the second from 1970 onwards with its adaptation and implementation through the activities of the West African Regional Mathematics Programme (WARMP) and the East African Regional Mathematics Programme. Yet to characterise the development in this fashion is too simplistic since at different times there have been offshoots, modifications and borrowings from different countries and even within them.

In the first 'stage' yearly writing workshops were held from 1962, first at Entebbe and subsequently elsewhere. Production of materials from them was exceptionally prolific. By 1969 a complete textbook series from primary one to primary seven (pupils' books and accompanying teacher's guides); a manual for teacher training, *Basic Concepts in Mathematics*; and two alternative series for secondary schools had been produced, providing in all 67 volumes of prototype materials.

But the quantity of these early materials was not entirely matched by their quality and relevance. They still remained somewhat too close to the American School Mathematics Study Group materials upon which they had been modelled. They were not derived from any significant analysis of aims or objectives in relation to the development of learners, nor based on a sufficiency of basic knowledge about the pupils and teachers and schools who would have to use them. Attempts to test and modify materials (although included in the programme) were perfunctory since there was a tightly structured writing and production schedule to meet. The fact that the materials which emerged, for all their faults, were usable in schools reflects the hard work and experience of the writers, but as many of the participants themselves readily admitted the original 'Entebbe' books needed considerable modification – and the further down the primary age range one travelled, the more they needed it.

In certain cases they never received this modification and found their way almost unaltered into school programmes, as in Lagos State, Nigeria. More typically in the 'second stage' they formed the basis for local modification and adaptation in the West African Regional Mathematics Programmes based in Accra and including Ghana, Sierra Leone and Liberia, and the East African Mathematics Programme for Kenya and Ethiopia. In these they were subject to varying degrees of revision and improvement, yet retained a number of the shortcomings resulting from their initial hurried drafts. Chief among these, I would argue, are a too heavy reliance on language, particularly descriptive terminology, a constant preoccupation with classroom and textbook centred examples at the expense of using the rich mathematical resources in an environment, and a sense of rigid, logical class-by-class progression resulting probably from the original division into year-based writing groups. As the years have gone by, much doubt has been cast on the approaches even by people closely involved in them.[5] But once foundations are laid it is very, very difficult to do anything but modify a programme and the original structure always shows through.

In both the first stages of the African Mathematics Programmes and the Regional Programmes which followed it, very considerable investment was made in both initial and in-service teacher training and international 'Institutes' designed to promote a cadre of university staff, teacher trainers and inspectors capable of carrying the momentum of the project. The fact that in the event the volume of training proved insufficient, relates (as I shall argue later) to the whole issue of priorities in teacher education and to the relationship between expectations in curriculum reform and means available. But no subject received more attention than Mathematics and no curriculum project then or since has received such massive support as the Entebbe programme and its successors.

In terms of adoption in syllabus and recommended materials, the success has been phenomenal. In five countries, all schools now use materials directly derived from the AEP. In Nigeria until very recently it has been very strongly reflected in the national syllabus guidelines and materials or derivatives are widely used at state level.[6] In other countries considerable indirect influence is apparent, particularly in teacher education programmes. Moreover, the international co-operation originally envisaged by the fathers of EDC is much in evidence and that 'nucleus of people knowledgeable in Mathematics curriculum' is already in being in some countries.

Personally, I have some very strong reservations about the apparent success of the 'Entebbe programme' and other parallel new Mathematics programmes of the 'sixties. I believe that the very speed at which they have been absorbed into the school system indicates an uncritical acceptance of the package because it is new and modern and fashionable and that there has been little serious examination of which aspects are relevant and which are not. I believe that there has been too much attention to ordering of content – which is an easy job – and too little in considering the process – which is a very difficult one. Consequently, more often than not we have exchanged old rote for new. Lastly I fear that because the Mathematics

38

Table 3 Production and application of APSP and SEPA Primary Science Units

TITLE	1	2	3	4	5	6	7
A Teachers' Guide to the APSP/Making a Start	▓	▓	▓	▓	▓	▓	
LOWER PRIMARY							
Introduction*/Arts and Crafts*/Construction*/Cooking*/Dry sand*/ Exploring the Local Community*/Plants in the Classroom*/ Playground Equipment*/Water*/Wet Sand*/Wheels/Woodwork*	▓	▓					
MIDDLE AND UPPER PRIMARY							
Biological Sciences							
Exploring Nature*				▓	▓		
Seeds/Small Animals*/The Water Book					▓		
Ask the Ant Lion*/Juba Beach					▓		
Mosquitoes*/Ourselves					▓		
Chicks in the Classroom					▓	▓	
Tilapia/Buds and Twigs						▓	
Physical and Chemical Sciences							
Making Paints*				▓	▓		
Colours, Water and Paper*/Sinking and Floating*/Torch Batteries and Bulbs/Changing Solids					▓		
Making a Magnifier/Friction/Estimating Numbers					▓	▓	
Making Things Look Bigger: Teachers' Handbook					▓	▓	
A Scientific Look at Soil*/Inks and Papers/Construction with Grass/ Powders/Chima Makes a Clock/Measuring Time: Part I					▓		
Bricks and Pots*/Tools for the Classroom*/Making a Microscope/ Balancing and Weighing/Sound: A Look at Musical Instruments/ The Moon Watchers*/Stars Over Africa*						▓	
Strangers in the Sky*/Using the Sky/How the Sky Looks/ Common Substances Around the Home/Measuring Time: Part II/ Pendulums/A Book About Pendulums						▓	▓
Liquids*							▓

Suggested class levels

Notes
(1) Two countries, Kenya and Ghana, have published modified versions of units. In Kenya all those units marked * have been re-issued with greater or lesser modification by the Jomo Kenyatta Foundation. Many of the units were originally developed at the Kenya Institute of Education.
(2) Some material has been incorporated into national syllabuses, schemes of work and recommended textbooks.
Extensive use of materials is made in Ghana, Sierra Leone, Nigeria (National Schemes: Primary Education Improvement Project and some State syllabuses), Kenya and Tanzania.
(3) Production of Teachers' Guides incorporating SEPA ideas has been undertaken in work-shops in Sierra Leone, Nigeria, Kenya and Lesotho.

Preface to an APSP Unit 'Juba Beach' (developed in Sierra Leone)

'During the months of January and February my class six children studied the beaches and sea at Juba. This book is a collection of writings, drawings and photographs of what they discovered.

'As a teacher I have observed that children truly learn when they try to solve questions which they themselves ask. In order for children to ask questions they need a diversity of materials to arouse their curiosity and a sense of freedom to question and explore their own potential. For my school, the beaches provide the materials. But it doesn't matter whether it's a beach or a river or an upland farm or a village market: the children will still want to ask questions and find out. Whatever is near the school the children can study, and because it is near the school and the children's homes it is important.

'I hope the following pages show that the general topic of beaches and sea integrated many experiences of learning. The children found and observed a wide variety of animals. They examined rocks and shells and sand. They tasted and tested water for salt content. They counted waves and the flow of rivers and talked to fishermen. The challenges were without limit.

'The children knew much about the beach environment before they began their study. The events of this unit encouraged them to find answers to questions. They wanted to learn and because of this they used and developed their skills – they measured, weighed, compared and counted, they kept notes and discussed their findings. For me, their own evaluations and this record book tells more about the progress of the children than any written examination I might have given them.

'Most important, the children had the satisfaction of discovering things on their own. Their discoveries built their confidence to look further into what is around them. This book is the result of the children's looking and experimenting, a continuous inquiry into their environment.'

Hawa Kamara
Teacher
Juba Army Rural School

programmes came first and were so well organised and established, with the neat sequential task of curriculum development so easy to define (despite its obvious size), there may have been a tendency to concentrate scarce resources upon an item which, on sober reflection, I believe now to be a lowish priority in the primary curriculum. But these are thoughts for 1978. The 'Entebbe Maths' in the 'sixties and for the 'sixties was a success story and one which laid the foundation for interest and expertise in curriculum development not only in Mathematics but in other subjects as well.

THE AFRICAN PRIMARY SCIENCE PROGRAMME (APSP) AND THE SCIENCE EDUCATION PROGRAMME FOR AFRICA (SEPA)

The second of the AEP programmes was radically different in both philosophy and structure from the first. The philosophy of the African Primary Science Programme derives from the experimental American curriculum projects such as the Physical Science Study Committee (PSSC) but the initial goals set at the MIT conference in 1961 indicate that considerable thought was given to needs and conditions in Africa.

The prime goal of the programme was to help develop processes of scientific thinking in children. It was not sufficient to describe the chain of cause and effect nor only to observe it. Wherever possible the pupil would intervene with his own thought, his own hands and his own will to learn.

The following criteria for selection of content were also set:

1 Wherever facts are presented they should be discoverable by the student.
2 Facts selected should be of critical importance to understanding of a principle.
3 Content should help to show how science proceeds through a method of discovery.
4 It must be cheap to do, cheap to find out, economical in time as well as money.

Following some preliminary work at Nsukka, Nigeria – the APSP was formally established in 1965, a preliminary conference held in Kano and initial writing workshops in Entebbe (1965), Dar es Salaam (1966) and Akosombo (Ghana, 1967). Both the pilot work at Nsukka and the outputs of the writing workshops owed a great deal in style and organisation to the EDC's American Elementary Science Study. Like it, the basis for development was the 'unit' – an enquiry based topic which might be used in any order and at more than one level. Prototype units were designed at the international workshops and discussed and modified in the field for the APSP was far more decentralised than the Mathematics programme. Science Curriculum Development Centres were established in Ghana, Ethiopia, Kenya, Malawi, Nigeria, Liberia, Sierra Leone and Uganda. These could test and modify units designed at international workshops (or by other centres) or initiate work of their own and present it for international criticism, modification and subsequent diffusion to other countries. Certain aspects of centres' work may have been less successful than others (there was a considerable and unproductive stress on making inefficient 'cheap' material such as bead microscopes) and some centres like Nsukka, Nairobi, Domasi and Njala were more active than others but the overall record in terms of creation of exciting relevant material based on children's experience is indeed impressive. Table 3 shows a list of units and details of their later modification at national level.

From 1969 the direction and administration of programmes was handed over to an African organisation (SEPA) with its headquarters in Accra, though training for Science Educators is offered under its auspices at Njala, Sierra Leone.

SEPA's role was originally seen as a clearing house for exchanging ideas and information about science curriculum development and as a means of supporting and strengthening national bodies in member states in their efforts towards improving the learning of science, but under effective direction, it has extended its interest and influence further towards interest in evaluation, child development and the relationship between the materials and approaches developed in science and the evolution of the primary curriculum as a whole. Most specifically, however, SEPA has concentrated its efforts towards developing expertise in teacher education in science and in the process of integrating units initially developed by the APSP into evolving national programmes.

The adoption of the APSP materials has been far less immediate and widespread than those in mathematics. There are certain obvious reasons. Science is a 'lower priority subject' especially when viewed through the distorted lens of selection examinations. There were other science materials in the field and other programmes. But essentially the APSP units have been slow to gain acceptance because both the method of their development (which offers choice and demands local initiative) and the philosophy of their content – so unequivocally enquiry based – demand radically new approaches. In some countries, such as Nigeria, Ghana and Kenya, developments have been very considerable but the process is necessarily slower and perhaps deeper and more lasting for that.

THE AFRICAN SOCIAL STUDIES PROGRAMME

The impact of the third programme initiated by the EDC, the African Social Studies Programme, is noticeably slighter than in the two other areas. The initial conference which launched it at Mombasa in 1968 produced a thoughtful and influential document which has done much on its own to stimulate interest and activity in social studies teaching and curriculum development.

The founding of the African Social Studies Project in 1969, the establishment of its headquarters in Nairobi and the international workshops (there were four) have done something to advance knowledge and interest through the designing of packs of source material, teachers' guides and trial units of varying quality. But funding has been significantly less than other programmes, dissemination of materials less effective and leadership less dynamic. For this reason and probably also because Social Studies is not an area where governments readily welcome international initiatives, support for the programme is distinctly lukewarm.[7] Yet though the African Social Studies Programme suffers from close comparison with its two elder brothers it has nevertheless already influenced practice and served as a forum for international exchange of ideas and can be seen as a contributory factor in the widespread change of emphasis towards study of man in his environment.

A statement of EDC philosophy

'The final criterion of our curricular style is this: it takes time. What the textbook can summarise in a page of results – life is cellular, cells have water and carbon, cells divide to multiply – our methods with the child's own work, with his own hands, with his own microscope and his own laboured arithmetic may take six weeks of classroom effort. We do not begrudge this time. We are not disturbed by slowness, for what goes slow can run deep. And school hours are not all of life. To stroll into reality, the detail of it and the context, to unravel and to uncover it is a better thing than to sprint past, reading the billboards of science.'

From 'The Curricular Triangle and its Style' by Philip Morrison, in W. Martin and D. Pinck, *Curriculum Improvement and Innovation*, Robert Betley, 1966, p 16.

Machinery for change

Subject initiatives were, perhaps, the first indication of widespread interest and activity in curriculum planning and development. They were closely followed by setting up the national machinery to promote and manage it.

EDUCATIONAL POLICY AND CURRICULUM CHANGE

Governments were used to the fairly simple process of changing a syllabus, but confronted with a new orthodoxy that it was desirable to engage in curriculum development, they were usually happy initially to see this potentially time-consuming exercise take place outside the Ministry, at University Institutes of Education or specially constituted curriculum development centres.

It seems odd, in retrospect, to see governments delegating so passively their most important educational function, but there were two main reasons for it at the time. The first is that nobody had really analysed and spelt out the interrelated series of planning and policy decisions which changing a school curriculum entails; the essential links between the processes of curriculum planning and implementation; the costs of change. Moreover we never look hard for what we don't particularly want to find, and governments' revenues and manpower were so highly committed towards programmes of quantitative expansion (particularly at secondary level) and subsequently towards keeping the machine they had created running, that few people were prepared to question advice which suggested that a certain new activity could be safely (and, hopefully, inexpensively) tucked away at a centre or institute.

Such advice was undoubtedly given since the predilections and experience of the aid donors and advisers who exercise, I would argue, a quite disproportionate amount of influence in deciding fundamental issues of curricular policy, strongly supported the idea of centre or project based curriculum development. In Britain there was no tradition of government 'interference' in matters of curriculum. In the United States most of the great curriculum projects in the 'sixties had been subvented rather than controlled by government and in both countries university personnel had been heavily involved, bringing with them, in almost equal measure, a power of creative innovation and an unacceptable academic arrogance which ignores realities in schools and distrusts anything 'political' as a threat to 'academic freedom'.

The result was therefore an initial policy towards curriculum planning which separated curriculum development from its implementation in schools and which ensured a rapid, but perhaps unnatural, growth, of new ideas and new materials. Later in this chapter we will examine the gradual growth of government concern to assume a closer control of the process.

PATTERNS OF CONTROL: (I) INSTITUTES OF EDUCATION

The name 'Institute of Education' has been used in African universities to describe institutes which do little except train secondary school teachers, but in the sense of a professional centre concerned with various aspects of quality both of teachers and the curriculum they teach, it was first used in Bakht Er Ruda in the Sudan in the 1930's.[8] Later the idea was strongly revived at the University of East Africa Conference in Mombasa in 1964 and the influential Institutes of Education in Uganda and Tanzania were founded which assumed an important national role in curriculum planning and development at both primary and secondary level. In West Africa two Institutes have been delegated important curricular functions at primary level: at Ahmadu Bello and Sierra Leone Universities (the latter not until 1968). Other Nigerian Institutes have exercised influence to a slightly lesser degree: Nsukka, Ife, Lagos and Ibadan.

I have questioned the degree of control which university institutes assumed, but there must be no minimising the contribution they have made to a more rational and systematic form of curriculum development.

A university based institute offers the possibility for greater objectivity and a greater preoccupation with overall purposes than may be possible in a hard pressed Ministry, together with the potential (and it *remains* a potential) for linking research findings with the practical problems of curriculum design.

In two other respects certain Institutes developed important machinery for curriculum planning. The first regards the essential task of co-ordination between subjects and between levels and it was the Institute at Dar es Salaam which first developed a structure which has served as a useful model elsewhere. This is a system of *horizontal* and *vertical* panels, thus a primary, secondary or teacher training panel (horizontal) which co-ordinates and moderates activities for a particular educational level together with vertical panels, say in mathematics, science or music which are responsible for the overall and systematic development of a subject. Sub-panels and writers' groups report to the vertical panel and the whole is co-ordinated by the Institute's professional board. A further development of this pattern of interrelated panels and committees is provided by the Boards of Studies system at the Ahmadu Bello Institute of Education. In this model the curriculum for teachers' colleges and the examination system for both schools and colleges are closely linked with school curriculum development.[9]

(2) CURRICULUM DEVELOPMENT CENTRES

In some countries University Institutes did not assume such initial importance in curriculum development. Instead curriculum development centres were set up, physically separate from the Inspectorate and possessing some degree of autonomy, yet at the same time firmly established under Ministry control. In at least one case there was a deliberate policy decision *not* to involve the University. This was in Kenya where the Ministry of Education's special centres in English, mathematics and science were brought together into a Curriculum Development Centre in 1966 and the whole amalgamated with the Kenya Institute of Education, a non-university body which co-ordinated standards in teacher education in 1968. Other important curriculum development centres were set up in Ghana (1967) and Zambia (1970). In Uganda a centre set up in 1973 assumed control of many of the functions originally undertaken by the Institute.

Which is most important?

Deborah is an excellent teacher. If she is withdrawn from school for two years to help produce a new language course eighty children will lose out. What a pity! But then half a million children will benefit. The arithmetic seems to be very clear.

Yet how many times have Deborah or her brothers and sisters been refused secondment on the ground that they could not be spared either because 'there was no money' or because Peter, who could *very* thankfully be released, was sent off instead.

Because the efficiency of a curriculum development centre is a direct concern of the Ministry, there would appear to be a much greater probability that the very considerable staffing demands which curriculum development makes should be recognised. Bodies such as the Kenya Institute of Education with some thirty full-time professional staff and the Zambia Curriculum Development Centre with about forty,[10] would claim, probably rightly, that they were still understaffed and often experience difficulty in securing the release of the most able teachers from schools and colleges, but the provision made for them is certainly more realistic than that available in University Institutes like those in Ahmadu Bello or Sierra Leone.

A Ministry Centre has also the opportunity to establish far closer links with the means and process of implementation especially in regard to publishing and distribution of materials, trial, follow up and evaluation in schools. Such opportunities are obviously present in Kenya and Zambia though they do not appear always to work out in practice, one reason in Kenya being that centre personnel are continually called on to perform routine professional jobs such as practical examinations for final year college students. The fact that this happens so widely and the fact that *in relation to the volume and importance of the work they have to do, curriculum centres are still understaffed and under-funded* indicates that there still exists a rather strange ordering of educational priorities.

(3) CURRICULUM UNITS WITHIN MINISTRIES

But even a Ministry Curriculum Development Centre can find itself in some sense isolated from the main machinery of educational planning and administration and thus acquire a certain sense of unreality. The mere physical separation of personnel can be a real source of frustration. Until 1977 the Secretary of Nigeria's Educational Research Council[11] had to battle his way through the appalling Lagos traffic from Apapa to Lagos Island if he wanted to consult with his Permanent Secretary or Chief Federal Adviser. The Director of Swaziland's Curriculum Research and Development Unit at Manzini must motor miles to Mbabane if he wants to see the Chief Education Officer. Others may have shorter journeys but they are still in danger of being classed as 'those people from the Centre'. It is interesting to find, therefore, that in certain systems there has evolved a tighter and more centralised system of control with curriculum units established and housed within ministries of education. Thus certain states of Nigeria such as Bendel and Oyo States have curriculum units within Ministry Planning Divisions while under the latest reorganisation in Ghana, the Curriculum Development Division has been established as one of the divisions in the Ghana Education Service. The former curriculum and courses unit situated some miles from Accra has been closed and its personnel transferred into the new division.

(4) TOWARDS GREATER MINISTRY CONTROL

The pattern observed in Uganda, Nigeria and Ghana represents the same trend – a gentle but firm assumption of increasing control by ministries of the policies and

Table 4 Curriculum control patterns in ten African primary school systems (1978)

	ROLE OF THE MINISTRY	ROLE OF UNIVERSITIES AND/ OR INSTITUTES OF EDUCATION	ROLE OF TEACHER TRAINING ORGANISATIONS	OTHER IMPORTANT INFLUENCES
LESOTHO	(1) Primary Education Panel moderates policy: seven subject panels work to it. (2) A primary curriculum unit has researched on situational analysis in primary schools. (3) National Curriculum Development Centre being established.	No university or institute role in Lesotho.	(1) National Teachers' College controls teacher in-service education and influences diffusion of curriculum innovation. (2) Pre-service education contains a one year internship programme. (3) National Teachers' College is represented on the Primary Education Panel and widely on subject panels.	(1) A proposal to establish 26 Teachers' Centres is still in development. (2) A system of model schools to help diffuse curriculum ideas has been attempted. (3) Certain parts of the leaving examination are common with Botswana and Swaziland.
SWAZILAND	(1) Ministry has both a Curriculum Coordinating Committee with a subsidiary Primary Curriculum Panel, and a Primary Curriculum Unit, with subject panels. (2) The Ministry appointed Senior English Inspector is in charge of the primary 'English through Activity' programme.	(1) University Agricultural Department closely linked with the schools agriculture project. (2) No other university or institute role in Swaziland.	William Pitcher Teachers' College has powerful curriculum influence via teacher upgrading course which sends out correspondence materials and recommends books and aids to teacher interns.	(1) Proposal made for Teaching Innovation and Diffusion Centres. (2) As for Lesotho (3).
BOTSWANA	(1) Curriculum a ministerial responsibility but extensively modified locally. (2) National Curriculum Centre being set up.	No university or institute role in Botswana.	College based teams in in-service training project operate with local curriculum committees (college staff member/in-service training member/local education officer/headmasters/teachers).	(1) Two teacher centres: Lobatse and Serowe. (2) As for Lesotho (3).
ZAMBIA	(1) Curriculum Development Centre within the Ministry is responsible to the Inspectorate. (2) Examinations controlled by the Inspectorate under separate department.	University Institute of Education now reconstituted as Department of Adult and In-service Training and no longer deeply involved in curriculum development except for dissemination of materials via in-service advanced courses for primary schools.	(1) Teachers' colleges assessed and advised by Inspectorate concerning dissemination of new curriculum. (2) Colleges also responsible for bulk of in-service training. (3) National In-service Training College has special responsibility for curriculum development training.	An Audio-Visual Aids Department has some influence on the production of new materials.
TANZANIA	(1) Special sections within Ministry for design and coordination of special programmes, inspection and evaluation for primary schools.	Parastatal Institute of Education is autonomous from the University and responsible for developing new materials within Ministry guidelines.	Teachers colleges involved in testing and modifying materials produced by the Institute of Education also in pre-service/in-service training of teachers in the new materials.	(1) Examinations are responsibility of National Examinations Council (ministerial sub-dept.) which co-operates with development of new curricular materials. (2) Itinerant teacher educators act as pressure group for curriculum reform, also implement new materials locally.

KENYA	National Commission for Educational Objectives within Ministry has provided broad guidelines to curriculum policy.	(1) Kenya Institute of Education, independent of University, is the major influence (1976 Education Act defines its functions). (2) Despite teacher education responsibilities, a major part of KIE's task is in developing, and diffusing curriculum materials (via in-service training). (3) For (2) comprehensive system of subject panels established.	(1) Coordination of college curriculum organised by KIE. (2) College representation on all main curriculum panels. (3) A number of colleges closely linked with TAC's.	(1) Teachers Advisory Centres set up, coordinated by Inspectorate and increasingly also by KIE. (2) To a varying degree, local panels and teachers groups exist sometimes coordinated by the TAC's.
UGANDA	(1) Curriculum policy decisions are responsibility of Ministry subject panels. (2) Exams set by subject panels administered by separate Examinations Division. (3) Curriculum Development Centre responsible for formal and non-formal education.	National Institute of Education, at Makerere University, moderates college curriculum/exams in cooperation with the Curriculum Development Centre.	Teachers' college role limited to diffusing materials in regular training programmes.	(1) An Audio-Visual Aids Centre produces curriculum materials. Ministry, University and Teachers Colleges represented on its board. (2) No local teachers centres.
NIGERIA	*Federal* (1) Overall responsibility for national goals and directions of curriculum policy. Policy documents issued and statements made. (2) Exam policy to some degree Federal responsibility. (3) Nigerian Educational Research Council coordinates research and curriculum development policies. (4) National Guidelines issued as result of conferences and workshops. *State* (1) State ministries establish syllabuses; moderate local exams and prescribe texts. (2) Some states have Curriculum Development Centres.	(1) Ahmadu Bello Institute retains some responsibility for coordination of teacher education, curricula and examinations in northern states. (2) It coordinated activities of the influential PEIP programme. (3) Elsewhere university influence largely centred on research and training.	(1) Both Federal and State ministries operate teachers' colleges which serve only to implement changes and distribute material. (2) Mobile teacher trainers particularly in northern states act as implementers and may contribute to local variations. (3) National Teachers' Institute (Kaduna) likely to exercise important future influence.	(1) Science Teacher's Association an important pressure group. (2) Teachers' Centres in some states.
GHANA	Ghana Education Service has one of its 5 Divisions concerned with curriculum research and development.	Faculty of Education at Cape Coast University has close ties with the Curriculum Research and Development Division of the Ghana Education Service.	National Training Council, in charge of teacher certification and in-service training, diffuses ideas and materials.	(1) Bureau of Ghanaian Languages influential in producing mother-tongue materials. (2) District Teachers' Resource Centres responsible for diffusion: design and production of materials being carried out more centrally. (3) Certain parts of leaving exams are common with Sierra Leone and Gambia. (4) West African Regional Mathematics Project (WARMP) and SEPA science have influenced primary curricula.
SIERRA LEONE	Ministry maintains overall responsibility for curriculum, but works largely through the Institute of Education.	(1) Institute of Education, attached to University with governing council including Ministry and University officials, has major responsibility through panels for curriculum development. (2) Sierra Leone Education Review (university sponsored) made important policy recommendations in 1974. (3) National Curriculum Revision Unit sited at the Institute. Curriculum conferences and national seminar on primary teacher education have been held.	(1) Resource centres located in teachers' colleges have been proposed. (2) Bunumbu Community College undertakes experimental work in ruralised curricula.	(1) WARMP and the science centre established for the SEPA programme have influenced primary curricula. (2) As for Ghana (3).

mechanisms of curriculum planning. The same trends are observable in both Zambia and in Tanzania where we have witnessed the gradual shift of power and responsibilities from a University organised Institute to a national one and from the Institute into the Ministry itself.

DIFFERENT AGENCIES, DIFFERENT ROLES

Table 4 indicates briefly the bodies currently responsible for primary curriculum control in ten countries. What emerges from any comparative analysis of the tasks of curriculum planning and responses to them is that no one centre or unit can adequately accomplish them all. Ideally structures within a country should –

– be closely related to decision making and planning including financial appropriation;
– be sufficiently autonomous to exercise a degree of flexibility;
– have links with sources of information concerning the system to be changed – e.g. research and survey;
– be closely linked with machinery for dissemination of information about changes and their implementation in schools;
– be involved in evaluation both of product and process.

Some of these functions are best performed by University Institutes, some by a Curriculum Development Centre, some by a Curriculum Planning Unit and it is therefore possible that functions which may hitherto have been seen as either wholly performed by this body or that may increasingly be undertaken in partnership. There are indications, particularly from Nigeria, that this is beginning to happen. Yet it seems nevertheless as inevitable as it is logical that the prime mover and co-ordinator of curriculum planning and development must be a national Ministry of Education.

Planning activities undertaken centrally

In a centralised education system, the setting up of machinery to undertake curriculum planning and development is no more than a means towards making possible the six processes I outlined at the beginning of this chapter and which in our ideal world should have happened logically at national level: laying a research base for change, deciding objectives, forming a strategy, developing materials, implementing them and evaluating both the process and the result – a clinical sequence which even the methodical Swedes[12] did not perform to their satisfaction.

Yet, as we have already noted, the sequence of events in Africa was neither logical nor ideal. There were too many outside pressures. Subject-based curriculum programmes thrusted in very insistently and very early in the game. Facilities and activities for gathering basic information (described in Chapter 2) were relatively few and late. Curriculum development programmes of some magnitude got going before ever attempts were made to chart national goals or directions for educational advance. Machinery for curriculum development was often set up and put in motion in advance of machinery for its co-ordination with other educational activities. Yet once the processes were under way and the machinery was set up there did come the realisation that national goals must be set, often coupled with the very welcome awareness that this process is far too important a one to be left solely in the hands of the curriculum developers themselves.

NATIONAL GOALS AND DIRECTIONS

The extent to which national goals for primary education have been consciously set and conscientiously followed varies in emphasis from country to country. There are two ways, not mutually exclusive, by which goals may be set and subsequently made public – through a political announcement of national policy and philosophy and its application to the school system and/or by seeking some form of consensus through a commission, review or national symposium. In either case the initial statement is merely the beginning of a long road. The goals must be debated and discussed until their true implications are appreciated, then their application worked out in terms of the curriculum planning and development decisions they imply at the various stages of the educational process. These include the selection of subjects and their emphasis, the way teachers are trained, how materials are written and presented, the content and conduct of assessment procedures and a host of other key decisions.

The most influential example of a political lead in curriculum policy is Nyerere's pamphlet *Education for Self-Reliance* published in 1967, a direct follow up of Tanu's Arusha Declaration. The content and implications of this document have been very widely analysed and debated as has the Tanzanian reaction to it, but a few short passages need perhaps to be quoted yet again if only to underline the very fundamental challenges it poses for curriculum planners. I have selected from a wealth of alternatives:

1 '. . . we want to create a socialist society which is based on three principles: *equality and respect for human dignity; sharing resources which are produced by our efforts; work by everyone.*'

2 '. . . This means that the educational system of Tanzania must emphasize co-operative endeavour, not individual advancement; it must stress concepts of equality and the responsibility to give service which goes with any special ability, whether it be in carpentry, in animal husbandry, or in academic pursuits.'

3 'It must also prepare young people for the work they will be called upon to do in the society which exists in Tanzania – a rural society where improvement will depend largely upon the efforts of the people in Agriculture and village development.'

4 'Schools must, in fact, become communities – and communities which practice the precept of self-reliance. The teachers, workers, and pupils together must be members of a social unit in the same way as parents, relatives, and children are the family social unit. . . . This is not a suggestion that a school farm or workshop should be attached to every school for training purposes. It is a suggestion that every school should also be a farm; that the school community should consist of people who are both teachers and farmers, and pupils and farmers.'

5 'Increasingly children are starting school at six or even five years of age, so that they finish primary school when they are too young to become responsible young workers and citizens. On top of that is the fact that the society and type of edu-

An impartial commission of enquiry
(Englishmen imported to tell Kenyans what to teach)

I am sorry for Mr Gordon Bessey. He must have suspected that his all British commission was hardly the kind of body that Kenyans either needed or were likely to listen to in 1972. Indeed the detailed, cautious, inconclusive report of the commission is probably now of more interest to outsiders like me than it is to the Kenyans.

I am told by some Kenyan cynics I fell in with that the commission was appointed largely to satisfy demands from one aid donor (was it the World Bank?). Such attitudes to both the giving and receiving of aid (and they are so common) spell the same dismal answer – an opportunity missed, for how much could have been achieved by a well-funded *national* commission.

Reminiscence from the Nigerian National Workshop on Primary Education

I was invited to attend as a 'participating observer' and the time I spent in the Social Studies group, I remember as one of the most exciting and productive in my educational experience, marred only by the fact that the conference had to end a little early because the money ran out. I remember thinking at the time that someone had got their priorities wrong. In retrospect I am sure I am right.

Opportunities to come together, to think, to plan, to chart the future are not occasions for financial economy.

cation they have received both led them to expect wage employment – probably in an office. . . . This problem calls for a major change in the content of our primary education and for the raising of the school entry age so that the child is older when he leaves, and also able to learn more quickly while he is in school.'

6 'One difficulty in the way of this kind of re-organisation is the present examination system. . . . There is no reason why Tanzania should not combine an examination, which is based on the things we teach, with a teacher and pupil assessment of work done for the school and community.'[13]

I have selected these six passages because they appear to me to call effectively for a rethinking of practically every aspect of the pre-1967 school curriculum in Tanzania – its underlying values, the structure, the balance between in-school and out-of-school activities, the content and pacing of the materials in relation to the age of the learners and the whole process and attitude towards evaluation.

Since the publication of 'Education for Self-Reliance', the process of transforming these goals into curriculum plans and curriculum practice has been taking place, somewhat languidly at first, but with increasing momentum. But 'old attitudes die hard,'[14] and nobody I have spoken to from Tanzania is under any illusion that the changes in content which have been undertaken in curriculum plans and examination policies necessarily reflect a change of heart among all teachers or parents.

The political lead provided to curriculum planners in Tanzania is present in varying degrees in other countries. In Zambia it is strong.

The President's statement 'Humanism in Zambia' (1967),[15] subsequent declarations at Mulungushi (1968),[16] Kabwe (1972)[17] and the cabinet pronouncement (1975) that schools must become production units, provide a general, but relatively clear brief for education planners and have been clearly reflected in the Zambian Education Review (1976).[18] Elsewhere, too, there have been significant statements: the Kenya Government Sessional Paper 'African Socialism and its Application to Planning in Kenya' (1965),[19] Seretse Khama's 'Education for a Nation' (1969),[20] a speech which deserves to be better known than it is, and the statement of the Imbokodvo National Movement in Swaziland (1972).[21] Development plans in these countries and others also carry statements of national intent. In one country, Malawi, the President has taken a somewhat extreme stand against 'modern methods' in education and has forbidden their use.

The second way in which national guidelines for curriculum policy have emerged is through conferences, reviews or national commissions. Education commission reports past and present have always addressed themselves in varying degrees of rigour to the analysis of educational objectives and it would be possible to collect an impressive dossier of high minded statements of intent. Of most interest to us, however, are those initiatives particularly concerned with defining and refining educational objectives and with laying down guidelines for curricular policy. We note the university-based Sierra Leone Education Review (1974)[22] and subsequent curriculum conferences in 1976; Kenya's 1972 enquiry and report 'Curriculum Development in Kenya' (oddly undertaken by an all British commission) and its current national commission on Education Objectives; Uganda's inaugural National Curriculum Conference in August 1976; Nigeria's National Curriculum Conference (1969)[23] and National Seminar on Policy of Education (1973).

The Nigerian Curriculum Conference and the National Workshop on Primary Education which followed it in 1971 are important for a number of reasons:

(i) Although some foreign observers were present at the conference and a few expatriate lecturers attended the primary workshop, all the decisions were made by Nigerians (a state of affairs somewhat unique for its time).

(ii) At the conference a successful effort had been made to invite informed opinion not only from the educational community but from many interest groups within Nigeria, an initiative which met with a splendid response and which led, with the help of some skilful chairmanship and competent editing to the production of a useful and sensible working document.

(iii) At the workshop the organisers had managed to unite informed educational opinion throughout Nigeria and to establish a productive working climate in which panels in six areas of the primary school curriculum: *cultural and creative art, languages, mathematics, physical and health education, science* and *social studies*[24] met and in the light of the goals set at the 1969 Curriculum Conference expanded and refined objectives in these areas and produced a series of guidelines which have since been used throughout Nigeria at university and state level as a basis for detailed curriculum planning.

There are many ways in which, in retrospect, we may find fault with the procedures adopted in Nigeria; lengthy time gaps between conferences and in the production of the reports; shortcomings in follow up and publicity (largely due to inadequate funding and staffing of the NERC); failures in articulation of content and approach between subject areas; an overloading of committees with university academics. But for all these criticisms there was still a serious and effective attempt to involve the best minds in the country in laying a foundation for curriculum decision making and to provide an instrument to ensure that detailed curriculum plans reflected this.

PROGRAMMES AND PROJECTS UNDERTAKEN

Once a curriculum development centre or similar body is established, it naturally sets about developing curricula, usually with some fervour. So, with considerable encouragement from overseas donors, the institutes, centres and units described earlier produced in the late 'sixties and early 'seventies a very impressive crop of programmes and projects, sometimes linked with programmes of syllabus renewal, sometimes more or less independent of them. In subject curriculum development, schemes in Mathematics, Science and English predominated, a number being linked more or less closely with the EDC's African Education projects described earlier, but some, like the UNESCO sponsored science project in the Bendel State of Nigeria, of different parentage and philosophy.

Multinational publishers also made a considerable contribution and investment to the process of subject curriculum development, in co-operation with institutes and centres, through the funding of writers' workshops in Science, Mathematics and later, Social Studies and in the production, on numerous occasions, of trial editions, particularly of language courses. This healthy contribution of commercial interests, which, after all, have experience and technical know-how which is often in short supply in ministries, deserves more recognition than it has received, especially since it does much to offset the squalid tale of the involvement by one British company at this time in corrupt monopoly state publishing ventures during the Obote and Nkrumah governments in Uganda and Ghana. Yet these examples, too, are significant, for they underline the unfortunate truth that the production and distribution of books to primary schools are important enough, financially, to attract the very largest species of shark against whom the professional at the ministry or in the centre (who is usually no more than an average sized fish) has little redress.

LARGER SCALE CURRICULUM PROJECTS

But piecemeal modifications of school curricula were often considered inappropriate, particularly in the light of new national policies and structures. Thus a number of much larger curriculum reform schemes were undertaken.

The first and probably the most influential of these grew from small beginnings. The *New Primary Approach* in Kenya derived from a research project carried out in twenty-five Asian schools in Nairobi, experimenting basically with the teaching of English (the Peak Course) but at the same time with new and active approaches to teaching young children.

The success of the scheme was rapid and spectacular, borne along by the enthusiasm of organisers and experimental staff alike and by the conviction that here was a programme far more relevant and exciting than anything Kenya had had previously (which it was). So the material spread into all Asian schools and, after modification, into selected African ones (the New Peak); from towns where supervision was easy and teachers well-trained to country where supervision was infrequent and teachers far less well-grounded. What had started as a 'new look' language course began to be seen as a new approach to teaching children based on a new and popular medium – English. A follow-up language course, the Safari Course, was devised, and programmes framed by the language section of the newly formed Curriculum Development Centre were to be integrated with those prepared in other subject sections. Training for English medium was made compulsory in all teachers' colleges and a government decision was taken, at political level, to provide for extension of English medium teaching to all schools in Kenya where there was local demand for it. Government took over field supervision of the project with eager help from the USAID. These were heady days when the wine was new.

Nowadays in Kenya nobody is quite so happy or so optimistic about the NPA, for though it survives in urban schools its extension proved to be full of problems. In the first place the scheme literally drowned in its own success. The extension went too far, too fast. Time available for in-service training was cut and cut again. Supervision arrangements broke down. There were pained complaints about pseudo-literacy or even of illiteracy in upper classes.

More fundamentally perhaps, people are asking themselves, 'Why did we all want English medium anyway?' and there is a rather bitter feeling around that perhaps all the enthusiasm, all the euphoria about 'new methods' ought to have been preceded by a sober consideration of 'new objectives.' Sadly indeed, the pendulum

Appropriate reading?

One of the things that really annoyed us in the Ministry was when the Publisher's representative used to go straight into the Minister's office and dictate letters which the Minister then signed.

But even that wasn't as bad as some of the titles which appeared on the 'recommended' lists (in a desperate attempt to clear old stock, I suppose). One English book was entitled *Mr Kneebones' Hobbies*. Another called *Toby and Bilbo* and recommended for Primary 2 contained passages such as the following: 'Toby's friends are coming up the path now. They are Don Donkey, Kitty Cat and Tom Cat, Perky Sparrow, Pip Puppy Dog, Gerty Cow, Terry Tortoise and Busy Bee.'

A visitor to Kagumo NPA 1964

'The teacher was not highly qualified but very much alive and specially trained in English medium teaching at Kagumo Training College nearby; the children had been learning English for six months. Everyone in the room seemed to be engaged; I have seldom seen children more eager to talk and learn and think. . . .

'The peak of the lesson was an exercise in mental arithmetic involving very simple addition of halves, quarters and units. The thinking was done in English and the answers came out in English right or wrong. The teacher queried one boy's answer, he stood in rapt recalculation, you could almost hear his brain working. "No, it is one and a quarter, sir," and he was right.'

From *Growing Up in East Africa*, by E. B. Castle, OUP 1966, p 211.

seems to have swung, as it does swing on the education clock, so far away from the New Primary Approach that even the integrated approach to lower primary teaching, which had been so wisely and effectively urged, is no longer reflected in the current Kenya syllabus.

Meanwhile at least one offspring of the NPA flourishes – the 'English Through Activity' programme in Swaziland, where I found similar activity and enthusiasm in schools, talked to a committed supervisor who saw her role entirely as getting her materials – including issues of English Ladybird books – to rural schools as efficiently as possible and of encouraging 'active learning', (but of what and why she took little heed). However, at the primary curriculum unit in the building next door, I encountered a growing unease, a growing preoccupation with purpose.

THE PRIMARY EDUCATION IMPROVEMENT PROJECT

A second and rather later example of a large scale curriculum project is provided by the Primary Education Improvement Project in Northern Nigeria which started in 1970 and until 1977 received considerable support from UNESCO and UNICEF. This extremely ambitious programme, co-ordinated by the Institute of Education at Ahmadu Bello University and operating in six (now ten) of the northern states, sought to effect a complete change of approach in primary schools, through new courses in either Hausa or English medium depending on the policy in operation in the states. Eleven centres were selected near to teachers' colleges or state capitals and in each six experimental schools identified.[25] Prototype materials were tried out in these schools with the help of field curriculum workers (mobile teacher trainers whose story we shall take up in a later chapter) and later refined and distributed in final form to a further eight hundred schools with a similar scale of supervision, in the hope that these would serve as a nucleus in each state for further dissemination to other schools. The materials developed by the project were happily in line with the national objectives and syllabus guidelines developed in '69 and '71. They were relevant, exciting and highly ambitious in the knowledge and skills they demanded of teachers. Despite attempts to recommend local materials, the per capita costs of the scheme were also high and there seems to have been a certain 'willing suspension of disbelief' about the local capacity to provide replacements for all the goodies originally supplied by UNICEF.

In planning terms the scheme was understaffed and the whole operation conducted at a headlong speed rendered necessary by the short perspective and the uncertainty of UNICEF funding.

I had been personally concerned (and I employ the word in both its senses) with this project in its early stages. It was therefore particularly interesting to visit, with my colleague, ministries and schools in two of the states concerned, Kano and Benue Plateau in 1976, to read current reports from other centres and to talk with colleagues at Ahmadu Bello – six years 'into' the project. Enthusiasm for the content of the materials – especially in lower primary classes – was still clearly evident and at state level there was considerable resolve to maintain aspects of the new curriculum and the closer supervision it entailed in at least some schools, despite the challenge of universal primary education which effectively meant that

On the treadmill

In the Kenya Institute of Education I meet excellent teams producing good materials in Language and Mathematics. They are cheerful, competent, overworked and understaffed. A series is in course of production and implementation in both areas, and once a programme is introduced in Class I this is the beginning of a seven year ride which cannot be slowed down or stopped.

In both subjects I am told that more time and more help is needed to spread the ideas, to run courses, to try out new approaches in different situations, to evaluate the success of the last step before embarking on the next, but the curriculum workers I met were disturbed that they were unable to provide what they knew teachers needed. Yet these men and women are well off compared to their counterparts in Ghana where subject teams had been given just nine months to produce new curriculum plans and to launch a new series of materials to fit a 'new content and structure of education' announced by the cabinet.

At a conference (Nigeria 1971)

First delegate: That Mathematics syllabus is too difficult. Rural children in the North wouldn't be able to follow it.

Second delegate: It's been tested. The children at the Lagos University Demonstration School have no difficulty with it.

Postscript (1979)
It was adopted. Rural children in the North could not follow it adequately. Poor teaching was blamed.

everyone had to try to do more with less. Moreover, a number of materials developed by the project have since been commercially published and are in use in Nigeria. Yet only a very modest proportion of its original grandiose objectives had been achieved. There had been no sweeping transformation of schools in the northern states in Nigeria and there *never could have been*.

HOW FAR AND HOW FAST?

Certain common elements in the New Primary Approach and the Primary Education Improvement Project – ambitious goals and policies, unrealistic time scales, high hopes and eventual very fragmentary success – may be traced in other big centralised projects throughout Africa. Indeed several schemes in their very early stages, like the current hurried reorganisation in Ghana, and the plans announced in 1977 for curriculum revision in Cameroon, carry in their very planning, like a Greek tragedy, the seeds of eventual disillusion.

At first sight the solution looks easy: attempt less, more slowly. But in practice this is very difficult to achieve. Subjects depend on each other. National objectives postulate certain contents. Parents demand others. Curriculum workers are resolutely opposed to excluding content and approaches which they know, with good teaching, to be within the grasp of a fair percentage of the nation's children. It can also be clearly demonstrated that the 'best' curricula as designed by centres in Ghana, Nigeria or Kenya are within the competence of the 'best' schools, teachers and children. So who wants to level downwards? Shouldn't targets always be set high so that we should have something to aim at? These are comfortable philosophies for middle class educationists with school age children of their own.

There are no instant answers to this dilemma, but two partial solutions present themselves. The first lies in increasing the efficiency of the curriculum development workers themselves through heightening their awareness of the growth points and problems in the schemes they are developing. The beginnings of preoccupation with educational evaluation described at the end of this chapter represents one response, the prospect of more widespread training, examined in Chapter 9, another. The second lies in the adoption of a more flexible and decentralised policy for curriculum planning and implementation.

Decentralisation and curriculum planning

The orthodoxy of educational planning and aid policy is subject to spectacular changes as world politics change, as the advice so confidently given and taken in former years proves not to yield the promised fruit, as old gurus are discredited and new ones rise to take their place. In the early nineteen-sixties they liked their policy centralised (and linked to manpower projections) and their institutions big. So there were big hospitals, big schools, big colleges, big curriculum development centres.

Now the song has changed. The World Bank sector review of December 1974, with the same olympian assurance[26] that formerly urged big units, centralised control and emphasis on the secondary sector, now advocated basic education, small institutions and decentralisation. 'Vector planning', another term currently in vogue,[27] suggests that we build unevenly using natural growth points within systems rather than devising elegant (and unworkable) master plans. We begin to accept that in education, as in economics, small can be beautiful.[28]

In this new climate new policies for curriculum development are much easier to envisage, for they support what I herald as a return to common sense. For as the somewhat disappointing fruits of big, centralised curriculum projects become apparent, as the essential human and uneven character of curriculum development comes to be appreciated, more and more systems are seeking alternatives.

Two different types of approach may be detected. The first is the willingness to mount genuine experimental projects (as distinct from 'trial' or 'experimental' schools in curriculum projects committed from the very start to widespread implementation), the second the building up of machinery for curriculum development at local level.

EXPERIMENTAL CURRICULUM PROJECTS

A conventional 'project school' modifies trial curricula but undertakes no fundamental changes. For these to be undertaken it is necessary to mount a separate 'experimental' project, but since children are not white mice it is necessary first to enlist enough parental support to allow people to give them their children to experiment on, and enough official support to ensure that in matters such as official examinations, children who have followed radically different curricula do not suffer. For this reason, although it is possible for an armchair academic like me to imagine a number of very profitable working experiments taking place involving length of schooling, age of entry and patterns of teacher deployment, in fact such controlled experiments are not common. But the potential of such 'working models' is well illustrated by those which have been mounted. Two in particular in Namutamba (Uganda) and Ife (Nigeria) have attracted continent-wide interest because they are examining issues of importance to practically everyone.

The *Namutamba Rural Education Project* started in 1967, is based on a teachers' college and involves fifteen primary schools near the town of Mityana, some fifty miles from Kampala. The project examines possible approaches towards providing more relevant locally orientated curricula for rural children and strengthening links between the school and the rural community.[29] To this end the formal school operates a single morning session of five hours leaving the rest of the day for projects undertaken by students which are seen as complementary to the in-class programme. These include written assignments of various types and a number of community-based schemes such as brick making for home improvement, apprenticeship schemes, young farmers' club activities and workshop practice. During the afternoon the school buildings are used for a variety of adult education and community purposes and teachers undertake further community work outside them.

Uganda, it hardly needs to be said, currently faces problems in translating the results of this experiment into practical action, but the results and experience gained have been well publicised to the obvious benefit of other systems in Africa.[30]

The *Ife Six Year Primary Project* demonstrates just how profitable a well-run and well-funded project can be. The project which started in 1970 in one experimental school, and in 1973 extended to classes in ten more, is administered from the University of Ife with the co-operation from the state Ministry of Education and with financial assistance from the Ford Foundation.

The main aims of the project as described by its organisers were as follows:

1 The project will make it possible to test the validity of the claim that primary education received in the mother tongue is richer and more meaningful than that received in a second language.
2 Solutions to the problems accompanying the adoption of a Nigerian language (such as Yoruba) as the medium of instruction will be stimulated.
3 It is hoped that the experiment will suggest a solution to the perennial problem of teaching English effectively to Nigerian children.[31]

The initial emphasis of the project was therefore linguistic and, clinically examined, it might have appeared that to carry on with current curricula, making the change of language policy the only variable, would have made for more easily comparable results. But since good teachers, like the project staff at Ife, put children first, they considered themselves to be in duty bound to devise the best possible workable curriculum for the school. Consequently the project became as concerned with curriculum issues as it did with linguistic ones. The whole operation and the monitoring of it was thus rendered more complicated, yet at the same time the experiment became far richer.

Using national and state curriculum guidelines as a basis[32] parallel texts are devised in both English and Yoruba, children in Yoruba medium streams being taught English as a subject from Class 1 – in the experimental school by specialist teachers, in the expansion classes by the regular class teacher. Approaches are somewhat more teacher-centred and consequently easier to handle by average teachers than parallel material from the Primary Education Improvement Project in the North, but interesting and relevant nevertheless. Copious reading material, cheaply produced, is made available to children and in one class I visited each child had ten substantial units to read in Yoruba, in addition to the English language text and supplementary readers. In all, the project has produced 400 trial publications. Per capita costs of material appear low, but the project is so small that production costs are minimal and a great deal of good will and free time has gone into material production and distribution.

Attempts at evaluation of the project continue, but in terms of establishing conclusively whether children 'learn better' through Yoruba or English, they are unlikely to achieve the precision which the Ford Foundation would like to see – largely because of the very richness of the project.

Subjective assessments are said to be less acceptable, but I offer mine, nevertheless, drawn from my own studies of the literature of the project (including one evaluation so far completed), from talks with project workers and brief visits to schools. I recognise that it may also be tinged with a note of bias, for I passionately believe with the project organisers that school and community are parallel and co-operative agencies in the education of young children, and that to establish

A true story from Ife (1976)

Tunde, aged 10, in the Yoruba medium class, had been asked in his Social Studies class to find out details from his father about a local festival. At first father was unwilling . . . it had nothing to do with school, he said. But Tunde persisted, father told him, and Tunde made his contribution in class – with great success. He went back and told his father. A few days later the father told a project worker, 'You know that was the first time I felt I had something to offer to the school.'

understanding, as well as to promote real creativity, children should begin reading and learning in the language they speak at home.

I would assess the project as follows:

1 It has shown how effectively a locally based curriculum unit can devise and produce trial materials using the strengths of both the university and the school system.
2 It has indicated that children in experimental Yoruba medium classes do not appear to suffer either in their knowledge of English or in their performance in a final state examination in English.
3 It suggests that children in these classes are better adjusted, more relaxed and resourceful than children in parallel English medium classes.
4 A great deal of useful information on the problems of both Yoruba medium and English subject teaching has been gained and a critical analysis of currently recommended English teaching material is still in progress.

Perhaps I have been over enthusiastic about this project, but there was something about the schools I visited, and I am no stranger to African primary schools, which seemed to me to provide a recipe for steady progress. The children could read the books, the teachers could understand the method, the parents could understand the children, the university understood the schools. Ford's money may have been in evidence, but Ford's men were not. It was all Nigerian from start to finish.

LOCALISED CURRICULUM DEVELOPMENT

A second and probably a more significant aspect of decentralisation is where a certain measure of local autonomy or local initiative is encouraged by central authorities.

In Nigeria federal authority is very naturally devolved to state ministries, but these are larger in size and population than many sovereign African states, so it is within states as well as within smaller nations that true devolution is to be sought.

Increasingly it is to be found and in a number of different forms. In several countries local 'curriculum implementers' of one species or another have been appointed and in the main they have proved to be conscientious and down-to-earth professionals who do an exceptionally useful job. In Tanzania they are called 'itinerant teacher educators', in Northern Nigeria 'mobile teacher trainers' (possibly an English translation of the former), in Ghana 'local subject organisers'. In each case they have proved a potentially effective instrument for channelling productive local suggestions and for achieving sensible modifications in centrally designed materials. Meetings and feedback sessions in which they share local experiences have proved very valuable.

In other areas teachers' centres are beginning to be set up, and I shall be discussing their current effectiveness and future potential in Chapter 6. While these are primarily still seen as centres where teachers come to learn things, there are some instances where in small measure local curricula and local materials are beginning to emerge. In Kenya, for example, interesting and original booklets on local history are being prepared at teachers' centres, supported in some cases by collections of traditional artefacts. This area is seen as only one of a number of possible future points of development, for plans are being discussed for setting up a linked structure of subject panels from national down to district and location level to give all teachers the opportunity to comment on materials and raise suggestions for new approaches. Indeed the Director of Kenya's Institute of Education looks forward to a time when a syllabus may be devised which, in addition to a national 'core', has specific defined areas where programmes devised at district or local levels will be developed and implemented. No one in Kenya underestimates the amount of thought still necessary to get these proposals from the discussion to the operational stage, but they are on the table and they are exciting.

In Botswana the principle of limited decentralisation was accepted as Ministry policy in the establishment of an 'in-service project', with support from the British Ministry of Overseas Development, based on the country's three in-service colleges with a co-ordinator at the Central Ministry of Education. It was envisaged that teachers' centres would be set up based on the three colleges and that these would combine in-service course work with active experimentation on new approaches. An initial memorandum from the Chief Education Officer elaborates the policy:

> 'At this initial stage the priority is to help teachers to adopt more enlightened approaches to learning. Naturally this will also involve a much more critical look at the existing syllabuses and there will be areas where it will be felt that curricular reforms consistent with enlightened teaching and effective learning are imperative. If so, any school or group of schools in consultation with the College and the leader of the in-service team may decide to depart from a particular syllabus or portions of it and develop in its place new material which after being tried out and improved upon may be passed on to other schools and colleges for use on a wider scale with the approval of the Ministry. This will be a definite contribution to a continuous process of renewal of syllabuses and closely linked and incidental to teacher education.'[33]

A further innovation in Botswana has been the setting up of local curriculum development committees. According to the Ministry memorandum their membership should be as follows:

1 the local Education/Assistant Education Officer (or Chairman)
2 a member of the in-service team
3 a member of the College staff
4 a Headmaster from one of the local primary schools
5 a teacher from one of the local primary schools

In Francistown, where the idea of a local curriculum committee has been most warmly adopted, the actual committee is considerably larger including head teachers of all local primary schools where new approaches are being tried. Its organisers look on the participation of these head teachers who have become very active as they become increasingly involved, as an indispensible and exciting part of the committee's operations.

The Ministry's circular suggested the following as possible roles for the committees:

1 Identification of problem areas in the current syllabuses;
2 Suggestions as to the necessary modifications;
3 Advice on the programme of work to be done in the schools;
4 Preparations for workshops, seminars and courses;
5 Assistance with displays at the Teachers' Centres where these exist and encouragement of displays in schools;
6 Encouragement of regular visits to the Centres by teachers and guidance and help to teachers with regard to sources of information and other material;
7 Such other functions as may become necessary.

In practice considerably more has been attempted in Francistown including suggestions for production of localised materials and in some cases their actual design and issue. A very important function appears to be the discussion and rationalisation of conflicting demands for materials made upon local councils and the drawing up of agreed minimum lists of equipment.

Policies in Botswana have not worked out as smoothly as expected. There have been personality clashes, difference of opinion on degrees of centralisation and devolution, but, quite apart from successes in individual subject projects, it has been shown that in at least one instance, a local curriculum committee can be made to work productively, a model well worth studying.

CURRICULUM DEVELOPMENT THROUGH IN-SERVICE TRAINING

One further interesting model of decentralised curriculum development is provided through the various new patterns of in-service teacher training which are emerging. The provision of opportunities here for introducing and monitoring new materials is now beginning to be realised and opens very exciting possibilities. I discuss it at some length in Chapter 6.

Machinery for evaluation

Essential in the process of curriculum reform is the control of two aspects of evaluation. They are:

1 The evaluation of *outcomes* through the examination processes and alternatives to them (both internal and external).
2 The evaluation of the *process* of curriculum planning and development.

(1) EVALUATION OF OUTCOMES

Curriculum planners would all agree that it is necessary to establish strong and efficient links between the machinery for curriculum development and public assessment. Indeed most would argue that both were part of the same operation. But they find it strangely difficult to do. In the first place the setting up of machinery for examination and selection predates the creation of means to plan and develop curriculum. So bodies such as the West African Examination Council

Straight talking (from Tanzania's Commissioner of National Education at the closing speech at a seminar on evaluation)

'You are now better equipped to carry out your challenging task of educational evaluation. Let us not, however, be complacent. . . . You will need the co-operation and the involvement of many types of people in carrying out your tasks. This raises the necessity of transferring what you know and will know about educational evaluation to other people in many other disciplines. This, I consider, is a vital task if Tanzania is to satisfy its need for qualified, experienced evaluators who are supported by an informed, critical and positively motivated public and is also to establish, on a long-term basis, a systematic, effective and efficient evaluation programme. For I believe educational evaluation, in its broad interpretation, is the sole means for ensuring the progressive and enlightened development of the people the educational system serves. Goals are often too readily set and aims too ambitiously expressed and unless a systematic (scientific) examination is made of the methods utilised to achieve these ends, there is the danger that progress may be slowed or even upset. . . .'

From Michael Kinunda's speech at the *African Regional Seminar on Education Evaluation*, Dar es Salaam, 1975.

are already institutionalised and, in considerable measure, resistant to change.

Nor do curriculum planners usually get any really dedicated help from administrators or politicians, for a single, centralised and not too complicated final examination ensures quiet rest for both Minister and civil servant.

Yet the issue at stake, is not merely the content of the final examination. It is its whole style and importance. For current examinations seem to carry with them a number of hidden assumptions:

1 that only the final product of the primary school system is worthy of serious evaluation;
2 that only knowledge or skills (such as language skills) of national relevance are worth testing;
3 that the only kind of learning worth seriously measuring is that which can be evaluated by making a mark on a card for subsequent ingestion by a machine (An awful corollary to this is that judgments made by human beings must be given less weight than electronically certified facts.)

Of deep concern, also, is the fact that in many countries machinery and criteria for final assessment of primary school children (with all the feedback that this brings into the school curriculum) are still dominated by the requirements of selection for Secondary School despite the obvious truth of Nyerere's statement that those capable of further education will readily identify themselves.

These issues are discussed later in greater detail, but even at this point they must be raised and current policies and machinery for assessment and selection set alongside those for curriculum planning and development described earlier in this chapter. For in some cases the one practically negates the other.

Currently in some areas, concern is breeding action towards designing better methods of testing and, more fundamentally, towards a shift in policy which places greater emphasis on regional and school-based methods of assessment. These, too, are examined in my next chapter.

Yet for all this, more co-ordinated machinery still has to emerge and I confess to experiencing a certain sour taste of insincerity when I hear educational leaders talking about promoting a relevant and dynamic curriculum for primary schools, yet notice that they are hastening most slowly in providing the assessment policy needed to enable this to happen.

(2) EVALUATION OF THE PROCESS

This aspect of evaluation is only just beginning to receive the attention it deserves. The word 'evaluation' is sagely introduced into most conferences by most speakers. The International Institute for Educational Planning held an important and, I understand, effective regional seminar on education evaluation in Dar es Salaam in 1975 which has led on to a certain degree of follow-up in a number of countries. An International Centre for Educational Evaluation has been established in Ibadan and, though currently very understaffed, has made a useful start in mounting long training courses in evaluation and in undertaking evaluation of curriculum projects at the request of their organisers (among which are the Namutamba and

Ife projects described earlier in the chapter). In one national primary curriculum unit (Swaziland) a full time evaluator has been included from the very inception of the work.

Yet apart from the obvious general fact that there is still insufficient concern about process evaluation and that there is a regrettable tendency for people to embark upon long and costly courses of action without carefully considering whether they are necessary or possible, there remain two major issues to cause concern in the countries I visited.

The first is that there still exists a widespread misunderstanding about the nature and purpose of evaluation. Formative evaluation (to use the current jargon), is so obviously more important than summative, since you need to modify things as they develop rather than wring your hands over them when they have failed. Yet an evaluation seems so often to be understood more as a sort of independent commission of enquiry undertaken at a fairly late stage in the life of a programme or project by 'experts' from outside whose findings may or may not be in straightforward language.

There is a need for such evaluators, but they are surely a very minor part in a much larger process, for evaluation is foremost an attitude of mind backed up by a series of techniques which may, indeed, be very simple and which affect all the workers from the start and throughout the project. The development of the APSP and SEPA materials provide, I believe, a very fair example of this kind of formative evaluation in action.

The second concern is that evaluation is largely a wasted exercise unless it leads on to some action. In a number of cases, however, there may be a tendency to regard it, rather, as a sort of libation to the gods – a project or programme acquiring a certain added respectability by being evaluated, but with no deep-seated resolve on the part of its organisers to make any substantial organisational or financial investment in change (after all to contemplate fundamental change to a primary programme once it is underway is an exceptionally costly business).

Yet in spite of these areas of concern, there is growing pragmatism and reality everywhere apparent in Africa among politicians and educationists – a measure of confidence gained and success achieved. This provides a firm basis for the new interest in evaluation and an earnest desire for its continued growth.

Issues raised in this chapter

Three issues are particularly relevant to this chapter: planning, balance and dissemination.

(1) THE ISSUE OF PLANNING

The issue of planning is complex since it involves far more than merely accepting new structures and new forms of co-operation – for in effect it involves recognising a new dimension of financial commitment at a time when money is short.

The following questions must therefore be asked:

To what extent are the real planning implications of curriculum development realised? If they are realised with their true implications in terms of money, manpower, materials and time, can the realities be faced? If not have we a long term alternative or are we doomed to continue dealing in unrealities?

(2) THE ISSUE OF BALANCE

We have recognised in this chapter the need for balance between the various processes involved in curriculum development and of balance between local initiative and central (including political) direction. This involves a very considerable degree of planning and administrative skill together with sufficient maturity at both local and national level to recognise what can be devolved and what should be maintained as a national concern.

(3) THE ISSUE OF DISSEMINATION

When activity is taking place rapidly under pressure and with scant resources, there is a tendency to neglect to tell anyone what is going on or to fail to find out whether the ground may have already been covered by someone else.

The need to spread the word both within and between systems is accepted in theory by almost every educationist within Africa. Yet still not enough takes place nationally or internationally (where there is an additional danger of conferences being high on rhetoric, low in practicalities).

An African Curriculum Organisation was set up in 1976 and has already proved that it has an important part to play in this process.

Notes

1 From 1962–65 I worked in the Ministry of Education in Uganda as Senior Inspector responsible for primary schools and their programmes. I had taught in a junior secondary school in Uganda but never in a primary school. I cannot recall ever learning or using the term 'curriculum development', though it was already current in universities. I don't imagine my condition was unique.

2 To be more precise: Ghana '57, Cameroon and Nigeria '60, Sierra Leone and Tanganyika (now Tanzania) '61, Uganda '62, Kenya '63, Malawi and Zambia '64, Gambia '65, Botswana and Lesotho '66 and Swaziland '68.

3 E.g. Ghana (1952), Eastern Nigeria (1957), Western Nigeria (1955). The Cabinet in Uganda had it in mind to announce a similar scheme in 1964 but the planning officer, J. D. Chesswas, sat up nights to prepare a detailed costing of the scheme which spelled out bankruptcy in such unequivocable terms that the plan was never launched.

4 Figures produced for a commission to examine Uganda school fees in 1967 also revealed wide internal variations. At worst there were districts like Teso where the total income (based on a wildly optimistic premise of 100 per cent fee collection) was only two-thirds the barest minimum expenditure required.

5 It should be borne in mind that the classic work of Gay and Cole in Liberia arose out of and was partly sponsored by the programme. See Gay, J. and Cole, M. *The New Mathematics and an Old Culture*, Holt, Rinehart and Winston 1964

6 Until 1977, when the Federal Commissioner for Education spoke out very strongly

against 'new mathematics' in general and its use in primary school syllabuses; what is meant by 'new mathematics' has not as yet been defined.

7 The programme received initial foundation support but it was hoped that major funding would come from member states. By 1974, however, only four had contributed and only one substantially.

8 And recently described in an interesting book by its founder: Griffiths, V. L., *Teacher Centred*, Longman 1975

9 . . . though the effects of nationally set Teachers Examinations and Common Entrance Examinations to secondary schools does much to negate the potential of this system.

10 In Kenya only about half of these will be involved in primary work. In Zambia about three-quarters.

11 Nigeria has federal and state ministries. The Nigerian Education Research Council, a federal body, co-ordinates and provides leadership in matters of curriculum policy. New sources of federal revenue have increased central control and with it have come plans to strengthen the role and increase the establishment of the NERC. Nevertheless the policy of Nigeria, and its strength, lies in developing a partnership in national and state curriculum planning.

12 Yet the introduction of the Swedish comprehensive school and its curriculum is still a classic case study in rational curriculum planning. From the first royal commission in 1946 through the passing of the law of 1969 to the final implementation of the curriculum plan in all nine classes has taken twenty-seven years and rolling reform continues. An excellent short description is contained in OECD *Innovation in Education – Sweden* and a more detailed account in Husen, T. and Boalt, G., *Educational Research and Educational Change*, John Wiley 1967

13 Nyerere, J. K., *Education for Self-Reliance*, Government Printer, Dar es Salaam, 1967

14 The title of an excellent article by A. Lema, (Tanzania Teachers' Journal 1971), in which he analyses the difficulty schools have had in understanding the full meaning of the President's educational philosophy. Some schools even introduced 'Self Reliance Periods' as if it were a subject, like cookery.

15 Kaunda, K., *Humanism, A Guide to the Nation*, Government Printer, Lusaka 1967

16 Kaunda, K., *Zambia's Economic Revolution*: *The Mulungushi Declaration*, Government Printer, Lusaka 1968

17 Kaunda, K., *A Nation of Equals*, Lusaka 1972

18 Republic of Zambia, *Education for Development*, Ministry of Education, Lusaka 1976

19 Kenya Government Sessional Paper No 10 of 1965 (Nairobi 1965)

20 Republic of Botswana, *Education for a Nation* – Address by His Excellency the President to the Botswana Teachers' Union Conference at Lobatse, 15 Dec 1969. Government Printer, Gaborone

21 *The Philosophy, Policies and Objectives of the Imbokodvo National Movement*, Government Printer, Mbabane, 1972.

22 The draft final report appeared in 1974. The final report, *All Our Future*, was published in 1976 and released for circulation in the following year.

23 Adaralegbe, A. (ed.), *Philosophy for Nigerian Education*, (Proceedings of the National Curriculum Conference held at Lagos in September 1969), Heinemann, 1972

24 A Home Economics Report was also prepared, separately, and issued as part of the final published document, *Guidelines on Primary School Curriculum*, NERC, Lagos, 1973

25 One bizarre omission to the plan was the lack of provision of any experimental schools near the Institute itself. The nearest centre was over a hundred miles away.

26 For an interesting critique of the sector review see Williams, P. (ed.), *Prescription for Progress, – a commentary on the education policy of the World Bank*, University of London Institute of Education 1976

27 The approach is well described in an influential paper by W. J. Platt, director, Depart-

ment of Planning and Financing of Education in UNESCO and summarised in the Seminar Report *Basic Education in Eastern Africa*, UNESCO-UNICEF, Nairobi, 1974

28 Schumacher, E. F., *Small is Beautiful*, Blond and Briggs 1973

29 A further larger scale project (hardly experimental) at Bunumbu in Sierra Leone will be examined in Chapter 8.

30 Described in a useful report by the German Foundation for International Development, '*Work-orientated Education in Africa*, Bonn 1972

31 See Afolayan, A. in Bamgbose A. (ed.) *Mother Tongue Education – The West African Experience*, Hodder & Stoughton 1976, pp 113–134

32 Project staff on a personal basis also contributed to the current state syllabus revision.

33 Kgarebe, A. W., *Interim report on the In-Service Project working in primary education*, May 1975–October 1975, Government Printer, Gaborone

Chapter 4 What shall they learn? (1) The official curriculum

In my next two chapters I shall attempt to compare the *official* curriculum in African primary schools with *actual* curriculum practice, and thus to contrast what official plans say should happen in schools with the realities of what actual schools and real teachers plan and provide. Starting from this distinction it is easy, and initially satisfying, to present a nice clear argument, supported by well chosen anecdotes, proving how wide and how unacceptable is the gap between the two.

In an article I wrote in 1970 I described the whirlpool of activity in the official curriculum: in syllabuses, in Institutes of Education, in curriculum centres, and I commented sadly that 'most of its impetus is at the centre, that some of it is circular, that its impetus decreases rapidly towards the perimeter and that the vast majority of primary schools lie in the stagnant water outside and are totally unaffected by its movement'.

This sort of imagery is amusing to elaborate but the argument derived from it can be dangerously simplistic. For one thing it is by no means easy to recognise an official curriculum and for another it is very easy to confuse a government's policy, a process which is growing and evolving, with static written evidence which may be out of date and even recognised as such. Often all sorts of local or national variations to an official plan are known, permitted and encouraged, while original documents gradually slip into greater degrees of obsolescence pending their next public revision.

My whirlpool analogy can prove equally dangerous in its generalisation for there are innovators to be found even in the most remote schools. Yet since this book abounds in generalisations I shall retain both the simple distinction between official and actual curriculum and the simple argument that the differences between them are wide and disturbing.

What constitutes the official curriculum?

We commonly and erroneously assume the syllabus document to be the core of any official curriculum in schools. It is only one of a number of instruments which express the official curriculum. These include: national public statements of goals

Aims of primary education (Sierra Leone 1974)

Many sensible and realistic statements of aims for primary schools have recently emerged from Africa. The following from Sierra Leone, seemed to me to be particularly well framed.

The primary school would aim for its students to acquire:

1 'Literacy in one or more languages, eventually to include literacy in at least one Sierra Leone language and in the official language, English;
2 'numeracy, i.e. computational skills in Arithmetic, understanding of certain basic mathematical principles, and ability to judge the quantitative results of certain decisions and actions;
3 'a rational outlook on natural and social events through observing and understanding the environments in which the students live;
4 'occupational skills at elementary level;
5 'positive attitudes toward themselves, their cultural backgrounds, towards work and the process of community and national development;
6 'positive traits of character and ethical values.'

From Sierra Leone Educational Review Final Report, 'All our future', 1976, p 7.

and intent (e.g. the Nigerian 'Seminar on a National Policy on Education'),[2] the legal and administrative framework of the school system, official calendars and time allocations, the syllabus and related descriptions of prescribed content, official lists of recommended books, and the content and style of the final and inter-mediate examinations.

If we look further we can discover yet more determinants like official policies concerning building, furniture and equipment of schools, contents of national radio and television programmes and the official syllabuses for teacher training.

Rarely do we set these prescriptions alongside one another and examine the total picture which emerges. Indeed, if we did so, we should certainly discover many ambiguities and overlaps. Consider just a few of the more common and more obvious ones. There are instances where the official syllabus recommends one type of content and emphasis (e.g. in language skills), while the official examination is clearly constructed with the intention of testing different ones; or cases in which the official aims of education extol the virtues of self-reliance and enquiry-based education, whereas the official syllabus contains an outline of content so rigid and overcrowded as to render any initiative almost impossible to achieve. An official teachers' guide may recommend project work and locally based enquiry, whereas the official timetable renders such initiatives impossible by dividing up the day into small fragments. Yet again the official syllabus and scheme of work may recommend the purchase and use of local materials gathered from the local environment when official administrative regulations preclude the headmaster from purchasing these and fail to provide him with any facilities for storing them once he has obtained them.

One thing is certain: to the head, the manager or education officer in school, the official syllabus often appears far less important than it does to the curriculum committee or the outside observer. Let us consider some of the chief influences which determine the official curriculum schools follow and assess changes which have taken place and trends which may be emerging.

THE STRUCTURAL FRAMEWORK OF THE CURRICULUM

The age at which children go to school, the amount of time they spend there and the disposition of that time have the very greatest bearing on the learning that is planned and provided for them.

Predictably, the basic patterns are inherited from colonial times and often (at some remove) from the English Board Schools of the early 1900's; hence the three term year, the five day week, the six or seven year cycle, the age five or six entry, the forty minute period. There are also some interesting survivals in terminology like 'standards', and 'monitors', both words still in common use throughout Africa, both harking back to the English era of 'payment by results' in the late nineteenth century. Until recently, nobody stopped to consider the rationale for these prac-tices. They were accepted uncritically as part of the school package in the same way as blazers, school caps and terminal reports.

But currently these traditions are being quite rapidly eroded, sometimes as a result of conscious rethinking of philosophies, purposes and priorities, sometimes in the face of dire necessity. The following changes in practice or intention are significant.

AGE OF ENTRY

Certain countries in our 1975–76 survey, Sierra Leone, Tanzania and Zambia, and others outside it such as Ethiopia and Somalia, are seeking to raise their minimum age of entry into primary schools. The purpose of this policy is twofold, first as a means of achieving a more effective link between education and employment so that school leavers are old enough to take up productive work when they leave school, secondly as a means of offering a basic education to a greater number of the nation's children and ensuring that they stay at school to complete it.

LENGTH OF COURSE

A parallel and significant trend of policy is a move in a number of countries to differentiate between a basic education cycle and a continuation cycle, the first aiming to provide basic learning skills, the latter emphasising prevocational studies and education for citizenship.

Predictably, where such policies have merely involved adding on a vocational junior secondary top to a general primary base as in Ghana and Nigeria, there has been little overt reaction to the proposals. Where there has been suggestion that the new 'basic cycle' will involve shortening the number of years available to children (in Sierra Leone, the 1973/1974 Educational Review originally suggested a two year cut from 7 to 5 years[3]) the reaction has been vehement. Yet over the past two decades we have seen reductions, in almost all countries surveyed, from eight to seven and sometimes even to six year primary cycles. These have been absorbed, often under protest, by the educational systems.

LENGTH OF SESSIONS

Yet another critical factor is the length of time children actually spend in class and the time of day they are there. Often under pressure of numbers, urban schools are adopting a shift system only too common in Asia and Latin America, but a new feature in African primary schools. In Botswana and Lesotho, for example, many lower classes, from Class 1 to 3, are working short two-and-a-half to three hour sessions, thus enabling teachers to split up very large groups.

Clearly all these structural changes are vital determinants of the official curriculum. An eight-year-old child does not learn the same thing at the same speed as a five-year-old child. You cannot teach the same amount in seven years as in six; or in four hours in the afternoon as you can in five hours in the morning. The lack of official recognition of these truths is disturbing. Syllabus makers appear to suffer from a sad tendency to measure curriculum content by what is contained in the syllabus and textbooks rather than by what is, or what can be, absorbed by the learners. Hence, to my knowledge, no school curriculum materials have been designed with older learners in mind and there has been an alarming tendency, when cycles have been reduced in length, not to reduce content. The reason, frequently given, and I shudder because I can remember advancing it myself on a history syllabus committee, is that since primary schooling is terminal for many children, they must cover the ground or remain forever ignorant.

Little concession either, is made for double shift or 'short session' pupils. In countries where the practice is officially, if apologetically, accepted, as in Sierra Leone, Zambia or Botswana, revised timings are provided in the official syllabus, but there exists no guide as to what the teacher is to leave out from an already overloaded syllabus.

What subjects, when, and in what language?

Writers on curriculum theory may expound on 'forms of knowledge' or 'realms of meaning', but to the curriculum worker and to the headmaster the issues to be resolved are as follows:

In what language do I teach?
What subjects do I include, at what stage?
What balance do I accord them? (principally decided by time allocation).
How far, and for what purpose do I attempt to integrate areas hitherto taught separately?
What is to be assessed, when and how?

LANGUAGES OF INSTRUCTION

The choice of language affects selection, integration and choice of curriculum content throughout the primary cycle, and is of dominant importance in planning for the first school years. Language policies for education are highly charged political issues and seldom if ever decided on educational grounds alone. When they are made, they are almost invariably subject to mistrust and misunderstanding by some sections of the community. It is virtually impossible to please everyone.

Stripped of some of their emotional overtones, the main issues in English-speaking Africa are as follows:

1 Language embodies culture. Teaching in the mother-tongue provides a vital link between home and community education on the one hand, and school education on the other.
2 Most teaching in lower primary classes and some in upper classes depends on linking learning with the local environment through the use of language, e.g. storytelling, social and environmental studies, the oral work which precedes reading; religious and moral education.
3 English is an official language in most countries and is the medium of instruction in secondary schools. Competence in English is an unquestioned asset both for learning and in employment. It is fully recognised as such by parents and children.

76

4 In some subjects and topics, particularly in Mathematics and Science, English language embodies western thought patterns and there is a risk that translation may lead to fundamental misunderstandings.

5 Language situations vary widely in countries and between them. In the three little countries in Southern Africa, Botswana, Lesotho and Swaziland, nearly everyone speaks the same mother tongue. In one big country, Tanzania, there is a widely accepted national language, Swahili. Elsewhere national language maps are exceptionally complex, ranging from large and clearly educationally viable groups like Hausa or Luganda through progressively smaller units to situations where numbers speaking the mother tongue are very small or very scattered.

6 There are consequently variations in the quality and availability of reading material in school and out and in the number of teachers who can speak the language and teach in it. Small language groups, e.g. Kalenji speakers in Kenya are thus very much at a disadvantage compared to larger groups such as Gikuyu.

7 The language of instruction in adult education may be different from that used in school. Adult education programmes have consistently used more local languages and the current realisation that formal and non-formal education must be more closely linked has, at last, awakened concern over this strange state of affairs.

In the face of these conflicting issues a choice has to be made. However the pressures are such that in many countries no clear unambiguous official statement is available. Rather, one encounters a sort of educational case-law built up. This, in its turn, may conceal considerable variation in practice. It should be an easy task to produce a comparative table listing official language policies. It has not proved so. Table 5 indicates the best available information I have at time of writing. Readers are invited to disagree.

Yet, though official policies may be difficult to pin down, trends are very clear. There is increasing use of the mother tongue or local 'language of the market place', as a medium of instruction, particularly in lower classes and consequently a movement, albeit slow and tentative, towards the development of a body of expertise in curriculum development and materials production in the mother tongue. The Curriculum Development Centre in Zambia, the Kenya Institute of Education and the Bureau of Ghanaian Languages, working in association with the Curriculum Development Division of the Ghana Education Service, are providing leadership in this field. This trend is reinforced by international opinion, particularly pan-African opinion, and it should be noted that both the Intergovernmental Conference on Cultural Policies in Africa (Accra 1975) and the Conference of Ministers of Education of African Member States (Lagos 1976) recommended the increased use of African languages as vehicles of instruction.

There is also an indication that certain countries, particularly Kenya and Ghana are becoming increasingly prepared to recognise more languages as media for the initial years of formal education. I believe that this trend will spread and that it is based on very sound educational grounds. Mastery of the code of reading is intimately bound up with oral competence in a language. Once the code is mastered it is relatively easy to transfer the skill to another language; but to learn to read in a

Table 5 Language teaching in primary school: ten African countries
  (a) Official medium of instruction
  (b) Languages taught

COUNTRY	MEDIUM OF INSTRUCTION IN PRIMARY SCHOOL CLASS							MEDIUM USED IN SUBJECT TEXTS (other than language subjects)	NOTES
	1	2	3	4	5	6	7		
LESOTHO								English (apart from some Sesotho religious texts).	Recent commission recommends extension of Sesotho medium.
SWAZILAND								English.	Schools following the 'English through acitivity' scheme use English medium throughout.
BOTSWANA								English.	Recent commission (1977) report recommends Setswana medium to Class 4.
ZAMBIA								English.	Currently nearly all schools use English but official policy is towards wider use of mother tongue.
TANZANIA								Swahili.	Swahili is the medium in all schools.
KENYA								Texts in Swahili have been prepared by KIE up to Class 4. All others in English.	Some schools, as well as most urban schools, are following the New Primary Approach which uses English medium.
UGANDA								Texts in Maths and Social Studies up to Class 3 have been prepared in 6 local languages. Otherwise English.	The syllabus recommends a gradual transition from local language to English depending upon linguistic and conceptual complexities of school subjects.
NIGERIA								Texts up to Class 3 have been produced in the three main languages. All others in English.	States with multiple languages (e.g. Plateau/Lagos) still use English medium. One small experiment uses Yoruba throughout.
GHANA								English.	The diagram refers to official school system only. Many private primary schools use English throughout.
SIERRA LEONE								English.	Recent policy statements imply a future use of mother tongues as medium in lower classes.

Key: ☐ African languages ▦ English

LANGUAGES TAUGHT IN PRIMARY SCHOOL CLASS							LANGUAGE(S) USED IN EXAMINATION	NOTES
1	2	3	4	5	6	7		
							Sesotho subject exam, all others in English.	Sesotho is the only local language taught.
							Siswati subject exam, all others in English.	Siswati is the only local language taught.
							Setswana subject exam, all others in English.	Setswana is the only African language taught.
							English. No local or African language examination.	7 African languages taught: Nyanja/ Bemba/Lozi/Tonga/Kaunde/Lunda/ Luvale.
							English subject exam, all others in Swahili.	Swahili is the only local language taught. Recently there has been much discussion about commencing English teaching only after Class 4.
							English. No local or African language examination.	TKK (primer) reading materials have been prepared in Kiswahili/Dholuo/Luyia/ Gikuyu/Lubukusu/Lulogooli/Kalenjin/ Ateso/Maasai/Kikamba/Kimeru/ Kidawida/Kigiryama. (Kisumari, Turkana and Kiembu in preparation).
							English. No local or other African language examination.	6 African languages taught: Lwo/Ateso/ Runyoro/Lugbara/Ruyankore-Rukiga.
							Hausa, Igbo or Yoruba subject examination. All others in English.	Northern states teach Hausa, west/central states Yoruba, south/ eastern states use Igbo. Nupe, Efik and Kanuri used in some local areas.
						MIDDLE SCHOOL CLASS 7/8	English. No local language examination.	9 local African languages taught: Ashanti Twi/Akwapim Kwi/Fanti/Ga/ Dagme/Nzema/Ewe/Dagbani/Kassem. Two others in preparation.
							English. No local or other African language examination.	Recommendations that local languages be used for Years 1 and 2 have not yet affected the curriculum.

Note: Variation in size of block indicates relative total time available for language teaching.

The anatomy of change (Kano State 1970–1977)

Hausa is spoken throughout the state, but in the sixties English had been used, often disastrously, as a medium in schools. It was introduced in the north of Nigeria as the result of the 'straight for English' policy, one of the many off-shoots of the Kenya 'New Primary Approach'.

In 1970, the State Ministry of Education wisely recommended a reintro-duction of Hausa medium in lower classes, but this proved far easier said than done. First the governor, a military man, demurred. This move, he claimed, would undermine the 'One Nigeria' policy. His fears were eventually allayed. However, appropriate teachers and materials had to be found; neither were easily forthcoming. Kano was short of teachers, and still is. Many teachers from the south of Nigeria were employed and they do not speak good Hausa. Eventually they were replaced, moved to higher classes, or learned Hausa.

Newly qualified teachers posed another problem. They spoke Hausa, but had very little training in teaching it. The staff available in teachers' colleges consisted in the main of dignified old gentlemen, veritable repositories of folklore and tradition, ever eager to discuss finer points of language with other scholars, but totally unequipped to teach reading methods.

Writers and the books they produced were of the same type, full of anti-quarian information and the archaic vocabulary that went with it. Nobody seemed to write books about what was happening in the 1970's.

Consequently, a new diploma course had to be set up, new teacher trainers prepared and new books written. The effort continues but change comes slowly.

language where the spoken word is not well understood is to invite pseudo-literacy of the kind so painfully apparent in many countries.

However, alongside the trends which reinforce the introduction of local language medium, no sign of weakening of emphasis in the teaching of English can be detected. Politicians, parents and educationists seem determined to try to have their cake and eat it. Theoretically this is perfectly possible. The experiment at Ife suggests that it is a myth to believe that early introduction of English medium (especially if it is badly handled) can be correlated with eventual better performance in English. Moreover I firmly believe that children cannot satisfactorily be taught to read in two languages at the same time and that they will be better English readers if they learn it after they have mastered the skill in their mother tongue.

Yet while the maintenance of a degree of competence in two languages is both possible and desirable, it can only conceivably be achieved following a reassessment of present curricular priorities, a recasting of a great deal of current material in school, and a new emphasis on teacher training. Very naturally, there has been a disinclination to face up to these very daunting issues with their massive implications on educational investment and, perhaps, a subconscious hope that the contradictions would resolve themselves. Unfortunately the language problems will not go away. They are central to curriculum planning and have to be recognised as such.

SELECTION AND INTEGRATION

Table 6 attempts to show comparative official time allocations contained in syllabuses in six countries – and alternative patterns within two of them, Nigeria and Tanzania. Further information concerning all ten countries in our survey is contained in Appendix 2.

As I have previously stressed, it would be unwise to place too great an emphasis on these official documents. Many of them are under review and some of them may be virtually ignored in practice. Yet they do indicate certain interesting patterns. They are very crowded. They place a predictable emphasis on language (particularly English) and on Mathematics, an emphasis which we shall see intensified in the actual curriculum. They offer very scant opportunity for children to express themselves in creative and cultural activities, while retaining a relatively generous allocation for physical education (a subject which in all my years as an inspector and teacher trainer I never saw convincingly taught outside college teaching practice). They also offer relatively modest time allocations for practical and pre-vocational subjects in upper primary classes, a feature which may reflect a lack of real conviction by syllabus panels to respond to the political creed that such studies are necessary and profitable for primary level children, but may also be born of a firm realistic assessment of the lack of money and materials to make such studies workable.

If we look back over the record of the last twenty years in our ten countries, we may detect certain common trends, unspectacular, but nevertheless significant.

The pattern of time allocations to subjects has changed with an increase in time

Table 6 Official time allocations by subject area: lower and upper primary classes in ten African countries

Key

1   Language

(a) ▨ English

(b) ▤ African language(s)

includes writing, reading, composition, grammar, poetry, drama and oral work.

2   ▦ Mathematics   includes arithmetic and number work

3   General science

includes nature study/knowledge, health education, nutrition, first aid

4   Social studies

includes civics, history, geography and environmental studies

5   Religious knowledge

includes moral education

6   Physical education

7   ▦ Cultural and practical activities

includes music, art, craft, needlework, domestic science, homecrafts, clay modelling, woodwork, gardening, agriculture and rural science

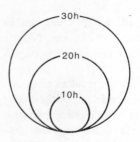

Hours per week spent on formal education (excluding time spent on roll call, recess and lunch breaks, assemblies and health inspection etc) See Appendix 2 for further details.

Notes
(1) Terminal class is Class 7 except in Nigeria and Ghana, where it is Class 6. Ghana has a 2 year middle school with a separate curriculum.
(2) Figures shown are taken from those most available in 1976 and all are from the late 60's/early 70's. A number of the countries shown are currently revising systems (e.g. Swaziland/Zambia/Ghana).
(3) Nigeria, being a Federation, has wide differences between states. The two here selected are taken from (1) the inspector's handbook for Northern States 1974 and (2) recommended time allocations in Lagos State.
(4) Tanzania, since the late 60's, has been undergoing widespread educational changes. Therefore two syllabuses are shown (1) the 1969 syllabus, used in 1976 in a majority of schools and (2) the 1977 Community School Syllabus.
(5) Volumes per subject do not take into account variations in the length of school year, which taken across Africa show much less variation than the lengths of study weeks shown.
(6) Some areas practise double shift schools (e.g. Zambia/Lagos State/Sierra Leone) which further modifies the school week.
(7) School and community involvement is occasionally permitted to modify time allocations shown.

Table 6 (contd.)

SOUTHERN AFRICA

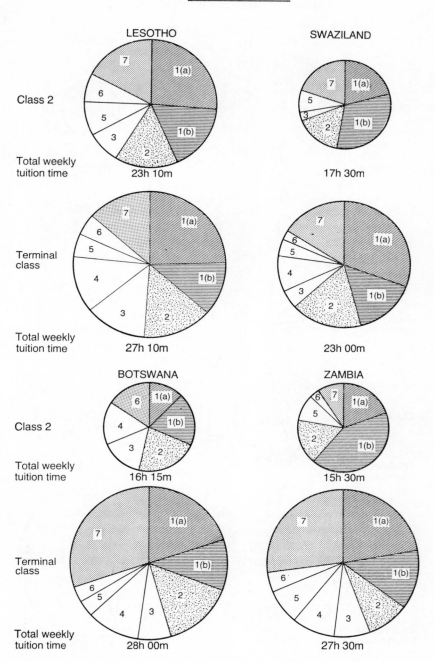

	LESOTHO	SWAZILAND
Class 2		
Total weekly tuition time	23h 10m	17h 30m
Terminal class		
Total weekly tuition time	27h 10m	23h 00m

	BOTSWANA	ZAMBIA
Class 2		
Total weekly tuition time	16h 15m	15h 30m
Terminal class		
Total weekly tuition time	28h 00m	27h 30m

Table 6 (contd.)

EASTERN AFRICA

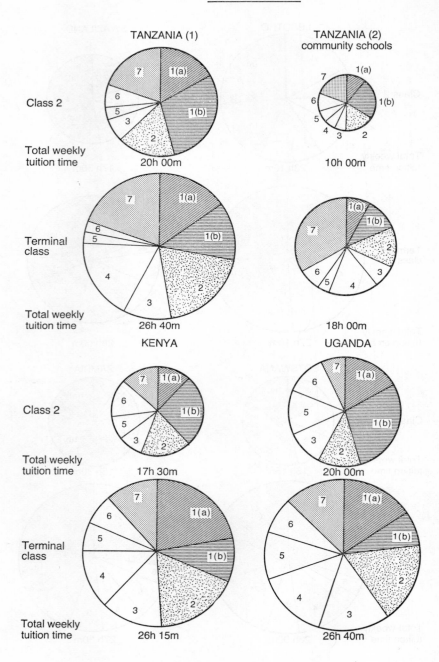

TANZANIA (1)

TANZANIA (2)
community schools

Class 2

Total weekly
tuition time
20h 00m

10h 00m

Terminal
class

Total weekly
tuition time
26h 40m

18h 00m

KENYA

UGANDA

Class 2

Total weekly
tuition time
17h 30m

20h 00m

Terminal
class

Total weekly
tuition time
26h 15m

26h 40m

Table 6 (contd.)

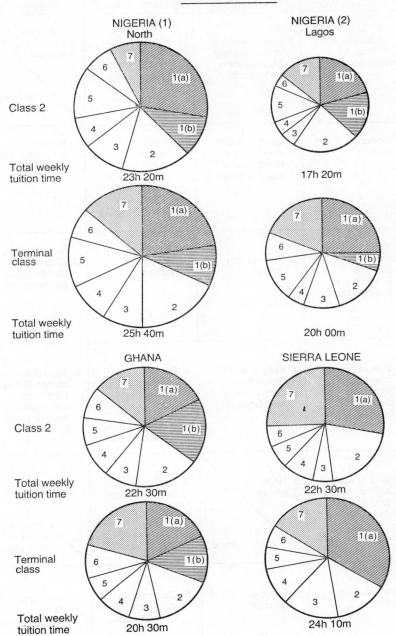

WESTERN AFRICA

NIGERIA (1)
North

NIGERIA (2)
Lagos

Class 2

Total weekly
tuition time

23h 20m

17h 20m

Terminal
class

Total weekly
tuition time

25h 40m

20h 00m

GHANA

SIERRA LEONE

Class 2

Total weekly
tuition time

22h 30m

22h 30m

Terminal
class

Total weekly
tuition time

20h 30m

24h 10m

85

Fig. B 'Activities This Week' – (Northern Nigeria). Extract from group work programme for two weeks (Year 1 Term 2) – *Primary Education Improvement Project*

Year One Term 2 Week 5 (Mon/Tues/Wed)	Year One Term 2 Week 5 (Thurs/Fri/Sat)	Year One Term 2 Week 6 (Mon/Tues/Wed)	Year One Term 2 Week 6 (Thurs/Fri/Sat)
1 Make wall story –Frieze for classroom.	1 Make masks + dramatic story. Use dressing up box too.	1 Kuka & ash. Model & paint food for food hotel.	1 Book corner Pre-reading games
2 Home corner Shop	2 Sand + water play for maths. Have special assignments.	2 Home corner Shop	2 Maths activities for subtraction
3 Blow & drip painting. Smearing + folding paper.	3 Pre-reading games.	3 Collage pictures.	3 Clay making stabile bases for next week
4 Make masks + dramatise a story. Use dressing up box too.	4 Kuka & ash. Model food, paint it, for food hotel.	4 Book corner Pre-reading games	4 Take down home corner. Set up food hotel, with menu, money, plates, food etc.
5 Sand + water play for maths. Have special assignments.	5 Home corner Shop	5 Maths activities for subtraction	5 Making stabiles Striking matches on paper to make patterns
6 Pre-reading games.	6 Collage pictures	6 Clay making stabile bases for next week.	6 Weaving or sewing.

Extra activity: card games   *Extra activity:* Making a book for book corner, choose topic

From: Activities for Lower Primary Classes, Institute of Education, Zaria 1974, p289

allotted to language teaching – especially English. Indeed as Dottrens noticed in his world survey of primary curriculum in 1962[4] there seems to be a bit more of everything included in a curriculum every time it is revised – a trend which is likely to be reinforced whenever syllabuses are designed by committees rather than individuals. Finally, we may detect a marked tendency to integrate subjects hitherto taught separately, a trend reflecting curriculum practice in Britain but also stemming from a desire to stress the relatedness of learning within a child's own environment.

INTEGRATION OF SUBJECT AREAS

The topic of integration is worth looking at in somewhat more detail. Few subjects are more hotly debated in curriculum committees. People get very emotional over the issues involved and discussion may tend to become polarised. At opposite extremes are the 'seamless web of learning' party who would appear to argue that integration is so noble in itself that it should be undertaken whether teachers can handle it or not, and the committed and dogmatic subject specialist with a bookful of behavioural objectives and forty pages of sequenced syllabus to back them up. I often find myself in the middle, accused of reaction by both parties.

In fact, moves towards integration in most countries have been cautious and sensible. Four different trends are observable. First a considerable, and, on the whole, successful attempt to introduce some measure of integration to programmes at lower primary level. Often official syllabuses and timetables reflect the influence and expertise of infant method specialists in ministries or from colleges of education. Sometimes, as in Uganda, a lower primary panel has been formed to coordinate approaches. Sometimes specific projects have helped to promote integration. The 'centres of interest' introduced in the New Primary Approach in Kenya, have been mentioned and this pattern was taken up in both Zambia and Swaziland with topics gradually refined and widened.

The Primary Education Improvement Project in Northern Nigeria has produced a programme for the lower classes where more formal subject-based lessons were planned to cover about half the teaching time, but complemented by a carefully planned activities programme based on group work.[5] These are only two examples selected from a rich bank of experience. Indeed, there is no country in English-speaking Africa which cannot boast some useful project in co-operative teaching at lower primary level.

A second focus for integration has been through the design of materials based on one subject discipline but specifically planned to feed across the curriculum. Later in this book I will argue the importance of this approach to develop skills of 'language across the curriculum', but in the lower primary booklets produced by the Science Education Programme for Africa (SEPA) we have a brilliant prototype for developing basic scientific and mathematical skills across subject boundaries. Their units on construction, water, dry sand, exploring the environment and many others have been taken up and adapted in Language, Social Studies, Mathematics and Science syllabuses throughout Africa.[6]

More directly, the cause of integration has been served by the formal incorpora-

Syllabus planning: Nigeria

In our Social Studies syllabus committees in Nigeria at both national and local levels, we made an honest attempt to achieve a real degree of integration. The processes involved a number of related steps:

1 Identifying the aims of the programme as a whole.
2 Examining and listing characteristics, needs and problems of learners at three stages: lower, middle and upper primary.
3 Listing themes and sub-themes (units) for each class of the primary school.
4 Developing each of the themes on a grid with the following headings: (a) Topic (b) Main objectives (c) Concepts to be developed (d) Attitudes and values to be inculcated (e) Skills and abilities to be acquired (f) Facts to be taught (g) Ways of learning and teaching (h) Teaching and learning materials to be used (i) Evaluating the learning.

Sometimes the rigidity of our approach tripped us up. Sometimes, too, our suggestions bordered on the impracticable. But what a change for the better, I kept thinking, when compared to old committee meetings I used to attend when we haggled over lists of topics for inclusion in a syllabus.

Conversation over coffee (National Workshop on Primary Education, Ibadan, 1971)

Hugh Hawes: This new Social Studies Syllabus they are designing seems a great improvement over the old History and Geography ones.
Nigerian colleague: But it is difficult to make and even more difficult to get taught properly.
Hugh Hawes: Why so?
Nigerian colleague: You have blue bits and you have yellow bits and it's going to be much easier for you to put them together one on top of the other so you have a blue and yellow syllabus. But you have to design a green syllabus. You also have blue teachers and yellow teachers. You will need to turn them into green teachers . . . and that will be even more difficult.

---

tion of subjects hitherto taught separately into new programmes with new names. Thus Science syllabuses may include material formerly taught under the separate headings of General Science, Nature Study, Rural Science and Health Education; Social Studies syllabuses incorporate what used to be taught under History, Geography and Civics. In Nigeria there has been an attempt to integrate Music, Dance, Drama and Fine Art under Cultural and Creative Art. Typical of the trend is the new panel structure in Lesotho where panels are grouped into five main areas: Language, Mathematics/Science, Social Studies, Practical and Cultural Activities and Religious Knowledge.

Such integration can be largely formal; in Lesotho, for instance, the evidence of real integration in between Mathematics and Science is very slight. On the other hand it may represent a genuine attempt by specialists in related subjects to sit down together and plan a programme which allows for separate activities but suggests common themes and provides examples of integrated lessons as in the Nigerian Cultural and Creative Art syllabus. Yet again it may be the product of basic rethinking and true integration founded on new objectives and a fresh approach as in the Social Studies syllabus now under development in Sierra Leone where an integrated programme with significant regional variations is being planned in a series of central and local workshops and where a special series of booklets on skills development (e.g. map making, note taking skills, creative skills) is being produced for teachers.

One other pattern of integration has, to my mind, considerable potential value since it maintains a useful and workable balance between an entirely subject-based curriculum, often fragmented and irrelevant to real life and an integrated curriculum which may neglect essential learning skills, or prove beyond the capabilities of the ordinary teacher to teach effectively. It involves the development of a restricted number of units of study based on themes which can be examined across the curriculum. In Lesotho for instance, a six week unit has been designed on transport. Another more modest project has been based on a school garden in Botswana. In the latter instance a whole timetable was freed for two days, this being in itself an innovation, and two classes, 6 and 7, combined to work in groups with their teachers and a local inspector.

I detect in such tentative experiments the germ of a potentially exciting innovation. They show the possibility of identifying themes vital to national development like 'saving our soil', 'clean water' or 'feeding ourselves'; of designing carefully selected units of material to cover perhaps two weeks' learning with teachers trained to handle them; of arranging the school programmes of studies so that they allow in every term, a period, two weeks or so, available for such common projects. These ideas are further elaborated in a note at the end of the next chapter.

To achieve any measure of integration requires a confidence and a breadth of understanding which teachers possess in varying degrees. Part of the art of curriculum development – for it is, indeed, an art and not a science – is to gauge the extent to which teachers are secure enough to forsake the safety and familiarity of the categories into which they have been accustomed to divide learning. This extent will inevitably vary and, in consequence, it may prove wiser to provide for alterna-

Fig. C Patterns of integration suggested by a school garden project in Lesotho

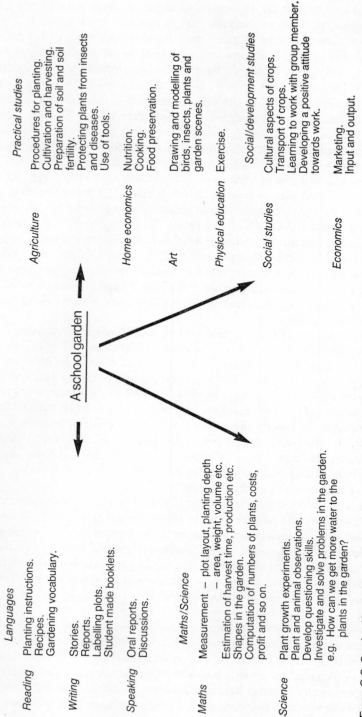

Languages

Reading Planting instructions.
Recipes.
Gardening vocabulary.

Writing Stories.
Reports.
Labelling plots.
Student made booklets.

Speaking Oral reports.
Discussions.

Maths/Science

Maths Measurement – plot layout, planting depth
– area, weight, volume etc.
Estimation of harvest time, production etc.
Shapes in the garden.
Computation of numbers of plants, costs,
profit and so on.

Science Plant growth experiments.
Plant and animal observations.
Develop questioning skills.
Investigate and solve problems in the garden.
e.g. How can we get more water to the
plants in the garden?

A school garden

Practical studies

Agriculture Procedures for planting.
Cultivation and harvesting.
Preparation of soil and soil
fertility.
Protecting plants from insects
and diseases.
Use of tools.

Home economics Nutrition.
Cooking.
Food preservation.

Art Drawing and modelling of
birds, insects, plants and
garden scenes.

Physical education Exercise.

Social/development studies

Social studies Cultural aspects of crops.
Transport of crops.
Learning to work with group member.
Developing a positive attitude
towards work.

Economics Marketing.
Input and output.

From: G.S. Soroka, 'A school garden in Lesotho', film strip produced by Department of
Education in Developing Countries 1967.

tive approaches within a system than to force patterns of integration on insecure and bewildered teachers.

Contents of subject syllabuses

It is neither possible nor practicable to attempt a critique of syllabus content in all subjects in African primary schools. The most I can do is to offer a very brief and personal view of some of the recent changes in emphasis drawing from the syllabuses of ten countries and to isolate a few of the new approaches which strike me as particularly interesting and exciting. In most cases I instance one or two well-designed syllabuses which exemplify these.

CULTURAL SUBJECTS – ART AND MUSIC

Main trends: Integration of separate subjects and inclusion of dance, mime and drama have already been noted (Nigeria). There is increasing emphasis on African musical tradition, including the making of musical instruments (Uganda and Kenya) and the gradual weakening of mission tradition based very largely on choral singing and religious music. New syllabuses (e.g. Lesotho, Uganda) show a greater diversification of materials and media in art and craft, and recommend many materials available in the environment rather than depending so single-mindedly on picture-making.

LANGUAGE

Main trends: More interest and importance is now attached to mother tongue teaching; improved design of materials for the teaching of language and reading (Zambia and Tanzania).

There is greater partnership and closer friendship between mother tongue and English teaching; development of complementary materials and approaches, particularly at lower primary level (Kenya and Ghana)

Greater efforts are now made towards identifying the purpose and function of language; to answer key questions such as 'what does the primary school leaver need English for?', 'what kind of skills does the learner need to develop in his mother tongue, at what stage, with what purpose?' (Nigeria)

There is greater concern for the role of language throughout the curriculum, particular attention being paid to the relation between language and activity methods in lower primary classes (Zambia and Swaziland)

MATHEMATICS

Main trends: The continent-wide adoption of 'New Mathematics' programmes has already been noted. Metrication and decimalisation of coinage have been introduced. In recent years the following changes have emerged:

1 a swing of the pendulum away from uncritical acceptance of 'New Mathematics' programmes, sometimes manifest in overt political opposition to them (Nigeria and Malawi), more commonly by a re-emphasis placed on the values and processes of basic numeracy, e.g. tables, measurement, number bonds (Swaziland and Lesotho).

2 a greater concern with the environment as a basis for the teaching of Mathematics in relation to examples which can be used, e.g. in measurement, sampling, graphs, as well as to the uses of Mathematics in everyday life (Botswana and Ghana).

RELIGIOUS, MORAL AND POLITICAL EDUCATION

Main trends: Christian Religious Knowledge syllabuses are rapidly developing joint denominational approaches (Lesotho and Uganda) and more slowly, but nevertheless steadily beginning to widen syllabuses, based on Bible knowledge and catechism, towards greater discussion of local and contemporary moral issues (Kenya and Zambia); local beliefs and customs are no longer excluded or contrasted with Christian beliefs. In some instances, Islamic Religious Knowledge under the influence of Egypt becomes more concerned with belief and less centred on mere learning of the Koran (Uganda and Nigeria).

Political education with syllabuses devised by national parties, is introduced in two States (Tanzania and Zambia). Community service is required in varying measure, from a very considerable degree of involvement (Tanzania) to occasional gestures such as National Tree Planting Day (Lesotho).

PHYSICAL AND HEALTH EDUCATION

Main trends: These subjects are sometimes planned separately, sometimes jointly. Physical Education has long shed approaches based on exercises and drill, for approaches based on training in skill and co-ordination (Kenya). More culturally based elements e.g. dancing, mime and movement are often now absorbed in Cultural Activities and Music syllabuses (Nigeria). Health Education may be less formally treated than previously, with activities woven into other subject syllabuses and stressed as part of the school programme as a whole (Ghana).

SCIENCE

Main trends: Syllabuses based largely on Biology are now superseded almost everywhere by 'General Science' syllabuses. Integration of Health and Agricultural Science with General Science as mentioned above prevails in many countries.

The basis for selection of materials varies between mainly *content based* criteria (e.g. what scientific knowledge and ways of thinking are most appropriate to the present and subsequent experience of the child), and mainly *process based* criteria (e.g. what thought processes are necessary for a primary child to develop and what knowledge and experience must therefore be selected to form a content from which this development can best be effected). The most sophisticated statement of a

Trying to understand

An African Primary Science Unit called 'Ask the Ant Lion' has been incorporated into the 'Primary Science' programmes in Northern Nigeria. Ant lions are infamous little creatures which dig pits and trap ants. Nobody has ever bothered much about them because they harm no one (except the ants). It is precisely for this anonymity that they were selected. Children are invited to find out how they trap ants, how they make their pits, what material they use. They are easy to find and children are fascinated by this unit. The following conversation, recorded almost verbatim, may give us cause to think...

Visiting expert: What's the use of that unit about the Ant lion?
Hugh Hawes: It makes children think.
Visiting expert: But what's the use of knowing about Ant lions?
Hugh Hawes (patiently): It's the process of thinking we are trying to develop, the content helps us to do this.
Visiting expert: I think I can see now, why you have put it in. Ant lions eat ants. Ants eat crops. Pest control is an important topic in a Science syllabus. I understand. . . .

He didn't, of course: and if he did not understand the rationale behind the process-approach, how much less would a primary teacher?

No people

I was once heavily criticised by a BBC producer for saying that early African history was boring in school because there were no people in it. He cut the remark out of the final programme lest it should offend the listeners.

There is, however, a good deal to what I was saying. Most children would rather learn about Julius Caesar who was a real person with a long nose, killed by his own friends because he had become a dictator, than study the rise of Meroe or Axum which have little interest to an eleven-year-old.

There are some syllabus makers, often expatriates, in all subjects, who would see anything African as desirable and anything European as irrelevant; the antithesis of the old Euro-centred approaches and equally ridiculous.

process approach comes from Nigeria where a modified version of a list produced by the American Association for the Advancement of Science has been suggested in the national 'Guidelines on Primary School Curriculum' to help evaluate coverage and approach in syllabuses and curriculum materials.

The following fifteen processes are listed:

observation, classification, communication, counting number relationship, measurement, raising questions, prediction, inference, formulating hypotheses, making operational definitions, controlling or manipulating variables, experimenting, formulating models, interpreting data, manipulative skills.

A very stimulating series, 'Primary Science', developed at the Institution of Education, Ahmadu Bello University, based on this approach, is now in very wide use throughout Nigeria.

There is some common ground between these two approaches to selection of materials for Science teaching, but they do result in radically different programmes: the content based approach is much easier to understand and interpret by the average teacher whereas the process-based approach often strikes much deeper towards the prior aim of making learners think more scientifically in a world where this process is increasingly necessary for survival.

SOCIAL STUDIES, HISTORY AND GEOGRAPHY

Main trends: Moves towards integration have already been discussed and some very creative Social and Environmental Studies programmes are being devised (Nigeria, Sierra Leone). But even in countries where History and Geography syllabuses have been maintained (Kenya and Botswana), considerably more local study is incorporated.

Gradually syllabuses are shedding that heavy load of world history, though a somewhat indigestible mass of early African history is often retained together with analysis of the structure and working of central and local government. Upper classes are often heavily loaded with current world affairs and the complicated workings of the United Nations and its agencies.

VOCATIONAL AND PRE-VOCATIONAL SUBJECTS

Some trends: Some excellent primary school Agriculture syllabuses now exist (Swaziland and Uganda).

Home Economics syllabuses, ever ambitious, are gradually now incorporating more elements of home-making, child care, nutrition (Kenya and Nigeria), while needlework assumes less paramount importance.

In one country (Kenya), a potentially profitable approach exists towards 'occupational education'. It is regarded as an area of concern, rather than a school subject. The specialists in the Institute of Education are hoping to devise means of feeding ideas and units related to skills training and pre-vocational work into other school subjects.

I would see this approach as being capable of useful application in other areas, e.g. Health Education or Development Studies.

TEACHERS' GUIDES

Occasionally official syllabuses contain very detailed advice for teachers and in one case (Botswana), a separate, loose-leaf file has been prepared for each grade, but in many cases it is the teachers' guide, or even the pupils' text which provides the real plan from which the teacher works.

The style and format of teachers' guides vary from the most detached to the most prescriptive. Usually teachers can expect detailed (possibly too detailed) help in English and Mathematics and sometimes also in Science and Religious Education, but often far less in local languages, Social Studies and cultural subjects, significantly enough, those subjects which are most closely connected with the local environment.

Can the syllabus work?

From the brief analysis in the last pages, I hope I have managed to convey the impression that a good deal of interesting, useful and imaginative content is being planned for primary schools. The picture, so beloved of third-rate politicians, of schools following inappropriate and European-centred syllabuses (hence not 'delivering the goods') is, and always was, a false one. But it is not true, either, to maintain, as some people do, that there is little wrong with the subject content and everything wrong with its implementation. Despite all of the official curriculum plans, there are many instances where the contents are inappropriate and still more where the plans themselves are largely responsible for the weakness in implementation. The following are some of my misgivings.

In the first place *these schemes often represent the experience and values of a middle class urban or semi-urban culture, at times totally alien to the rural child.* In some smaller countries such as Lesotho and Swaziland schools may even use materials designed for other African cultures. The English course used in Lesotho and designed originally for Rhodesia provides a particularly obvious example.

The syllabuses are heavily overloaded particularly in upper classes. Furthermore they are exceptionally ambitious in the language, skill and concepts they expect young children to acquire. A recent diagnostic test (1976) devised by the Mathematics section of the Curriculum Research and Development Division in Ghana reveals serious problems at all levels in comprehension of the language content of the Mathematics syllabus.

Comprehension of recommended English readers in upper primary classes is undoubtedly poor, probably appallingly so.[7] Certainly the reading content of the recommended book for Class 2 in Sierra Leone which I saw being used with very young children in Freetown schools is far above the average reading level one might expect for six-year-olds in London who speak English, not Creole, at home.

The introduction of abstract concepts into Social Studies and sometimes into Science syllabuses at a very early stage presupposes a level of cognitive development

Railway matters (Lesotho 1977)

I am taking a lesson in Class 6 in a school half-way up a mountain in an attempt to find out how well the children understand their English reader. The passage is about a schoolboy who goes on an outing and drops his bag out of the window of a railway carriage.

We are not doing well – the point of the passage seems to elude the class. I ask how many of them have ever seen a train. Three. How many have ever travelled on a train? None.

There are just two and a half kilometres of railway in Lesotho.

Extract from a teachers' guide (Nigeria)

Required for one Science lesson: Class 3

'live insects,
earthworms,
a frog or toad,
a lizard,
an aquarium with live fish,
a cat,
a dog or other mammal,
preserved specimens of each of the above,
a needle,
a spirit lamp,
a cooked piece of meat'.

I was particularly struck by the requirement for a preserved cat or dog. The rural teacher might find some difficulty here. As to whether a preserved aquarium is required, or merely a preserved fish, the text is unclear.

which Piagetian research would suggest to be beyond the average capacity of Swiss children. Since comparative studies from Africa seem to reinforce the evidence from all over the world that children pass through much the same stages, we can confidently predict that they mean just as little to the children of Kenya or Zambia[8].

Equally unrealistic are the demands made by syllabuses on teachers. Sometimes they contain more material than any human being could teach in the time recommended. Sometimes they presuppose background knowledge which teachers do not possess; very often they demand approaches and attitudes quite at variance with those held by an average teacher. Consider the case of a teacher brought up in the hard school where right answers were rewarded by praise and wrong answers by the cane. Now he is being invited to learn along with the children in Science, to admit ignorance (he the headmaster!), to reward discovery learning when neither he nor the children know the answer. Small wonder that he seldom responds to the challenge.

Demands on teachers, both in preparation time and materials to be collected may also be unrealistic. Sometimes materials are just not available or too expensive to afford, but often curriculum panels, drawing on experiences from college demonstration schools and materially rich urban contexts, place far too great reliance on the collection and use of 'waste' materials or require large amounts of apparatus to be made by teachers. Where and how they can do this in the conditions which prevail in many rural areas is rarely specified.

Finally teachers' guides are very frequently of a length and format and in a language which make them very, very difficult to comprehend by the average teacher. Research on the readability of guides to teachers is lacking, is needed and would be relatively easy to design and execute.

The rigidity in tone and approach of the syllabuses and materials is also a matter for concern. Often an introductory section mentions that the teacher *may* select and *may* concentrate on certain aspects in preference to others; sometimes it gives an indication that regional variations in content *may* be acceptable in certain cases. On the whole, however, there is little positive incentive for the teacher to select or diverge. The ground is there to be covered.

Moreover there seems little practical recognition of the fact that teachers vary, in their knowledge, in their experience and in their confidence. To manage such a spread of ability is one of the most delicate tasks a curriculum planner has to undertake, yet there *are* means, too seldom explored, of providing extra support for weaker teachers and extra ideas for innovative ones. *Moreover, the curriculum plan and materials are still firmly linked to a class by class progression and to teacher-centred learning.* The syllabuses are labelled Class 1, Class 2 and so on up the ladder. The books are graded and individual lessons often numbered and sequenced. Very little attempt is made to suggest alternatives in the syllabus plan or teachers' books, very little attempt made to design or recommend more flexible materials such as reading or number cards, and this, despite enormous variations in ages, abilities and background of children. Few serious attempts have been made to devise diagnostic tests in reading and number for the purpose of indicating relative attainment of learners.[9] *Added to this, plans and materials are still remarkably classroom orientated.* Relatively little indication is given of the way that the school environment can be exploited for teaching. There are seldom any references to

Table 7 National primary leaving and secondary entrance examinations: styles and patterns in African countries (1978)

COUNTRY	FUNCTION OF EXAMINATION	LANGUAGE OF EXAMINATION	
LESOTHO	There is one exam which functions both as a device for certificating primary school leavers and to select for secondary school entrance.	English in all papers except Sesotho.	
SWAZILAND	As above.	English in all except Siswati.	
BOTSWANA	As above.	English in all except Setswana.	
ZAMBIA	As above.	English in all papers except Zambian languages.	
TANZANIA	As above.	Swahili in all except English paper.	
KENYA	As above.	English in all papers.	
UGANDA	As above.	English throughout both exams.	
NIGERIA	As above, but separate entrance exam used in federal institutions and by some states. Other states organise their own selection methods.	English in all papers.	
GHANA	Exam used only as device for secondary selection. Certification of primary school leavers organised locally.	English in all papers.	
SIERRA LEONE	Exam principally used for secondary selection, but also important for primary certification.	English in all papers.	

SUBJECTS AND (no. of) PAPERS	TYPE OF EXAMINATION	NOTES
Verbal ability (1) numerical ability (1) Sesotho (2) English (2) social studies (1) mathematics (1) science (1).	All exams objective type except English/Sesotho which each have one essay paper.	Results are weighted: English, Sesotho, science and social studies 50 marks each; maths 60; total 260.
4 subjects required: English (2) Siswati (2) mathematics (2) general knowledge (divided between science and social studies paper).	All exams objective type except English/Siswati which each have one essay paper.	Results of all papers weighted evenly.
4 examination subjects: English (2) English (1) mathematics (1) mathematics (2) Setswana (1) general knowledge (1)	All exams objective/multiple choice except one English 1 and Setswana which are essay type.	Regional Testing Centre results weighted: English 1, English 2, maths 1, maths 2, general knowledge 50 each; Setswana not included; Total 250. English 2 and maths 2 set by the Centre — others by ministry subject specialists.
verbal ability (1) numerical ability (1) English (1) mathematics (1) science (1) social studies (1) Zambian languages (1).	All exams objective/multiple choice type including language papers.	As well as National Selection cut-off point in aggregate result, regional cut-off points are measured against regional availability of secondary school places. Zambian languages not included in aggregate to avoid penalising Asian/all-English schools.
Swahili (1) English (1) mathematics (1) general knowledge (1).	All exams objective/multiple choice including language papers.	Important swing in selection methods, away from simple exam towards performance testing of cumulative achievement on more decentralised regional basis, compensating for areas of disadvantage.
English (1) mathematics (1) general paper (1) (history, geography, general science)	All exams objective/multiple choice type.	Results of all papers weighted evenly.
English (1) mathematics (1) general paper (1) As for Kenya, general paper contains history, geography and general science questions.	All exams objective/multiple choice type.	Some degree of Ministry control in weighting results to compensate for inequalities between minority groups.
Leaving exam: English (2) arithmetic (1) general knowledge (1) Secondary entrance: mathematics (1) English (1) quantative aptitude (1) verbal aptitude (1).	All exams objective type except English 2 in leaving exam which is essay type.	Certain states may organise and employ other criteria for selection.
English (2) mathematics (1) verbal aptitude (1) quantative aptitude (1).	All papers objective type except English 2 which is essay type.	
English (2) mathematics (1) verbal aptitude (1) quantative aptitude (1).	All papers objective type except English 2 which is essay type.	Examination shared between Sierra Leone and Gambia with common criteria.

co-curricular activities and the important part which they might play in the whole curriculum of a school. Typically, for instance, a Physical Education programme concentrates on P.E. lessons, making little reference to games and sports, while Language and Cultural Activities syllabuses stress classroom drama but ignore potentials for clubs and community activities.

As yet, little emphasis is placed on learning initially planned in school and subsequently carried out in the community, such as home garden plots in Agriculture and Health Education projects. Sadly, when such activities do occur, they are heralded as innovations and labelled 'community education'.

Finally, I am always depressed at *the apparent lack of concern in our syllabuses and teachers' guides for the poorer educational contexts*. If you have forty children and desks for all of them, a set of recommended texts and a full complement of teaching time, the syllabus is for you and the texts help you. If you are teaching a heterogeneous mob of children in an afternoon session with little or no equipment, the advice given is clearly not for you: you are a 'sub-teacher', teaching a 'sub-class', The official curriculum plan washes its hands of you. Yet, you are well aware that you and those like you, well outnumber your more fortunately placed colleagues.

Examinations, selection and the official curriculum

The curriculum of the last two years of primary school is inevitably dominated by the final public examinations a child takes. Although schools and teachers I visited may not always have been able to produce copies of the official syllabus, everyone had copies of previous years' questions and were assiduously preparing children to sit for the current examination.

WHAT KIND OF EXAMINATION?

Table 7 indicates patterns of examinations in ten different countries.

Although some attempt is made to design an instrument which serves the needs of primary school leavers as well as secondary school entrants, the main official purpose of the exercise, and practically the only purpose which interests teachers or children, is to select entrants for secondary school. This purpose is amply reflected in the design, setting and weighting of the examinations. The following facts are worth noting:

1 Examinations are heavily weighted towards Language and Mathematics. Except in Tanzania, English language papers tend to be more heavily weighted than local language papers. Frequently, indeed, local languages are not examined or not counted in the final mark to determine selection.
2 English language skills are also necessary in all other parts of the examination. In cases where a verbal ability test is set, it is set in English. Mathematics, Science and Social Studies questions often require considerable speed and accuracy in English comprehension.
3 Certain subjects in the primary school curriculum, notably practical and cultural subjects are not usually assessed externally.

4 Those involved in setting the examination may lack direct experience of primary schools and their curriculum. They think, perhaps, more in terms of what knowledge and skills they would hope to find in a secondary school entrant rather than of those one might expect from a child who had successfully completed a primary school course. They may, therefore, only be marginally concerned with the effect that the examination they set has on teaching and learning in primary schools. There are even strange cases where primary syllabus panels have little or no direct link with examiners and where conflict exists between what the syllabus recommends and what the examinations examine.

5 Examinations are designed very largely to secure ease of marking since skilled markers are limited, and to ensure that, as far as possible, justice is seen to be done and that instances (and accusations) of nepotism or corruption are kept to a minimum. Multiple choice questions, easily machine marked, are therefore greatly favoured. Where essays are required in language, they tend to be marked to a fairly rigid marking scheme.

6 All examinations are competitive. Sometimes there is a fixed pass mark and leavers receive their certificates graded as I, II, or III; sometimes passes or grades are adjusted to fit places available in secondary school, but in either case, everyone knows that there are just so many secondary school places, and many, many more aspirants for them.

The level of marks required for entrance to secondary school is a very closely guarded secret and seldom officially revealed. In many cases, especially in Mathematics, it may be very low indeed. Thus we frequently have a pattern where a relatively difficult examination is set to conform to the entry standards someone hopes may be achieved, where a large number of candidates do very badly on it and some of the least bewildered are then selected for further education.

'THE BACKWASH EFFECT'

The effects of the examination on the primary school curriculum, described by Somerset as the 'backwash effect', are massive and on the whole disheartening. King comments on the effects in Kenya; his remarks would apply with few local variants to nearly all the countries visited in our survey:

> 'It appears, as a general finding, that there is much cynicism amongst primary school teachers about the possibility of innovation in curricula when teaching is under its present constraint. A number of teachers have of course been exposed to discovery methods, the principles of new maths and new science; there is, however, a strong countervailing trend in which pupils know from their CPE texts what are the answers, the definitions of the scientific laws, and increasingly regard as a waste of time proving by rudimentary experiments what they already know. Inevitably perhaps the present style of objective test concentrates on the general rules and definitions, and the pupils resent time not spent on revising these. Additionally, few primary schools have the equipment or facilities to carry out scientific experiments as the syllabus suggests.
> On the mathematics side one of the most serious charges, parallel to the lack of interest in the writing of English, is that some of the skills such as the careful construction of graphs and geometric figures are no longer considered important by

Miscellaneous information

The following are culled from Science and General Knowledge papers in two countries. They are typical of the kind of factual information which may be expected of children and could be paralleled elsewhere.

Nigeria (1974)
The mountains in Algeria are called:
A. Drakensberg   B. Fouta Djallon   C. Atlas   D. Ethiopian   E. Adamawa

Lagos was conquered by the British in:
A. 1949   B. 1851   C. 1871   D. 1901   E. 1939.

The diagram represents a cockroach. The structure marked I is:
A. a spiracle   B. an antenna   C. a proboscis   D. a leg   E. a cuticle.

Lesotho (1975)
In which layer of the skin is fat stored?
A. hornified layer   B. epidermis   C. dermis   D. malpighian layer   E. subcutaneous layer.

Which of these teams won in the Sturrock League Soccer finals in 1974?
A. Bantu F.C.   B. Manjantja F.C.   C. Maseru United F.C.   D. Linare F.C.
E. Mattama F.C.

students. In the actual examination all the figures are provided and it is only necessary to infer from inspecting the graph or drawing which of four alternatives is the correct one. Furthermore, a casual inspection of some of the children's workbooks in Standard 7 will reveal in most subjects lists of question numbers at the side of the page and then merely the corresponding answer letter, a, b, c, or d.

However, it is some of the non-examinable subjects which would appear to fare worst in the primary school at the moment. These are Swahili, domestic science and handicrafts, practical agriculture and religious knowledge.'[10]

Moreover, this is only half the story. The examination is set and marked in such a way that it excludes by its very nature from Science and Social Studies papers any questions based on the local environment. As a result, environmental study is virtually neglected in the curriculum in the years when it could be most meaningful and most beneficial, especially to school leavers.

The multiple choice questions, mentioned earlier, besides restricting the extent of the subject matter, often limit the range of intellectual skills which can be tested. In theory, items can be devised to test the more sophisticated thought processes listed in Bloom's *Taxonomy* such as knowledge of trends and sequences, or skills of analysis, but such item writing demands not only a high degree of skill, not often available, it also requires a considerable sophistication in language and comprehension skills which second language learners are unlikely to possess. It is by no means surprising, therefore, to find that the vast majority of items in Social Studies and Science papers demand straight recall of specific facts and that teaching is adjusted accordingly: in one paper analysed in Botswana out of fifty questions, forty-nine required only recall of factual information.

Finally, because the examination is set on knowledge and abilities required for secondary school entry, and because all children do aspire to such entry, it forces teachers to cover material with their pupils whether they are able to understand it or not; the very antithesis of sound pedagogy.

NEW APPROACHES, NEW IDEAS

Concern over the effect of terminal examinations and of their efficiency is widespread throughout Africa. While a few voices, mainly from the safety of universities, call for their abolition, the majority of practical opinion recognises that examinations are inevitable and that three tasks are necessary to improve both their efficiency and their effect on the school curriculum.

The first is quite simply to set better papers, to make sure that panels who evolve objectives and plan the content of the primary school curriculum assume control of the evaluation process, at the same time to reconsider the weighting of subjects and revise the languages in which they are set. Already considerable improvements in papers in language and mathematics have been effected by the West African Examination Council's Test Development and Research Unit, and by the Regional Testing Centre in Malawi. But it is still apparent that many current 'verbal ability tests', together with most papers in Social Studies, Science and General Knowledge are in urgent need of review. In at least two countries, Kenya and Botswana, such a review is already underway and CPE papers in Kenya already begin to show considerable improvement over those analysed by Somerset in 1974.[11]

The allegory of the swimming pool

Hugh Hawes: How then do the children of Africa pass through their first school?

Socrates: I would have you imagine a swimming pool. It is long and the bottom slopes downwards. At the one end it is very shallow and at the other end it is deep.

Into this pool plunge rank after rank of children chained together. They are of different heights: some are short and some are tall. At the edge of the pool stand guardians with spears. They force the children forward at a steady pace. After a time the shorter children become submerged and the number under water increases as the ranks go forward.

Hugh Hawes: What happens to these?

Socrates: Some drown and are hauled out of the pool and left on the edge. Still more are forced to walk on underwater, oblivious of the world outside. By the time they reach the end of the pool they are too exhausted to climb out.

Hugh Hawes: What of the tallest children?

Socrates: They reach the end of the pool without difficulty but very slowly for they must march in step with their weaker and shorter fellows.

Hugh Hawes: The end of the pool, then, represents the final examination, the lines of children are the pupils of different ages and abilities, the guardians, I suppose, are the textbook writers, syllabus makers and educational administrators.

Socrates: Just so.

The second task is to assess the effects, present and potential, of the examination style and content on the school, and to redesign examinations with these effects in mind. One relatively manageable task would be to use the computers currently employed to sort out lists and marks for item analyses of marks scored in individual questions, thus building up a profile of strengths and weaknesses in the subject analysed.

Much more fundamental, however, is the issue which concerns the existing format of the examinations. It may well be that machine-marked multiple choice type questions may prove inappropriate instruments for measuring or achieving desired curricular goals such as content or skills in Environmental Studies. In this case I believe that it is by far preferable to accept the lack of consistency which we all know exists in papers marked by people, rather than suffer the strangling constraints on what and how we teach forced upon us when papers are marked by machine.[12]

The final task is to reconsider the virtual monopoly of the final examination as the instrument of selection. Already, and much publicised, we have the Tanzanian alternative whereby cumulative records of performance and teachers' reports have been used alongside examination marks to determine who goes to secondary school.[13] It has always seemed to me that in pupils' day to day work and more specifically in their exercise books, we have a reasonable body of evidence which can be evaluated, probably in the school, moderated, probably by other teachers and headmasters and allowed to count in some way towards the success of pupils. In this way, provided they are given guidance on the type and volume of work expected, schools could be brought back into the mainstream of assessing their own pupils' work instead of being totally dependent on the success or failure of the guessing games they play with the examiner.

It may be appropriate to end this section with a quotation from H. C. A. Somerset whose research on examination and selection in African schools has done so much to clarify problems and suggest solutions:

> 'If the Certificate of Primary Education tested material which was firmly within the grasp of primary school teachers: if it tested the ability to reason and understand relationships of cause and effect; and, if, above all, it tested relevant and practical knowledge, it would be at the same time both a more efficient and equitable instrument for selecting secondary school entrants and also a more useful preparation for those for whom primary education is terminal. The two goals are not incompatible.
>
> In *Education for Self-Reliance*, Nyerere has written: "We should not determine the type of things children are taught in primary schools by the things a doctor, engineer, teacher, economist or administrator needs to know. Most of our pupils will never by any of these things. . . Our sights must be on the majority." If we wish to make a reality out of Nyerere's vision, the place to start with is the secondary school selection examination.'[14]

Issues for debate

Underlying all the decisions, all the choices which have to be made concerning an official curriculum, all the conflicting influences and all the necessary compromises, three familiar issues can be recognised:

What curriculum is to be selected?
Who is going to make the choice?
How is this selection to be expressed to the users?

Choices of language, decisions regarding objectives, content, the priority accorded to them and the criteria for determining them all have to be made, renewed and periodically revised. Side by side with these come decisions regarding curriculum control, in particular those related to the degree of flexibility to be permitted and encouraged in relation to choice of language, of content and of evaluation. Currently, in many countries, debate centres on whether some kind of core curriculum with permitted options should evolve, as suggested in recent reports from Zambia,[15] Botswana[16] and Lesotho,[17] and if so of what nature that core should be.

But who makes the choices, establishes the criteria and decides the priorities? Who co-ordinates and resolves conflicts? It must have become clear to us by now that a committee of different subject specialists trading off time and contents with each other is an unwieldy and potentially dangerous body.

But what can be suggested to replace them? A small primary curriculum steering committee, perhaps. Would it be heresy to suggest that such a committee need not be composed entirely of educationists and *should not* be composed entirely of specialists in curriculum development.

Finally how are such official plans to be expressed and disseminated? In only one country I have recently visited, Kenya, was I able to buy a syllabus in the bookshop. Yet a statement of national intent concerning the learnings planned and provided for a nation's youth is surely a document which should be available and one which needs to be open to public criticism. Could we not look forward to an era where our syllabuses for instruction in schools were as carefully drafted, as well produced and as widely read and discussed as our development plans for education?

Notes

1 Hawes, H. W. R., 'Primary School Curriculum Development in Africa – Hopes and Facts', *Journal of Curriculum Studies*, Vol 2 No 2, November 1970, p 108

2 Held in Lagos 1973. The recommendations were later incorporated into *Federal Republic of Nigeria – National Policy on Education*, Ministry of Information, Lagos 1977

3 The final report of the review still recommends a cut, but only from 7 to 6 years: *All Our Future*, 1976, p 7

4 Dottrens, R., *The Primary School Curriculum*, UNESCO 1962

5 Indications (and they are based on no more than the subjective judgement of observers) would suggest this to be one of the major success stories in lower primary teaching in Africa. Perhaps they got the mix between prescription and initiative right.

6 These titles have been developed and modified from the APSP booklets – see Table 3.

7 Our own entirely random unscientific attempt to gauge comprehension during recent visits to primary schools appears to suggest that more than half the children in these classes would not adequately understand the books in front of them. Gradually more reliable evidence begins to back this up e.g. from surveys attempted in 1977 by the Ministry of Education, Botswana and the Distance Teaching Centre in Lesotho.

8 See *The Development of Science and Mathematics Concepts in Young Children in African*

Countries, report of a regional seminar arranged by UNESCO–UNICEF. UNESCO/UNICEF, Nairobi, 1974

9 Some *are* beginning to emerge. I have recently encountered reading tests from Nigeria and Botswana and mathematical tests from Ghana.

10 Court, D. and Ghai, D. (eds), *Education, Society and Development*, OUP Nairobi 1974, p 127

11 Court and Ghai, *op. cit.*, pp 169–173

12 Issues of cost will certainly be raised whenever such arguments are advanced. Depending on circumstances estimates vary, but to my surprise I discover that in general the difference in costing between the two modes may be slight.

13 See Dore, R., *The Diploma Disease*, Unwin 1976, pp 117–121

14 *Education, Society and Development in Kenya*, *op. cit.*, p 182

15 *Education for Development*, Zambia, 1976

16 *Education for Kagisano*, Botswana, 1977

17 *Primary School Curriculum Change in Lesotho*, 1977

Teacher-centred learning (West African style)

The teacher is telling a story in Yoruba, but not in the way I, an Englishman, would tell it. She is dancing it, singing it, acting it. She tells with her face, her voice, her whole body. The class is completely caught up in the action: toes and shoulders wriggling in sympathy. There is a song involved; the whole class joins in without invitation. As we all dance forward towards the next episode, I realise that for one brief hour we have escaped from the drab monotony of the Oxford English Culture. (This is a win–dow. What is this class? That is a window. First row? That is a window. Musa? That is a window – Good, now all together. . . .)

A headmaster with a problem (Sierra Leone 1976)

The class is working – and working hard – on a verandah. Conditions are difficult. The house is in the centre of the village and there seems a very real danger that the goat will eat your Mathematics books. I am greeted warmly by the headmaster.

Hugh Hawes: How are you getting on?
Headmaster: Fine, we only have one problem.
Hugh Hawes: What is that?
Headmaster: We haven't got a school.
Hugh Hawes: Why is that?
Headmaster: Well, the inspector came and noticed a hole in the roof and told us to mend it. So we took the roof off but then it rained very hard so the walls fell down.
Hugh Hawes: Has the inspector come back?
Headmaster: Not yet.

Chapter 5   What shall they learn? (2)
The actual curriculum in schools

What determines the actual curriculum

To step out of the curriculum centres, the institutes or the ministries into the schools of Africa provides such a contrast that it is easy to caricature the differences. It is also treacherously easy to fall into facile and unproductive stereotypes, to categorise the curriculum in schools as 'teacher-centred' and 'formal'. Often it is both, but there are so many exceptions, so many degrees of variation that generalisation often invites misunderstanding.

We should also be wary of accepting unquestioningly the 'romantic' values implied in these labels.[1] There is only one valid measure of success of a curriculum: the learning which takes place. Apart from the obvious fact that certain kinds of learning may be most appropriately learnt directly from a teacher, there are many contents in Africa where 'formal' and 'teacher-centred' approaches are the only ones which can rationally and effectively be used. Indeed, I have sat in many classes dominated by the art and personality of a teacher, where the whole class was carried forward to new understandings.

In Chapter 2 and subsequently, I have stressed the enormous variations in context which exist in African schools, between countries, between urban and rural conditions, between and within individual schools, and the way that these various elements so critically affect the learning experiences a school offers. As I look back over visits to schools in recent years, the impressions, the differences, the experiences come crowding in.

I picture richly rewarding learning environments: I walk, unnoticed, into a creative activities period in Jos (Nigeria) where the children remain too absorbed in their various tasks to look up at a stranger, however unfamiliar. I am shown over a large and productive school garden in Lesotho by the teachers and pupils who created it. I meet an eager mob of fifty Class 2 children in Swaziland and a large lady who had taught every single one of them to read, determined collectively and individually to hold me in the classroom until they have proved it true. I recall being earnestly explained the breeding cycle of rabbits by pupils in a Class 6 in Machakos (Kenya) where the classroom floor appeared almost ankle deep in the creatures.

I can tell of many schools and many teachers doing an exciting job under very difficult circumstances: a school set up in abandoned, corrugated iron railway sheds in Ghana with no partitions, hot at midday and unspeakably noisy during rainstorms, yet well equipped with a cheerful co-operative staff, an open plan school, Ghana style; an overcrowded school in Lesotho where teachers had evolved their own brand of team-teaching, one teacher imparting information to a class of 120, followed by groupwork where two teachers and a student supervised written work;

a school down the road from them where Class 1 and 2 teachers who finished teaching at lunchtime had organised afternoon sessions on remedial reading for older children; another in Francistown, Botswana, in temporary classrooms, with walls made of hessian and children organised into 'family groups' playing reading and number games under the guidance of older children.

By contrast I retain pictures of those dull, soulless lessons, the daily lot of so many children throughout the world:

A Science radio lesson with poor reception and without accompanying teachers' notes;

A Mathematics class working through sums with half the children in a state of total incomprehension and getting all the examples wrong, while others spend fruitless time doing sum after sum on a process which they had mastered weeks previously;

A Civics lesson largely devoted to copying from the blackboard a diagram on the hierarchical structure of the ministry of education;

A singing lesson where the class intoned a version of 'Bobby Shaftoe' with words apparently modified by some early missionary;

A handiwork lesson where children were mechanically engaged in a task (making brooms) which all had already mastered before they ever came to school.

At the bottom end of the educational scale I remember so very clearly the instances – and there were far too many of them for my peace of mind – where the school had virtually given up in the face of difficulties. Classes abandoned by their teachers, children enslaved by their headmaster to do his work and not the school's and those endless revision classes with or without the benefit of 'students' guides' of one sort or another.

These impressions, so varied, so vivid, serve to underline the enormous variety in actual practice in African primary schools. But actual practice is somewhat different from actual curriculum. Practice may be intended or unintended. Curriculum is learning which is planned and provided for a purpose. Plans and purposes of schools and teachers may differ from those of ministries and the experts they employ – and may indeed be more realistic. Of course the gap between the official and the actual curriculum varies in nature and extent, but certain types of variations are common enough to warrant generalisations. Consider some of these.

TIME ALLOCATIONS

Time available in schools is almost invariably less than time allocated in curriculum plans. Quite apart from the leisurely beginnings and ends of terms, the examination time, unexpected holidays, and festivals, requests for children to parade or sing or help with community work, there are the apparently inevitable absences of teachers: the headmaster to collect salaries, the senior teachers to mark and supervise examinations or attend panels, the married ladies to nurse sick children or to have babies. These absences are part of life in an African primary school and no number of official circulars will alter the situation. Consequently, syllabuses and teachers' guides which depend on the full official time allocation for their completion, and many do, are doomed to failure, whereas a shorter and more manageable core, with optional and enrichment materials for better endowed schools and better teachers would ensure that minimum content was taught.

LANGUAGE OF INSTRUCTION

Whatever the syllabus says, the teacher and the school to some degree choose their own language medium. The official policy will influence that choice and so too will the school and community perception of what language medium is most likely to help towards secondary entrance, hence pressures towards more English medium and earlier English teaching in some areas. But the main determinant will usually be ease of communication: what language the teacher can teach and what language the children can best understand. As a result, all sorts of patterns emerge, including lessons which go on in two and sometimes three languages. To insist on a dogmatic policy is unworkable. It may prove more feasible and profitable to set standards of language competence to be achieved at certain levels and leave room for different paths to these common goals.

BASIC SKILLS

Syllabuses and those who frame them may talk of 'all round education' but schools are in no doubt about their curriculum priorities. These are Language and Mathematics. The emphasis on them is apparent even on the most casual visit to schools. Obvious indicators are the books schools or parents buy for children and the priority in which they buy them, the volume of work in exercise books and the care with which it is corrected as well as the actual, as distinct from the official, allocation of teaching time. Emphasis as between local language and English teaching varies according to national patterns and policies, but a survey would most probably reveal the English text as the most commonly possessed book in most schools.

These priorities are pragmatic and sensible. Teaching the 3 R's is what schools do best, and what no other form of education can do in their stead. It would seem entirely appropriate if official syllabuses, official materials' production schemes and official policies of implementation ensured, like the schools, that wherever else economies were made, the teaching of language and number and particularly the former, received adequate attention and adequate funding.

EXAMINATIONS AND PREPARATIONS FOR THEM

I have earlier discussed the critical importance of examinations and selection as a determinant of the actual curriculum in schools. Subject selection, content and methodology are to a great extent, dominated by their influence on upper classes and no one who is aware of social and salary structures in Africa, or who has had children of his own in the system, would expect otherwise. Even in a socialist

Philemon's results (A story from Zambia)

The headmaster stood up behind his desk. Although he greeted them cheerily enough, they noticed that he was twisting a new piece of white chalk nervously between his fingers. The boys knew from long experience that this was a sign of trouble.

'Good afternoon, boys. I've now received the acceptance from the head-master of the Secondary School. I am afraid that some of you are going to be disappointed, but you know that there are not places in the Secondary School for everyone who passes Standard Six. With only two exceptions you all did very well in your qualifying examinations and I am very proud of the school's results, but, I am sorry, only twelve of you have been accepted for Form I.'

There was silence in the classroom. No one moved, or said anything, because each one of the boys sitting there was quite certain that he would be one of the lucky twelve to be chosen. It was only when the headmaster had finished reading the list of names that the hubbub started. The twelve lucky ones jumped up laughing with relief and went wild with joy, the others shouted angrily, stamping their feet and banging the lids of their desks. The only one to remain quite still was Philemon. He sat like a man stunned by the sudden news of death. Slowly he rose from his seat and went over to the headmaster who stood twisting the piece of white chalk between his fingers.

'Mufundishi, you didn't read my name. You know me, Mufundishi, I'm your boy Philemon Nalusanga. You always told me that if I worked hard, one day, I would go for Secondary. You know I am going to be a doctor, Mufundishi. You know my Standard Six certificate won't get me any job at all. Mufundishi, what am I going to do now?'

The headmaster was an honest man, so he just didn't say anything.

Extract from Merfyn Temple's 'From Chipapa with love', an open letter to President Kaunda, Zambia, January 1974.

A revision lesson (Botswana 1975)

It is the afternoon session and very hot. I enter a Class I with hot, sleepy six- and seven-year-olds and a hot, sleepy teacher. The children have exercise books and scraps of paper. At a rough estimate 50 per cent can write a few words, 50 per cent cannot.

Hugh Hawes: What are the children doing?
Teacher: They are revising for their examination.

country like Tanzania, however committed one may be to the abolition of privilege in society, there is no arguing with the fact that young people with secondary and higher education can expect life to bring them a richer and more interesting experience than it does to the primary school leaver.

But to consider only the final selection examination, is to see only half the picture. Although the tyranny of 'promotion examinations' has mercifully decreased in the past decade, in many countries yearly and termly examinations and preparation for them account for a quite disproportionate amount of school time and teachers are virtually ignorant of how and why and when to test. Few approaches would produce more positive results on the actual curriculum in schools than review and re-training in this field.

While there are certain examples of examination paranoia in final classes which are unproductive and unnecessary such as the 'mock' examinations and endless preparation for them, it is idle to deny the influence of the examination or to discourage classes from working towards it. As I have already indicated, the critical question we must ask is how we may design selection procedures which encourage sensible teaching and learning.

Where do the official and actual curricula meet?

I have indicated that a wide and unacceptable gap exists between central plans and local realities. As a generalisation this is all too true: however there are areas where the gap is narrow or narrowing and others where it hardly exists. This happy state of affairs happens, mainly I believe, when two conditions are satisfied.

The first of these is when the teacher is asked to do a manageable job, where he is working within his intellectual capacity and has that confidence which proceeds from really knowing more about what he is teaching than the children do. Such confidence is further strengthened when there is positive and practical help available to the teacher in the form of clear sequenced teachers' notes with practical advice. The large volume of sound (if somewhat stereotyped) English teaching in lower and middle classes and the solid and sensible teaching of basic arithmetical processes are all, I believe, a product of such a sense of security, as are the generally more creative attitudes and approaches of teachers in the lower classes of primary schools.

The official and actual curricula are also brought close together whenever there is genuine interest and enthusiasm on the part of the teacher (which is almost invariably communicated to the children). This is noticeable when short term goals can be identified and seen to be worth reaching and may well account for the very impressive efforts by schools in agricultural, sports and music competitions. But it is most evident whenever a teacher has developed a real interest in some school subject or area of the curriculum, often the result of some form of limited subject specialisation by the teacher. Sometimes this is officially encouraged. More often it is not, for administrators would have a manoeuvrable teacher, and any form of specialisation decreases manoeuvrability. Yet it is doubtful whether this argument outweighs the benefits a teacher gains from being able to concentrate his interests. For if he considers himself in some small way a specialist, not only can he spend a good proportion of his time teaching what he likes and probably, therefore, understands better, but he also has more of a chance of keeping up to date on his chosen subjects, particularly if he has support, as many of the teachers I observed had, from local subject advisers, associations or selective in-service programmes.

One popular myth needs, perhaps, to be dispelled at this stage. That is the belief that teachers and children 'don't like getting their hands dirty'. Indeed I detect a genuine and growing support for Agriculture[2] in schools, evident from pupils and their parents, whenever leadership is given by an enthusiastic teacher, and I have met a number of these, giving freely of their own time and sometimes of their limited funds as well. The assessment of practical subjects and their funding remains a problem, but the negative attitudes towards Agriculture, which I remember so clearly in the years just preceding and just after independence in the countries where I worked and travelled, seems virtually dead. Instead there comes the realisation, surely necessary all over the world, that every African, whatever else he is, is also a food producer and must learn to be an efficient one.

HOPES AND FACTS

'Objectives are like targets,' says Richmond,[3] 'the nearer they are, the easier they are to hit.' In this chapter I have attempted to draw a distinction between the targets we set and our ability to hit them.

No one expects every one to hit these targets in the middle, but at least they should be in sight and the marksman should be provided with a gun that shoots straight. The fact that many syllabuses and teachers' books are full of relevant and challenging content and that in every country schools can be found where interesting and exciting work is in progress, must not obscure the central problem. *To the average teacher in the average school the official curriculum plan is unattainable.* He just can't hit the target however hard he tries.

Unless and until more knowledge is gathered concerning the aspirations, capabilities and limitations of schools and the people who work in them, and until sufficient flexibility is built into syllabus planning to allow for the necessary variations that are inherent in planning and providing learning for different people in different contexts, the gap between prescription and reality will remain an unconscionably wide one. Perhaps those of you, my readers, who are involved, like me, in curriculum design, might join me in a New Year's resolution to keep our wishful thinking in check and face reality more consistently. Those of you who are teaching and training teachers for school, I would invite to rebellion. It is high time that more of you spoke up in protest against us whenever we invite you to do that which is impractical or inappropriate. Out of our argument, a better and more workable curriculum could emerge.

The realities of curriculum choice – perspectives from Lesotho

Analysis of context and goals, of comparative trends and approaches to curriculum change provides valuable data for a curriculum planner. A knowledge of appropriate theory and the techniques of curriculum development gives him certain tools to work with. Yet in the last analysis there are always hard decisions and choices to be made: which learnings are worthwhile, which are appropriate, which should be emphasised above others.

In 1977 I visited Lesotho and worked together with colleagues in the Ministry of Education to recommend a possible strategy for primary school curriculum change in conjunction with the setting up of a Curriculum Development Centre funded by the World Bank and a parallel UNICEF programme to assist in the processes of syllabus and materials production and implementation.

The plan which has emerged from my visit and subsequent discussions is based on needs and conditions in Lesotho, but certain issues are of wider relevance.

DETERMINING AIMS AND OBJECTIVES

We envisaged the following processes as necessary:

1 'To reconsider, re-emphasise and publicise national aims for primary education and to spell out broad implications of these for the curriculum.

2 'To refine these further by attempting to specify what it is hoped that a Mosotho child should *know*, *feel* and have the *skills to do* as a result of a full primary education and at each stage during that education.

3 'To identify *priorities*: minimum learning needs for *all* Lesotho children who have attended primary school. To consider the broad implications of these priorities on the selection and balance of the curriculum.

4 'To identify issues vital to national development which can be woven into the fabric of curriculum materials for different subjects at particular levels or at all levels using the spiral approach. (We would have in mind issues such as conservation of national resources, self-reliance, population education, health priorities, concepts of nationhood and the use of appropriate locally based technology.)'[4]

Such statements derive from the meetings of a specially convened working party on national objectives, but as a preliminary to this a national debate on the purposes of primary education has already taken place in 1978, culminating in a widely publicised and widely representative National Seminar on the Content of Primary Education.

DEVELOPMENT THEMES

The concept of 'development themes' was central to our thinking. Once these were identified, suitable approaches could be considered for different ages and stages in the curriculum and 'topic webs' produced.[5] Thus a theme on population education would be centred, perhaps, on 'our family' in Class 2 and 'people and food supply' in Class 5. In respect of materials production:

'Once a theme (e.g. conservation of soil) is agreed upon it is up to all subject writers to ensure that it is woven into the content of materials produced; made the subject for reading passages in language, for problems in mathematics, for field surveys in social studies and for practical demonstration in agriculture.'[6]

Two interlocking cycles were recommended to cover the seven year primary course:

'*Cycle 1* concentrates on *basic skills* and extending from Grade 1 to Grades 4 to 5 (depending on standards of children). In this cycle emphasis would be on achieving acceptable standards of oracy and literacy (in Sesotho), though *oral* English is also introduced, together with adequate numeracy and other basic elements: i.e. co-ordination of eye and hand; simple powers of observation and reasoning based on the home, school and local environment; personal health habits and positive attitudes appropriate to the age of the child.
Cycle 2 is a *continuation cycle* extending from Grade 4 to 5 up to Grade 7. Here two elements are emphasised.
(i) Environmental Studies in which the child learns more about his or her environment and actually takes part in activities such as gardening and home science which help to control it and make it productive.
(ii) Further acquisition of learning skills: including further mastery of language skills (*literacy* in English is now introduced) and of skills in mathematical and scientific thinking.
In both cycles the fostering of sound moral, religious and patriotic attitudes are conceived as permeating the whole of the curriculum.'[7]

A non-competitive literacy test (in Sesotho) is recommended to be taken at the end of the first cycle or any time thereafter prior to the final examination since *mastery of literacy skills is seen as the first priority in primary school education in Lesotho* – 'if learners are to profit from further opportunities for education in or out of school.'

Central also to the recommendations was the concept of core, optional and enrichment materials. *Core materials* refer to topics studied by all Basotho children at a particular level. *Optional materials* would be of three types:

1 'Choices by schools and within schools of practical and cultural activities appropriate to local manpower and conditions. Thus one school might offer drama because a teacher was interested, another pottery because a local potter was available to help and because clay was readily available. Limits of choice should be indicated, but schools should be encouraged to offer local plans for approval.
2 'Choices within subjects e.g. alternative units in science and social studies to suit different interests and different local conditions. Alternatives would be offered in the curriculum plan but there would also be opportunity for many other alternatives hopefully designed at teachers' workshops.
3 'Interdisciplinary units.'
'Small numbers of units which cut across traditional subject boundaries could be designed – one such unit on transport having already been produced. Schools who had the interest and expertise should be encouraged to make a reasonable investment of time in teaching such units in place of separate optional topics.'[8]

Enrichment materials were seen as being produced mainly in connection with the teaching of basic skills and would include additional topics and materials in Sesotho, Mathematics and English chosen so that they deepened children's understanding of core topics and including supplementary readers, apparatus, assignment cards, games and radio broadcasts.

The design of the new syllabus and the programme of materials production was to reflect these three categories. At the same time both syllabus and materials would emphasise that the primary curriculum is seen as something much wider than a mere list of topics to be covered in class. As our report indicated, besides denoting objectives, content and possible means of evaluation (probably entitled 'how do we know what they have learnt'), the syllabus and materials were also to call attention to:

1 'The way that the subject is taught through the life of the school e.g. health habits, games, school government and self help in building and decorating etc.
2 'The way that the subject taught in school can be related to life in the community, e.g. community health, social service, home vegetable plots etc.
'Such sections should not be inserted as footnotes but rather as important component parts of the syllabus – under headings: *In The Class; In The School; In The Community.*'[9]

As this book goes to press (1979) these recommendations feed into the process of curriculum development in Lesotho. Assuredly some will prove more valuable, some less so, some unworkable. They are all part of that continuing process of gaining experience in rational curriculum planning which forms the theme of this book.

Notes

1 See Lawton's excellent analysis of 'classical' and 'romantic' traditions in his book, *Social Change, Educational Theory and Curriculum Planning*, ULP 1973, pp 22*ff*
2 By agriculture I mean a varied teaching and learning programme not merely cultivating large quantities of a single cash or food crop in order to raise funds for the school or feed it. This may be politically and economically necessary, but no twelve-year-old is likely to be overwhelmed with enthusiasm for the hard and repetitive work it entails.
3 Richmond, W. K., *The School Curriculum*, Methuen 1971, p 185
4 H. W. R. Hawes, *Primary School Curriculum Change in Lesotho! UNICEF's Commitment in Context*, Consultant's Report, April 1977, p 21
5 See page 90 for an example of such a topic web built round the school garden.
6 Consultant's Report, p 69
7 Report, pp 23–24
8 Report, pp 66–67
9 Report, p 66

Chapter 6 Proposals into practice (1)

Changing people and their attitudes

In the early days of the 'curriculum revolution', when our enthusiasm was matched only by our arrogance, many curriculum workers in Europe, America and Africa seemed to take for granted that, since their new ideas were such very good ones, they would be widely and rapidly accepted by schools. Now sadder but wiser, we are prepared to admit that the implementation of curriculum change is a complicated business. A considerable amount of thoughtful literature is emerging to help clarify our thinking.[1] Implementation *involves a series of related tasks*: so the dissemination of ideas is the first necessity to prepare people to accept change, understand what it involves and why it is worth making. In a centralised system the dull and docile will always go along with new policies, but no change can be properly interpreted or adequately sustained without support from active thinkers and innovators at different levels in a system. Next it is essential to agree a workable *strategy* for implementation based on conditions as they are, not as we would wish them to be. Only then can the *process* of implementation follow. This involves not only the introduction of new practices into a system, but their consolidation and continuation after the first enthusiastic impulse has worn off.

Implementation is *capable of different strategies* which may and should be used to suit different circumstances. Havelock[2] suggests three categories: *the research and development and diffusion model*, where an idea or practice conceived at the centre is fed out into the system; *the social interaction model*, where change proceeds through formal and informal contact between groups; and the *problem solving model*, where individuals are themselves involved in initiating, developing or modifying aspects of a programme at local level.

Such distinctions are valuable only, I believe, once we realise that they are not alternative, but, rather, mutually supportive. To achieve implementation is a long, slow, uneven task. We need to exploit every means at our disposal to achieve our goals.

Implementation policies *are very difficult to assess*. Whenever we say a system has 'adopted' a new curricular practice we are making all sorts of value judgements. Sometimes we may apply relatively simple yardsticks, such as whether the school has or has not received the newly recommended material and whether it is using it. More often, however, we wish to assess teachers' and pupils' attitudes and understanding. But whatever criteria we use, we cannot conceivably make valid judgements unless we spell out what we are attempting to achieve and try to measure whether we have achieved it or not. Some form of planned evaluation is therefore essential.

In the very simplest analysis, the task of curriculum implementation can be said to involve two main processes: first *changing attitudes* of policy makers, administrators, teacher trainers, supervisors, teachers, parents and ultimately (the sole goal of the process) learners; secondly providing the *materials* and *administrative means* to make this possible.

The two tasks are interrelated but in this book we separate them and look in this chapter at the first and most difficult task.

New demands on teachers and planners

The nature of the demands which new programmes may make on teachers has already been discussed. They involve acquiring new knowledge and attitudes to learning including a degree of flexibility often uncomfortable to an insecure teacher and foreign to an authoritarian culture, more work and more thinking for everybody: and thinking in itself is hard work.

The demands upon those involved in the management of implementation are equally great and often overlooked. Even the most straightforward programmes based on centralised planning, trial in project schools and eventual diffusion throughout the system involve considerable organisation and have far reaching financial implications.

With any model, however limited, implementation proceeds unevenly and involves participation at local level, a degree of flexibility in plans and among planners, a measure of decentralisation of control and the development of management techniques at local as well as at central level, together with the communication and the partnership which make all these possible. To undertake this kind of management requires considerable knowledge and close personal relations between central and field workers, qualities only bred of confidence and maturity of judgement which can only come with time. Significantly it is in Kenya where both experience and investment in curriculum development have been greatest over the past fifteen years that policies towards devolution in curriculum implementation are furthest advanced.

Spreading the word

One initial difficulty is that effective communication is just not one of the strong points in African systems of education. All too often headmasters, teachers and parents are ill-informed about intended changes in primary curriculum programmes.

There has always been some awareness of this problem and the publication of simple informative magazines such as *The Teacher* in Uganda, has been regarded as one means of overcoming it. More recently, however, I detect a considerable

Different country – same problem

Reflections on the Keele Integrated Study Project 1968–71:

'Three conclusions can be drawn:

First, the pressures on teachers involved in innovation to revert back in traditional content and methods are strong. These are only partly due to the nature of the innovation. They are also the product of the way the teaching role is traditionally defined. The innovating role seemed insecure. The assessment of standards of work was difficult. The new content was strange. Enquiry methods often seemed too time-consuming. . . .

The *second conclusion* was that involvement in innovation was both wearing and stretching. The crucial stage was not the introduction of the project but its establishment once these strains began to tell. This strain was increased by the exposure of the innovating teachers to outside observation. Innovations have to be evaluated. The teachers have to report back, be observed and accept visitors. As more time and energy is expended there is more exposure to critical evaluation. The pull of the traditional is combined with the strain of the new.

The *third conclusion* follows from this combination of strain and exposure. Successful establishment seemed to depend on the teachers investing enough in the innovation to overcome that already built into the traditional role. This was itself dependent on the resources made available by the school.' (And by the local authority.)

Extract from Marten D. Shipman's 'The Role of the Teacher in Selected Innovative Schools in the United Kingdom' in *The Teacher and Educational Change: A New Role*, OECD, Paris 1974, pp 205–206.

increase in concern. It is significant that the public debate on policies and content of education mounted in Zambia in 1976 has aroused much interest in other African countries. There can be no doubt that the people themselves in Zambia felt they had something to say: some 1,500 contributions were received, more than 1,100 from individual members of the public, the remainder submitted by local, district and provincial seminars, parent-teacher associations, teacher associations, church organisations and other bodies, including schools themselves. A large number of these responses had direct bearing on school curriculum.

Yet there is little doubt that in most countries a good deal more could be done to get people talking and thinking about proposed changes. Publicity materials could be increased and certainly better designed: teachers' magazines, newsletters, circulars could be shorter, better laid out, perhaps less patronising in tone. Moreover, there seem to be all manner of missed opportunities to communicate and discuss proposals with teachers and headmasters. Alongside the usual diet of methodology and administration, in-service courses could profitably include discussions on policy. Visits of inspectors and college tutors might well be occasions for staff discussions on new plans and projects. Better use could be made of radio and newspapers.

Experience is beginning to show us how necessary is even modest investment in such programmes. *Without information there is distrust. Where distrust is rife, innovations falter and fail.* Teachers and schools are of necessity partners in the business of curriculum reform and partners must set forth on an enterprise with an understanding of what it is about, and a certain confidence in the policies they pursue.

Teacher education – a first essential for implementation

There is no conceivable way in which curriculum implementation can be divorced from the process of teacher education. The teacher in school interprets the objectives and content in the curriculum plan and manages the learning situations through which intention is transformed into actual practice.

Over the last twenty years, we have come to draw a distinction between the initial and continuing training of teachers. The terms 'pre-service' and 'in-service' have been commonly used; they are, in fact, misnomers, for a substantial proportion of entrants to 'pre-service' training have always been drawn from the ranks of those untrained teachers who perform such an important and unrecognised job in African primary schools. Currently, however, distinctions between initial and 'in-service' training are becoming more difficult to recognise, as new alternative patterns evolve through the use of sandwich courses, internship schemes and multimedia courses. Currently, too, the whole weighting between different modes of teacher education is coming under review, as the realisation of the vital necessity for in-service education to professional survival forces us, somewhat reluctantly, to question the investment we make, in time and money, in initial training. As the perspective on teacher education widens to span the whole career of the teacher and as the work of teacher-preparation courses becomes far more closely linked to the

One day courses – Uganda 1966

When I was working at the National Institute of Education, we organised two-day meetings throughout Uganda to explain the newly issued primary syllabus. On the first day, a Friday, we held seminars of local education workers to discuss the problems and priorities of implementation. These were a modest success. Next day, Saturday, we held open meetings for teachers to explain and discuss the syllabus content, ending up with an open lecture in the evening by a speaker of some distinction. The response to these meetings was overwhelming. We would expect a hundred teachers only to be met with three times that number, partly, I feel sure, because we had, ourselves, taken the trouble to come from the Institute.

On one occasion, our Director, then the acting Vice-Chancellor of the university, travelled out over one hundred miles to meet and lecture to a remote teachers' group – an action immediately noted and long remembered. It is easy for an overworked ministry official or a self-important lecturer in education to think of his teacher-colleague as a sub-professional . . . easy and very dangerous.

Help and support

John passes his School Certificate and thereafter embarks on a three-year full-time teachers' college course. In it he learns how to operate the new curriculum and tries it out during his teaching practice. He passes out with distinction and enters teaching.

During the next five years, however, he finds he can expect little help or support. He is 'trained'. All the limited resources in the country are directed towards untrained or older teachers.

Yet in sober fact John desperately needs help. He is often bewildered, sometimes even frightened by the job he has to do. Conditions in his school are far more rigorous than he experienced during teaching practice and the new curriculum full of unforeseen difficulties and ambiguities. He becomes disillusioned, abandons his good intentions, opens a shop and buys a share in a taxi. He is effectively lost as an agent of innovation.

Suppose the system had invested *less* in John's initial training and *more* in keeping in touch with him during the first critical years. Or suppose his course had been redesigned so that its later half had been school-based and not college-based. Would we have lost him and all those like him?

---

work in schools, so its relationship to the tasks of curriculum development and implementation becomes more evident.

In this chapter, however, though I find the distinction increasingly difficult to maintain, I draw an arbitrary distinction between in-service and initial training of teachers as agencies of curriculum implementation.

In-service training and curriculum implementation

THE SHORT COURSE

The tried and trusted way of introducing new curricula is by offering a series of specially organised courses for teachers. Every country and every project attempts such programmes; in Kenya I found the verb to 'in-service' in current use. A teacher who had attended a course on the new material was thus 'in-serviced'. The extent and length of such 'in-servicing' vary enormously from one day, one evening, one weekend to longer residential courses, their length often depending on limitations of money and manpower rather than on the real needs of the programme.

For 'in-servicing' is expensive. Once a country faces the full commitment of the nationwide introduction of a new course, as Tanzania did, for instance, in its New Mathematics Programme in the late 1960's, the size of the task becomes apparent. In the first place, the staff for the in-service courses has to be trained, often a lengthy process. In a large country this may involve mounting courses and workshops both centrally and regionally. Next, courses need to be organised nationwide for all teachers at least every year or, if possible, more frequently. In a subject such as Mathematics these courses can only begin to be effective if we think in terms of a week or ten days for each of them. Those who supervise the teachers cannot be left out: heads, supervisors and inspectors must also be retrained. This process has, moreover, to be repeated yearly for six years. As the years go by, staffs change and work augments as it may prove necessary to run additional courses for newly-transferred teachers.

Such programmes are massive undertakings and in Tanzania it transpired that nearly all the money available for short courses barely sufficed to meet the needs of one single subject. To mount a series of nationwide courses for many subjects at the same time seems virtually impossible in terms of money, manpower and time available for the teachers who attend them (for remember that currently the teacher is a generalist who teaches all subjects). Yet syllabuses tend to change all at once; new ideas and concepts have to be learnt all at the same time: hence the dilemma which faces both the planners and the teachers.

Key questions for curriculum planners are two: how much is it possible to invest in in-service courses for curriculum implementation, and how far is it necessary to spread provision across subject areas, or, alternatively, to concentrate on one or two and ensure that these, at least, are covered adequately.

The key problem for the teacher can be summed up as follows: how can I learn all they want me to learn in such a short time when I am already tired of school and

Does it matter?

In Ghana, in-service courses are planned to run throughout the year. Teachers leave their classes to attend them. Several people I have talked to are horrified at this proposal. 'Who,' they say, 'will look after the children if the teacher is away?' How much does this really matter? What if the children get an extra holiday, or become engaged in a community project, or are taught something useful by someone in the village? . . . the alternatives are endless and often exciting. Yet we always seem to assume that because children are not slogging through the syllabus they are not learning.

need my holidays? Are they yet again going to ask me to do the impossible and then blame me for not doing it properly?

Faced with these mounting demands, most countries have attempted to increase funding and facilities available for courses. In Ghana seven former teachers' colleges, one in each region, are to become devoted entirely to in-service work. Elsewhere in-service units are attached to colleges, and in Botswana where this is done 'outposts' have been set up in remote areas. The college 'in-service team' travels to these periodically and mounts courses from them for local teachers. Radio is also used to some effect offering programmes for teachers. Later in this chapter I shall discuss the potential offered by more ambitious multi-media schemes for teacher education which, although mainly intended for the initial training of unqualified teachers and for the upgrading of lowly qualified ones, afford at the same time an important vehicle for curriculum implementation.

Concern for improving the content and efficiency of courses available for teachers also begins to be apparent and few areas need more attention. Too many in-service courses are still very sorry affairs, vague, 'how-to-be-a-good-teacher' courses, often patronising in tone and sometimes providing a living example of those didactic methods they so earnestly urge teachers to avoid.

Gradually, however, practice and experience help us to make the most of the limited provisions available: we learn that when time is limited priority contents have to be most carefully selected and most strictly applied;[3] we learn that courses must, of necessity, be linked to the new materials distributed during the sessions, thus giving teachers the means to interpret them in their schools; we realise that the direct 'carry over' from courses is limited in time, hence follow up becomes essential if impetus is to be maintained; we find that two stage courses, where one set of 'master tutors' initiates tutors for local courses must be limited in scope and very carefully and meticulously planned; we know that teachers retain more knowledge and enthusiasm if people work together with them rather than preach at them.

All these and other simple truths we begin to learn, and would come to accept quicker if there were more continuity among personnel involved in curriculum planning and development. Yet one lesson from experience is pre-eminent: the limitations of the 'course' as a method of curriculum implementation. The course introduces you, the teacher, to new material: it tells you in more or less detail how to use it, but you actually *use* the material in your school with your children. Day by day, week by week, problems arise, problems the course organiser never warned you about, problems the innovators probably never imagined. It is on the job, it is in the schools themselves that you need the help.

Local agents of implementation

The realisation that help and advice to teachers in their schools is central to the success of curriculum implementation has led to the development of different

Conversation in a state ministry (Nigeria 1976)

Hugh Hawes: What moves is the state making to help implement its new primary syllabus this year?
Permanent Secretary: We are increasing the inspectorate.
Hugh Hawes: By how much?
Permanent Secretary: We are reducing the ratio of inspectors to schools from 1 to 50 to 1 to 30.
Hugh Hawes: But will this give you the closeness of supervision you require?
Permanent Secretary: Not sufficiently, but already these increases impose additional commitments in salary, housing and transport loans. My resources are stretched to their limit. What more can I do?

A local professional association

Discovering one highly effective association of local Science teachers in Sierra Leone reminded me yet again how productive local subject associations can be. I remember coming across a particularly effective one in rural Uganda which had transformed approaches to teaching young children in member schools. They met weekly and paid a shilling subscription. 'We are Infant Methodists', the Secretary informed me.

---

means to enable this to happen. Four approaches may be identified: increased investment in supervision, the encouragement of teachers' groups, the development of teachers' centres and the strengthening of the professional role of the headmaster in schools.

MOBILE TEACHER TRAINERS AND ALTERNATIVES TO THEM

One of the most significant innovations in educational supervision has been the emergence in different countries of the various types of 'curriculum implementers' mentioned in Chapter 2. Possibly the largest investment has been in the mobile teacher trainers (MTTs) in the northern states of Nigeria.[4] Their job was to help in the introduction of a very ambitious set of materials into schools, to provide feedback and to train teachers both in the experimental and dissemination phases of the project. As I have already indicated, the goals which were set them and their teachers were too ambitious to be fully attained in every subject. However, striking transformations were and are being achieved particularly in levels and subjects where the task is both manageable and popular as it is for instance in Creative Activities, oral English and, in the hands of some teachers, Science.

Reasons for the success of the MTT as an implementer lie in the scale of staffing, the type and quality of supervisors employed and in the feeling engendered among the MTTs that they are part of a team taking part in an interesting and productive enterprise.

Each MTT usually has responsibility for only six schools. So he gets to know his schools and his teachers very well indeed. Since he is not an inspector and has no fixed status in the education hierarchy, he can thus easily gain the confidence of those he works with.

Previous experience of MTTs varies: some are expatriate VSO's, young trained teachers with some primary school experience. The Nigerians, and these are in the majority, are seconded teachers, headmasters and college tutors chosen for their ability and enthusiasm. A particularly productive move has been the institution of a Diploma in Infant Methods in the Ahmadu Bello Institute of Education, a number of whose graduates are now employed as MTTs.

Significantly, as the project develops and large scale implementation proceeds, based on state ministries, there have been some local success stories and, by contrast, other areas where the scheme is dead or dying. Some states have clearly decided that the very considerable investment necessary in the appointment of a large supervisory cadre is not justified particularly in the face of universal primary education. Others have failed to introduce the co-ordination mechanism necessary to ensure the discussion and feedback required to keep enthusiasm alive. Yet where both the people and the organisation are made available, very striking results have been achieved not least, to my mind, because central curricula are not only adopted but gradually adapted to suit local needs through the constant intervention of these knowledgeable and enthusiastic field workers.

While some areas have invested in special cadres of 'curriculum implementers', others have attempted to meet the same need by increasing their primary inspectorate on the grounds that this action achieves the same object of providing sympa-

Comments from a centre warden (Kenya 1975)

These short extracts are from the Annual report of the Centre Tutor, a seconded primary teacher. They do not do justice to his Centre's activities but they do give us an insight into the enthusiasm of its organiser and the potentialities of his centre.

'. . . The year 1975 has been a very busy year to the TAC staff and the sub-centres staff. There were several meetings held for the sub-centre staff concerning the changed syllabi and courses were run accordingly. Despite the difficulties encountered, much has been achieved in the course of the year's activities.'

'. . . We had several meetings which led to a compromise of constructing the sub-centres through Harambee basis. Due to the nature and extent of some divisions, it was suggested wise to have two sub-centres/meeting places – for such divisions.'

'. . . 1,226 teachers were in-serviced on various courses especially on the changed syllabuses. Among these are the sub-centre staff who were in-serviced on the content and scope of the changed syllabuses. They in turn in-serviced the teachers in their respective divisions guided by their A.E.O's. Hence an estimated number of about 4,500 were in-serviced in the other divisions excluding central Division which is near the TAC. Therefore, an estimated number of about 5,726 teachers were in-serviced on changed syllabuses and other subjects in Machakos District.'

'. . . The TAC staff collected traditional materials and enlarged the history illustrated pamphlet. The staff has also made another pamphlet on Science Equipment. These pamphlets are very useful to teachers. We have also made more teaching aids and displayed them in the TAC. More teachers visited the TAC this year than last year. They drew teaching aids, constructed teaching aids and read the library books.'

'. . . While the teachers visited the TAC to draw/make teaching aids, other teachers visited the TAC seeking professional help. Most of the teachers needed professional advice on how to implement the changed syllabuses. I enlightened the teachers who needed advice and they were very grateful.'

'. . . The centre staff acknowledge the sincere assistance rendered by the DEO's office and the Principal's office. Indeed, the DEO has provided the TAC staff with transport and much has been achieved through this assistance.

We at the TAC hope that the year 1976 will be very prosperous and I am in the process of setting very high goals for the year.'

thetic supervision for teachers. I cannot accept this view. In the first place there is, often, the need for an *unsympathetic* inspector, a tough professional who can ensure that scarce resources are adequately used and can discipline those who misuse them. In the second, I can see no way in which an inspector who controls funds, determines postings or recommends promotion can 'get close' to teachers, however sympathetic he may be.

I believe there is a necessity for two groups working hand in hand towards the same goal of improving educational quality: a smaller group of inspectors and a larger group of curriculum supervisors.

TEACHERS' GROUPS AND CENTRES

I suspect that one of the most effective instruments of curriculum implementation may prove to be the teachers' group or association, possibly with orientation round a single subject. The very successful Caribbean Mathematics Project has indicated the value of working groups sharing a common interest and involved critically in the implementation and modification of new materials (Havelock's problem solving model) and we have at least one success story to note at secondary level; the work of the Science Teachers' Association for Nigeria.

Unfortunately such groups have been slow to emerge at primary level though I encountered a very successful example in an association of some twenty schools based in Freetown. Here weekly workshops were held and conscientiously attended. SEPA booklets were tried out and local material devised. A further useful development has been that eight school centres ran a weekly and highly successful 'Discovery Science Club' for children in upper primary classes.

If we looked we should certainly find a small number of similar initiatives to this, but they are rare, partly through lack of support or positive guidance and partly, as I indicated earlier, because the modest degree of specialisation on which they best thrive is normally not encouraged.

The idea of teachers' centres gets more publicity, possibly because it seems likely to attract overseas interest and aid. In the United Kingdom the teachers' centre, local, widely patronised and run in great measure by the teachers themselves, has been one of the apparent success stories in the implementation of new approaches in primary schools. But because a teachers' centre works wonders in suburban Manchester is hardly a guarantee of its success in rural Zambia. Certainly the potential of teachers' centres in Africa is considerable; for this reason I have included a note at the end of Chapter 7 to emphasise the potential richness of the services such centres could provide. Furthermore there is certainly a belief in most countries I have visited that some form of local professional base is necessary, but how this is to be provided and what priority it is to be accorded is still usually in doubt.

Certainly the purpose of such a policy must be clarified at the outset. There is little use in establishing a centre first, in the hope that it will attract custom – rather like hanging up an empty beehive in a tree, hoping that a swarm will settle in it. Centres in Botswana, funded by British aid and established somewhat on the beehive principle, are manifestly underused. To operate as a major instrument for curriculum development and implementation, the programme for teachers' centres must be very carefully organised: they must be used continually and effectively, which implies accessibility on the one hand and multiple use by many different categories of people on the other. All this spells very considerable investment.

In Kenya such investment has been made.[5] It is linked with a UNESCO/UNICEF assisted scheme, set up in 1970, to increase the primary school inspectorate. Originally centres were set up in a variety of institutions including schools and district centres, but experience seems to suggest that those based on training colleges (currently eleven centres) have been the most successful. Present policy aims to strengthen these links and entrust the Kenya Institute of Education with the co-ordination of policy for teachers' centres. Success of these centres varies and no one in Kenya sees them as more than an alternative means of helping in curriculum implementation. At worst the centres are isolated and ineffective especially when the local administrators, inspectors and teacher trainers who form the steering committee squabble among themselves. But when they work properly, they are impressive. Often their influence can spread very wide, as in the Siriba centre where they have designated eight local 'pilot schools'. Teachers' centre and college staff visit these on certain specified days and they serve as a focus for all other schools in the area.

At Machakos we find an even greater commitment to diffusion. This centre has established ten sub-centres, in some cases built by voluntary *harambee* effort. Staff of sub-centres are not full-time; however, the District Education Officer has agreed to increase numbers of staff to schools where sub-centres have been located, so that teachers in these schools can undertake the additional duty of providing professional help to their colleagues in neighbouring schools. Each sub-centre has a local policy committee. The overall scheme is headed by an executive committee which includes representatives from the teachers' college, parents and teachers from the district.

Centres like Siriba and Machakos provide useful services: more than enough to justify investment in them. They run courses, workshops and discussion forums in the centre itself as well as in the schools; they organise the production of pamphlets in local history and geography; they have established collections and photographs of local artefacts and display prototypes of locally produced aids and materials. They offer a library service for teachers and workshop facilities for the making of aids. The centre staff is at hand to offer advice to teachers.

Kenya faces difficulties, not with these, but with other centres (and I suspect they are in the majority) where the enthusiasm is not present, where co-ordination is lacking and where, consequently, the services are not provided. The Director of the Kenya Institute sees his problem very clearly as one of co-ordination and training.

HELP AND ADVICE IN SCHOOLS

Despite the assistance which can be given by the course, the mobile teacher trainer or the teachers' centre, the most available and often the most effective means of help for most teachers are their more experienced colleagues. This implies the need to train headmasters for professional as well as administrative leadership, to recognise the importance of subject resource teachers for schools or groups of schools, to provide in-service opportunities for these, and, whenever possible, to staff schools in such a way that not everyone teaches every hour of the day so that experienced men and women *do* have a chance to help their colleagues.

Opinion is divided on the importance of these issues. Some countries, some people, some projects recognise the need for such emphasis and would account it a priority, as I do. There are others who would argue that to give such people extra time and extra responsibility is to invite them to misuse it. This attitude, and it is very prevalent, worries me more than I can say. I see the growth of quality as nurtured from outside by all the means I have described earlier in this chapter but rooted, nevertheless, in the school itself. If the headmaster and senior teachers are unable or unwilling to provide the professional leadership that only they can give, it is high time we considered it a priority to help them assume it, rather than sitting back and deploring their shortcomings.

Initial training of teachers

(1) CONVENTIONAL APPROACHES

The implementation of curriculum change and the continuation of the new approaches in schools depend not only on the retraining of teachers, but also on knowledge, skills and attitudes fostered during initial training. Indeed, the relationship between initial training of teachers and curriculum development must be close and constant.

Most initial training of teachers still takes place in college courses, usually of considerable duration. Teachers emerging from such courses might reasonably be expected to have a solid grounding in the new curricular approaches. Those involved in curriculum development might reasonably be expected to work in closest co-operation with the colleges, using them as sources of expertise on primary school curriculum planning, as agencies for locally based research and survey about the context for curriculum, as institutions through which contacts can be established with the realities in schools. We might reasonably expect the development of college and school curriculum to be very closely linked at every stage, and the process of curriculum development and implementation in colleges to march in step with that in schools.

In every country I have recently visited there was an earnest desire that in these matters reason should be satisfied and almost everywhere a wry, even bitter realisation that it was not.

The curriculum of pre-service education in anglophone African countries is in serious need of revision and has been so for years. Its shortcomings are well known, often deplored, yet surprisingly resistant to change, though individual examples of enlightened practice exist. The problems faced in different countries vary and I suspect the difficulties I describe may be more acute in West African

Proposals for a new curriculum for teachers' colleges (Sierra Leone 1976)

The National Seminar on Primary Teacher Education recommended that the new college curriculum:

Should be mainly professionally orientated;
Should be designed as an *initial training* for teachers which would lead on to various forms of *further training*;
Should be flexible enough to accommodate teachers of various levels of entry and experience;
Should reduce overcrowding and stress the central position of *learning skills* both for students and teachers,
Should contain elements which will lead teachers to a more enquiry based approach to:
   (a) the children
   (b) the materials they use in schools
   (c) the communities in which the children live.
One means of achieving this will be through projects based in college and carried out (at least in part) outside it.
Should 'include studies of local and national development in Sierra Leone as a major component based on a methodology which stresses the process of enquiry into development rather than merely learning about it';
Should develop qualities of maturity and self-reliance through the life of the college;
Should 'take cognizance of and relate to other forms of education within communities';
Should stress teaching of (and in) local languages;
Should recognise the teaching of communication skills 'as a first curriculum priority in the allocation of time and resources in the college curriculum in staff development, in-service policy, research work and curriculum development for primary schools'.

From the Report of the Seminar on Primary Teacher Education (1976), Institute of Education, Sierra Leone 1977.

systems than in the East, but to some degree the following worries concern all countries.

1 Colleges and their curricula are remote from the realities of schools. Information about real conditions and real problems appears incomplete: students are prepared for what should be, rather than what is. There seems to have been little conscious attempt to base the curricula or its priorities on the task which teachers should undertake in schools.
2 College curricula are monstrously overloaded, often with academic content, some of which is of doubtful value to the teacher in his classroom.[6] Particularly in West Africa, examinations tyrannise the curriculum. An inevitable corollary is that professional content is undervalued and study skills necessary for a teacher to survive in a changing educational world, often virtually neglected.
3 Within the professional content of the course, the study of educational theory is often irrelevant and academic, ignoring local problems and realities. Studies of local and national development and the teacher's role within it are often virtually ignored.
4 Links between colleges, curriculum development and in-service programmes may be a good deal less close than they should be.
5 Within colleges, the actual curriculum and the actual practice may indeed prove even less relevant to the needs of schools because qualifications and experience of college staff often leave much to be desired – largely because rewards and living conditions are unattractive, but also because it proves difficult to find staff with suitable academic qualifications on the one hand, and experience of primary schools on the other.

Put alongside one another, all these shortcomings add up to a strong indictment of the present system. Something is undoubtedly rotten in the state of teacher education. Everyone can smell it, and in nearly every system some action is contemplated.

One obvious remedy is a staff development programme which I consider at the end of this chapter, a second is to undertake a very radical revision of college curricula including assessment procedures and the balance between in-college and in-school training. Such a rethink is being undertaken in Sierra Leone initiated by a national seminar on primary teacher education (August 1976). The seminar made important recommendations on goals and structures (towards more flexibility and a measure of local autonomy to suit local needs and conditions), on staff development, on examinations and assessment (towards less reliance on external control, more emphasis on local assessment including self-assessment), and on the co-ordination of teacher education (including greater involvement of colleges in in-service education).

The recommendations on the college curriculum have been summarised on page 132. Taken together they spell out an entirely new emphasis: more professionally based and far more related to the needs of schools and the community.

In respect of the college role in research and curriculum development, the seminar stressed the need for partnership between the colleges and permanent staff of the institute and ministry and recommended the design of a strategy and permanent machinery so that such links may be assured.

It further recommended, 'that consideration be given to introducing studies of curriculum development into programmes of professional training to enable serving teachers to participate effectively in the process', and noted that 'the effective participation of colleges and college staff in these activities will require a more generous allocation of staff availability of funds and provision for the release of staff on secondment where necessary.'

Anyone can make wise recommendations, particularly when they are minding other people's business. The significant quality of the Sierra Leone seminar is its composition. Those invited to the seminar and who subsequently approved the recommendations were representative of all those parties whose co-operation was necessary to ensure that it worked. They included the Minister of Education who gave the opening address, all concerned ministry officials, the Director and his staff from the Institute of Education, University department heads, principals and vice principals from colleges, together with field inspectors of schools and two overseas consultants.

I was one of these and helped, mainly, to tidy up the report. I thus had the very productive experience of watching co-operation at work. No one underestimates the logistical and financial difficulties of changing the orientation of teacher education in Sierra Leone, but I was left in no doubt that significant change will eventually ensue, simply because all those who were grappling with the problem had taken the wise step of sitting down together and discussing what they wanted and why.

From such consensus, change emerges.

(2) ALTERNATIVE PATTERNS OF TEACHER EDUCATION

Another means of effecting change in teacher education is through a fresh look at its whole pattern and structure with a much greater emphasis on full-time supervised experience in schools. Increasingly, countries in Africa are turning towards these new patterns, chiefly, let us be frank, because they offer a chance to train or up-grade more teachers more cheaply, but also because they may offer real professional advantages.

One new pattern, the community colleges, in Sierra Leone and Tanzania, will be considered in a later chapter.

Two further trends may be separated. On the one hand distance teaching techniques in various combinations of correspondence, radio and linked residential courses are being increasingly used for initial training of unqualified teachers and for up-grading the lowly qualified. Large programmes have operated in Uganda, Kenya, Zambia, Botswana and Swaziland, with the largest of all now based on the National Teachers' Institute at Kaduna in Nigeria.

Parallel to these, we note those programmes mostly for initial training of school leavers in which periods of full-time college training alternate with or complement periods of full-time teaching in schools. Already such programmes are in operation in Lesotho and some states in Nigeria, and contemplated in Sierra Leone and Zambia.

Although these two types of programme may have been conceived in the face of financial and manpower pressures, I am convinced that they are potentially more effective than full-time initial training. They offer a way to link teacher training very closely with real conditions in schools; at the same time they provide a very powerful instrument for curriculum development and implementation. Consider the potential already inherent in two programmes in operation in Southern Africa.

THE CASE OF THE SWAZILAND IN-SERVICE PRIMARY TEACHER TRAINING PROJECT

This project which is based on William Pitcher Teachers' College, Manzini, enjoys support from three United Nations agencies[7] as well as from British aid. Its objectives are threefold: to provide training for one thousand two hundred unqualified teachers at present working in primary schools; to organise it so as to cause the minimum disruption to the staffing of schools; to use such training for the improvement of curricula and methods, not only among the trainees, but also in the schools in which they work.

The actual training comprises three six-week courses in college, eight correspondence assignments in each of five subjects every year and tutorial supervision of the trainees at their school which is regular and exceptionally effective. Length of time between courses varies somewhat according to the needs and abilities of individual students since it is dependent on successful completion of the prescribed number of assignments.

The success of the project is immediately evident to any experienced visitor. Its records reveal an enviable pass and retention rate. Assignments are regularly and conscientiously done and visits to the schools indicate that the regular contacts maintained between project staff and students have often transformed not only individual classes and teachers but also the whole school atmosphere. Moreover, the college clearly has the potential, through this contact, to act as an agent for the dissemination, trial and modification of curriculum materials. In certain subjects, notably Mathematics and Science, it is doing just that. Moreover the students are very suitable agents to pioneer a new curriculum. They are experienced but not highly educated or trained and they teach all over Swaziland; thus they adequately represent the 'average teacher' in the average school.

The Swaziland project has many features to favour its success: excellent direction and staffing, adequate funding and good communications. Yet none of these conditions are impossible to replicate in a larger system especially once a measure of decentralisation is accepted. What impressed me so greatly in the Swaziland project was the central role a college and its tutors could assume in the process of implementation.

THE CASE OF THE NATIONAL TEACHER TRAINING COLLEGE, LESOTHO

The National Teacher Training College opened in April 1965 and, with the phasing

Letter from a trainee teacher (Swaziland 1976)

'I wish to thank the tutors who were teaching us at the In-Service Teacher Training. Before I went to the course, two tutors came to advise us to go and learn there. I told them that I could not imagine myself going to learn. But they told me that some aged from 55–60 are learning. They said that I should go and try for once, and if I failed only then should I leave it out. I then agreed to go and try for once, but I told them that I would be happy if I could be in the first group.

Then it really went as I wished. When I got there for my first course, the materials were all new to me and were also above the level of my standard. But I sacrificed myself with all my strength to try, though difficult was to me, I almost got mad because of education height that was new to me. But I sacrificed myself completely so that I should not prove to be the worse ignorant. The English lessons were new to me as I had never learned them at school before, especially listening skills and comprehensions etc. I can say all the lessons were new.

Though Education was hard I eventually found myself understanding it because the tutor could explain a lot. I thank the patience of the tutors in uplifting the uneducated to the high education.

In fact there is a lot of things which I learned at William Pitcher, while learning. I did not know that even clouds had their names. I did not know also that even the earth was divided into many parts. Even though I cannot remember everything I learned, I would be able to recognize some, whenever I'd come across them. I wished that this education had come early while I was still young. But I am thankful that I can be able to know what is going on at this time.

I thank the present tutors and the former ones for their patience in teaching us. I am so very grateful for what you have done for me.'

Quoted in 'The In-Service Primary Teacher Training Project in Swaziland' Newsletter, International Education Reporting Service, Geneva, No. 14 1977, p 5.

out in 1977 of smaller voluntary agency colleges, now serves as the single source for initial and in-service training in Lesotho.

The college operates a three year course with the second year entirely spent in schools. The students, styled interns, are supervised in their intermediate year by specially designated supervisors in groups of schools (currently twenty-six groups).

At present, supervisors are Peace Corps teachers, but plans exist to train Basotho at the University. A scheme has been put forward for the construction of small centres at each of the intern sites. These would serve as bases for supervision of initial training students and in-service students up-grading through a series of credit earning courses, also as centres for all other in-service provision in the area.

The Lesotho project is not so far advanced as that in Swaziland and suffers from greater logistical problems, but already there is ample evidence that the presence of interns and upgrading students in schools linked to a programme of full-time supervision provides a means of professional improvement which can and already does, affect serving teachers as well. If the proposed centres are built, the programme will be further strengthened.

Lesotho is undertaking a full scale curriculum revision which started in 1977. The National Teacher Training College, its students and their supervisors are seen as playing a vital part in the diffusion stage of the project.

Who trains the implementers?

As one might expect, the different means and modalities of implementation described in this chapter, hardly fit neatly into Havelock's three categories described at the outset. To be sure, most countries in Africa favour a research-development-dissemination and diffusion model, often very short on research. But in practice implementation proceeds unevenly. At local level plans sometimes become transformed into reality through interaction between members of a teachers' group, the activities of a mobile teacher trainer or inspector, the personality of the teachers' centre warden with his sub-centres, or the influence of the local curriculum committee (Chapter 3).

Moreover when centralised diffusion programmes take place, their success depends almost entirely on the quality of the agents they use. An in-service course is of no value if the teaching is in the hands of some pompous ass with a lecture full of platitudes about child-centred education and no practical help to offer the classroom teacher. Hence the importance of training becomes apparent, for all those who make implementation possible: the curriculum developer, the teachers' college tutor, the mobile teacher, the inspector, the headmaster.

Table 8 indicates some of the initiatives already being undertaken.

Despite the impressive appearance of this list the shortcomings of the alternatives are manifold. In some systems and for many groups of workers, adequate training is just not available. Elsewhere it is insufficient. In many countries considerable reliance is placed on overseas training. I have done my share and know well the feeling of inadequacy when offering courses for Zambian inspectors or Nigerian teacher trainers out of the context in which they operate.

Table 8 Training facilities for curriculum implementation (1970–78)

TYPE OF COURSE	LONG	SHORT
1 General courses relating to primary education (attended by various categories of workers e.g. inspectors, teacher trainers, heads etc.)	Graduate or postgraduate: Postgraduate Certificate with Primary Option (University of Sierra Leone); Bachelor of Education with Primary Option (Makerere/Nairobi/Cape Coast). Non-graduate: associateship courses (Ife/Ibadan/Nsukka).	Various, including 'teacher vacation courses' supported by British aid.
2 Subject courses in primary methodology (attended by various categories of workers)	Non-graduate/graduate: SEPA Science Educators' Course (Njala/University of Sierra Leone). Non-graduate: diploma courses in Hausa and Infant Methods (ABU); one year course on ZPC (English Medium) (NISTCOL Zambia)	Wide variety including many sponsored by overseas aid.
3 Training in techniques of curriculum development	None. A correspondence course is planned by African Curriculum Organisation (with West German aid).	IIEP Seminar of Systematic Curriculum Development and Evaluation (Ghana 1975); training courses sponsored by West German aid (Tanzania 1977); counterpart training (part time) by USAID assisted project (Swaziland).
4 Training in techniques of evaluation	Postgraduate: MA in educational evaluation (International Centre for Educational Evaluation, Ibadan)	Periodic courses organised by ICEA (Ibadan); IIEP Seminar (Tanzania 1975).
5 Training for teacher trainers	Postgraduate: MA in teacher education (Nairobi). Non-graduate: Associateship courses (Part 1 and 2) in teacher education (National Institute of Education, Makerere).	Various, including teacher training 'institutes' in science and mathematics organised by African Education Program, SEPA and WARMP; also recent national courses in Sierra Leone (1975) and Botswana (1977).

6 Training for inspectors and supervisors	No specific courses, but see (1) and (2).	Various e.g. Northern Nigeria (1971), resulting in production of a handbook for inspectors; Lesotho (1977); also special programmes for ITEs (Tanzania) and MTTs (Nigeria).
7 Textbook and materials production	Graduate and postgraduate courses contain communications options.	Periodic courses in materials design (e.g. Zambia/Uganda); writers' workshops (e.g. Lesotho).
8 Special training for heads of schools	Headmasters' Institute (Benin) leading to associateship (Ibadan).	Wide variety, including those sponsored by overseas aid (e.g. Lesotho).
9 Training for teachers' centre tutors		Training and attachments organised by Institute of Education, Kenya.

Note

The above are examples of training provided in *Africa* for personnel involved in curriculum implementation. No attempt has been made to provide an exhaustive list. Countries and institutions mentioned are cited as examples only.

Long courses refer to training of six months or over in duration.
Short courses refer to training of less than six months.

Further investment in training I would regard as an essential first step towards a greater measure of success in implementation strategies and considerable thought needs to be given to its design. Just as patterns of training which combine practical on-the-job experience with theoretical courses seem to pay dividends in teacher education, so the same approach would seem ideal for 'implementer training'. Correspondence studies, day release, linked series of short courses all have their applications; so too does the sandwich course, and, since I have been much involved with designing such a pattern for the training of post-graduate teachers, I offer some suggestions towards its application in the training of inspectors, teachers, tutors, mobile teachers and other implementers in a note at the end of this chapter.

One cadre closely involved in curriculum implementation and commonly forgotten when professional courses are designed, comprises the educational administrators. They control money, distribute materials, post staff and often plan in-service courses. Unless they become aware of the purposes of new curricular programmes and the problems presented by them, they may well hamper change rather than assist it. By the same token the 'professional' curriculum worker who fails to understand limits imposed by costing, can prove equally dangerous. The material and administrative factors related to curriculum implementation are considered in my next chapter. In the present one I am concerned with stressing yet again that curriculum implementation involves professionals and administrators alike. All must know what is going on and receive training appropriate to their task.

Three important issues

Three issues underlie the argument put forward in this chapter. The first is the need to develop a feeling of *shared endeavour* between all those working towards implementing new programmes – to make teachers as well as inspectors, teacher trainers and curriculum workers feel responsible for its success or failure. The second is the need to *reward workers* within the system for helping it grow and develop rather than merely for obtaining certificates and passing examinations, and to offer a viable career structure through which the good headmaster, inspector, curriculum worker can remain involved with the all important tasks of maintaining and improving quality in primary schools. Recently Kenya has introduced a new policy in which contributions to raising quality through local research, participation in curriculum work and even involvement in community activities may be recognised for promotion purposes. Elsewhere schemes begin to emerge for higher level training for the primary specialist. Too often, however, the promotion ladder still leads the primary specialist out of his field and into secondary education.

The final issue, and it is linked with the two former ones, involves the *maintenance of impetus* once the first effort of implementation has died down. How do you maintain interest – keep changing and evolving? Only, I am convinced, once you have some permanent machinery and some form of practical control over your own curriculum. If your task is to implement the Government's curriculum, you may accomplish it and rest. If you have some responsibility, however circumscribed, for improving *your* standards in *your* schools then the effort becomes a continued one.

The role of local curriculum committees was mentioned in Chapter 3; that of teachers' groups and centres in this chapter and I return to the problem in the concluding part of the book, for it is central to my theme. Curriculum change and implementation depends on people. People respond best when they are involved rather than ignored.

Suggestions for an implementers' course (sandwich style)

PREAMBLE

The following proposals do not relate to any existing course, present or projected. They are put together as a result of my experience with a number of related courses. They represent, I believe, a workable and cost effective way of training which could adequately blend theory with practical experience.

PROPOSALS

Duration: Fourteen months.
Allocation of time: Eight and a half months' field work. One month's leave. Four and a half months' residential course arranged as follows:

Fig. D Implementers' course: allocation of time

1	2	3	4	5	6	7	8	9	10	11	12	13	14

Residential courses, a two months' course at the beginning and the end of the training and a two week mid-term course.

Work experience. Leave is taken at some time during this period.

Venue: Residential courses may properly be held on a University campus during vacation time. Universities need to become involved in such practical exercises.
Staffing: A combination of university and experienced field staff could be used. Overseas aid may contribute to staffing but should not dominate it.
Programme: The residential courses embody relevant knowledge, theory and methodology but are very closely linked with the practical component, planning activities to be carried out during practical periods and discussing them in the second residential course. The 'mid-term' fortnight concentrates on interim discussion and evaluation of practical tasks.
  During the work experience component, special planned activities are carried

out including a major research/survey project. Such projects are carefully chosen so that the combined findings benefit the national curriculum programme as well as the students themselves.

Supervision: Supervision of on-the-job training is carried out by experienced field workers e.g. senior inspectors, tutors, ministry of education workers who hold briefing discussions with project organisers.

Evaluation: All components of the training are evaluated and lead to a final assessment of the student. The course itself is also evaluated periodically by students and staff and thus modified.

Recognition: The course must lead to recognition equivalent to a year's full-time study, preferable through the issue of a university diploma or other appropriate qualification.

Overseas training: If overseas training is desired it can most profitably take the shape of an additional two or three months' comparative tour strengthenened by seminars and written work. Such a component may be included prior to or immediately after the final residential course.

Notes

1 E.g. J. G. Owen's *The Management of Curriculum Development*, CUP 1973; OECD *Handbook of Curriculum Development* 1975 or J. A. Ponsien's *Educational Innovations in Africa* Institute of Social Studies, The Hague, 1972

2 First described in 1969 in Havelock, R. G., *Planning for innovation through the dissemination and utilization of knowledge*, Ann Arbor, Institute for Social Research, Michigan, 1969. For an easily available commentary, see Huberman, M., *Understanding change in education: an introduction*, UNESCO/IBE, Paris 1973.

3 A recent project in Indonesia has used computer analysis to identify top priority tasks and hence content in a national in-service programme.

4 The Itinerant Teacher Educators in Tanzania (the MTUU programme) also represents a very large national commitment and investment.

5 A very ambitious scheme in Ethiopia for teacher resource centres, the Awraja Pedagogical Centres, has been in operation since 1976. The handbook prepared by the Ministry's Curriculum and Supervision Department in 1977 lists 45 such centres.

6 Indeed in Nigeria it may contribute to his leaving it. The Grade II Teachers' Certificate is designed to attain some form of parity with the academic standard of the School Certificate. Hence in some Northern States one sees advertisements (I remember one from the Customs and Excise) specifying minimum entry requirements as School Certificate *or* Grade II Teachers' Certificate.

7 UNESCO, UNICEF, UNDP

Chapter 7 Proposals into practice (2)
Administrative and material considerations

Even if people are ready, willing and able to implement new policies, they cannot do so unless certain administrative financial and material criteria are met. We need:

1 Administrative machinery which ensures that adequate communication takes place and that, provided they are reasonable, the demands for manpower and its deployment made by a curriculum can be satisfied;
2 A policy for school building and furnishing which is consonant with reasonable demands made by the curriculum;
3 Facilities for the production of suitable materials at suitable costs and in adequate numbers;
4 Efficient systems of ordering, distribution and storage of such materials so that they actually get to schools and remain there;
5 Financial control which is efficient and at the same time flexible enough to allow for necessary regional and local variations.

The right people in the right place

In Chapter 2 I discussed the human context in which the curriculum operates. The administrator's problem is to ensure that children and teachers are brought together in such a way that teachers who know the job they have to do are put into a position where they can do it properly. If a poor girl is asked to teach in a language she does not speak well, to attempt subjects which she has not been trained to teach, or to face enormous classes, she is unlikely to perform satisfactorily. If the continual transfer of teachers plays havoc with the continuity of a school, programmes will not be followed through.

Sometimes, particularly when demands made by curriculum planners are less than reasonable, problems are unavoidable. However, administrative shortcomings do exacerbate the situation and are, by all accounts, very frequent.

Recent interest in school mapping[1] provides one profitable means of ensuring that there is an adequate distribution of pupils in schools; the presence of effective local administrative and consultative machinery undoubtedly helps to ease staffing problems. To some degree, most African countries have made recent moves to

A cautionary tale from Nigeria (or Kenya, or Zambia, or Uganda)

Musa, a headmaster, receives a visit from an assistant inspector who tells him that the school is ill-equipped to teach the new curriculum and recommends books and materials to improve its standard.

Smarting under the implication that he is not doing his best, Musa sets off to the Education Office to secure money or materials to implement the recommendation.

Here, he is told:

1 That no report has yet been received from the inspectorate;
2 That the education office had not been informed of the visit;
3 That, anyway, no funds are available;
4 That, even if there were money, the books recommended by the inspector are not in stock.

Musa is annoyed, but not surprised. He has long known that his superiors don't communicate with each other. He consoles himself by visiting a friend or two around town – his class remains untaught for the day.

Open-air working

Anyone who does it regularly learns to see open-air teaching in its proper perspective. The school compound provides any number of opportunities for practical work, especially in Mathematics and Science. There are certain activities, like drama, which are usually most successfully conducted outside and certain times when the shade of a tree offers a welcome release from a stuffy classroom.

But consider the case of the teacher and the class who have

no classroom
no shelter from the weather or the onslaught of insects
no work space
no storage space
no adequate display area except that provided by the portable blackboard.

How far can such pupils meet the demands made on them by the new syllabus?

Such demands are being currently made on many millions of children and their teachers.

establish or re-establish mechanisms for local control and consultation, but a wide gap and a good deal of distrust often remains between the administrator, the inspector, the headmaster and the voluntary agency worker (where these still operate), a gap often accentuated by the existence of different career structures. The Ghana Teaching Service (now the Ghana Education Service) was established in 1974, partly to heal such divisions. There is no doubt, moreover, that increased investment in common or complementary training, as suggested in my previous chapter, could also help to emphasise the essential interdependence of educational services.

School buildings and furniture

One area commonly regarded as 'administrative' is the building and furnishing of schools. Variations between contexts have already been noted and are inevitable, but there is much concern that what money *is* available should be efficiently used.

One necessary priority is for consultation in the planning of schools and their furnishings, an operation which must take into account the enormous variation in means and materials available to the people who build them, from the Nairobi Municipal Council or the Shell Company in Port Harcourt, to the Ujaama Village in Tanzania or the Food for Work Project in Lesotho. It is therefore necessary for those who plan a curriculum to make suggestions for the type of building and furniture needed to implement it, but it is also necessary to think in terms of alternative styles and costings to suit different communities, and essential that these requirements be presented in such a way that they are understood and used. It is inappropriate to supply a poor rural parents' committee with a blueprint for a permanent urban school or to suggest ideal types of furniture for lower primary classes in situations where they cannot be made or may be too easily stolen.

Every context is different, which is why co-operation and consultation at local level is so important – but, in fact, at no level does sufficient discussion take place. There are, for instance, certain essential features which ought to be included in all new buildings and are within the capabilities of all but the very poorest communities. Without them an efficient primary curriculum is not easy to operate, particularly at the lowest levels. Yet at this very moment any number of schools are being planned and built without them.

These features include:

1 *Adequate space for movement*, so that children are able, physically, to change their groupings during a lesson. Young children need floor space to work on indoors or on covered verandahs. Yet rooms are often so congested that they permit of only one kind of grouping, facing the teacher. In some situations, now mercifully becoming rarer, furniture is immovable. 'Taking the children outside', advice much beloved of teacher trainers and inspectors who do not have to do it, works only for some topics and at some times of the year.

2 *Classrooms that lock*: most good teaching and learning depends on continuity. Many of the activities recommended in new syllabuses in Language, Mathematics, Social Studies and Science, emphasise co-operation in the arranging of displays

and the making of models. Good lower primary teaching depends on a classroom environment which has to be built up over the term.

All these activities assume that you can lock up your classroom and leave it, for once a cow has trampled over your model village, you are unlikely to build another. However, we still encounter new classrooms built with a half wall and roof, often by agencies and communities who could well afford other designs.

3 *Large flat working surfaces*: any number of activities recommended in syllabuses require space for writing, drawing, experimenting, construction and model-making. Many such tasks are difficult to accomplish without the appropriate surface.

Yet often new buildings, especially those designed by community effort neglect to provide it. For the young child a cement floor provides such a surface. For older children flat topped desks and tables are needed – not sloping ones with holes for non-existent ink-wells!

4 *Storage space*: so much good teaching depends on having the equipment you need ready to hand when you need it. Stocks of equipment are built up over the years, some bought, some made, some acquired. New syllabuses usually contain sensible and imaginative recommendations of things to buy, things to acquire and things to make. All these need to be stored.

The construction of a classroom store is relatively cheap and easy if it is incorporated into the initial building. Yet many plans produced by central and local administrations neglect to provide for storage.

5 *Adequate blackboard and display space*: The small square blackboard is adequate for the pedagogue presenting a problem to a class. Most other teaching and learning activities require more space for demonstration by both teacher and pupils as well as plenty of room to display children's work. All this can be relatively simply and easily provided. Even when money is very short, thin wooden battens at two levels fixed round classroom walls provide the opportunity to display a vast quantity of work, to fix up pockets for work cards or to mount charts and reading material.

It is disturbing to find many new classrooms still designed on the 'pedagogue principle' with a single small blackboard and no other facilities for display or demonstration.

6 *An adequate staffroom*: while syllabuses commonly suggest co-operation between teachers making all manner of demands on teacher preparation, school buildings rarely provide an adequate place for teachers to meet or work. A typical six class school is just that: six classes with a cubby hole for the headmaster and a vestigial store.

To these six necessities, many others may be added depending on local conditions and syllabus requirements, particularly in respect of practical aspects of the curriculum.

Once implications for building and furnishing policies are realised, the issue of priorities must be faced. I believe the provision of permanent lockable classrooms for every class to be the first building priority for schools, just as I am convinced that reading books and writing materials are the first equipment priority. The provision of furniture, especially for lower classes, comes considerably lower in the scale. In conditions of poverty it is possible to learn on the floor provided you have something to learn from.

Materials selection and production

In Chapter 2 I sketched some of the problems relating to supply of equipment and the consequent deficiencies and differences in provision between countries and within them. Not surprisingly these revolve around the now familiar issues of efficiency and relevance.

Efficiency involves securing a realistic allocation of funds to buy equipment, persuading those who recommend it to bear the realities of implementation in mind and ensuring that the most equipment is available for the least money. It also involves establishing and carrying out a system of priorities both between subjects and within subject areas, a process involving considerable discussion and, in my experience, a number of heartbreaks in subjects such as needlework and art where costs often have to be cut below what everyone admits to be an adequate minimum.

Choices are always painful. Prices of equipment have risen dramatically since 1974: government subsidies and parental purchasing power has not, on the whole, kept pace with it. Hence what can be bought for each individual child in 1978 is considerably less than it was in 1970. The following are among the hard decisions which have to be made.

BOOKS VERSUS ALTERNATIVE MATERIAL

Often the problem is to restrict the purchase of books and allow sufficient outlay on other teaching equipment and on consumable materials for children. Everyone likes books; they are easy to store and to account for. They provide visible evidence of learning to parents; children are proud to possess them. Nevertheless many curriculum workers I have met question the priority of supplying them to younger classes except, perhaps, for Language. Their argument becomes very forceful once one starts looking at alternative ways of 'investing' the money. You can probably transfer the whole verbal content of an introductory reader onto a few wall-charts, while all the Mathematics content of your first books fit onto cards at a fraction of the cost of providing texts. With the 'change', a quantity of material can be purchased: newsprint, crayons, card, scissors, flashboards, all of which offer much wider opportunities than anything that can be contained in a single book.

Even at middle and higher levels of the primary school there are reservations about the priority value of books in certain subjects. Is science the kind of subject pupils can learn mainly from a textbook or is there not a far better case to be made for investing in adequate guides for the teacher and materials which children can use to help them in discovery and then in recording their findings?

CLASS TEXTS: HOW ESSENTIAL ARE THEY?

The greatest item of expenditure a school makes is almost invariably on class

Reading all round us

I am continually surprised by the pockets of impressive language teaching to be found in every country. You visit a school like so many others: a bare compound, mud walls, rickety furniture. Then suddenly you step into lower primary classrooms alive with interest and colour: furniture and parts of the classroom labelled, supplementary reading books made by children, charts made from magazine pictures with writing beneath them, a mobile hanging from the ceiling, a corner full of miscellaneous objects collected by children, a class model on the floor.

Is it the young teacher straight from college who is usually responsible for these situations? Not in my experience. Ages, training and level of education of such good teachers vary as widely as the contexts in which you find them. Certain qualities they share: a sense of duty, a liking for kids and, nine times out of ten, a competent headmaster.

A poor investment

When a headmaster or parent goes shopping for books he always has to make choices. Sometimes it is a matter of choosing between desirable alternatives, but sometimes books are marketed which seem to offer little of educational value.

High on my 'non-priority lists' I would put texts in lower primary Social Studies and Science. Often attractively illustrated with pictures of 'our family', 'our school', the market, domestic animals or common plants, such books manage only too successfully to spread the false message that you learn about your environment by reading about it and not by observing it.

textbooks. In an increasing number of countries, it is being realised that children can profitably share texts, particularly in lower classes, thus releasing purchasing power for other materials. It is particularly important that additional graded reading material be provided in language courses. Children can so easily memorise the class reader without mastering the reading techniques it seeks to teach! Different alternative schemes exist to provide variety at minimum costs. In Kenya specially packed boxes of graded supplementary materials have been prepared by the Institute's language section. In Benue State, Nigeria a 'hidden library scheme' is in operation. Each parent buys a different book for his child from a prepared list and children exchange them. Elsewhere recommended lists have been drawn up and bulk orders placed. Still, the provision of variety at manageable cost, remains a problem to be solved by most systems. I would look forward to seeing widespread experiments with the production and use of attractively designed cards in place of books in Language, Mathematics and Science. These offer all manner of advantages in variety and flexibility. Provided they are produced in sufficient numbers, costs should not exceed that of books. Yet apart from a somewhat half-hearted attempt to introduce an international course, the SRA, into upper primary classes in Swaziland, no country has, as yet, taken an initiative, possibly because the design of card systems which are properly graded and attractively yet durably produced requires a considerable initial investment in expertise as well as money.

WHO BUYS HOW MUCH MATERIAL?

I have already expressed concern over policies which leave book purchase entirely to parents. Not only do they preclude the purchase of class and group materials which are essential for sound teaching, but they also effectively ensure that social inequalities are perpetuated in the classroom. But to rely on government provision for all equipment may mean having to make do with the barest minimum. In poor countries like Lesotho, discussion centres on the best method of sharing the cost with parents either through some agreed equipment fee, or their buying some basic texts for children, leaving it to the school to purchase other essential teaching and learning material. In either case it is realised that such a decision should be made carefully and in consultation with competent professional and administrative staff, and not left, as it so frequently is, to the arbitrary *fiat* of local officials, headmasters or managers.

QUALITY AND COSTS OF MATERIALS

Most books in African primary schools are produced by multinational publishing groups usually through local subsidiaries. For these companies primary school book production is big business and they have built up a wealth of experience and contacts worldwide, with the result that their products are often cheaper and their services more efficient than local enterprise or quasi-government publishing ventures.

Yet many of us who work in primary curriculum development have considerable reservations about the standards of production of many of the texts they market

Perfectly unbound (Kenya 1976)

The headmaster of the rural school in Kenya is very angry and delighted to find someone to listen to his complaint – in this case a colleague from the Kenya Institute and myself.

He dives into his store and comes out with two Mathematics textbooks, one old, torn and dirty, the other new and shiny.

'Look how they used to make books,' he shouts. Selecting one page from the middle of the old book, he suspends the book from it and waves it to and fro triumphantly.

'Now look at this!' He seizes a page from the new book which comes out in his hand. The book falls to the floor and promptly disintegrates. I recognise the new binding technique, too frequently used now. It is called 'perfect binding'.

Children as producers

On my recent travels I have come across a significant number of instances where school children are emerging as materials producers.

Already well-established is the practice of making books in infant classes and then using the children's own writing practice as additional reading materials. But what about using older children to produce materials for younger ones:

Writing and copying out stories and reading cards;
Making and cutting out number and reading games;
Making toys for the youngest children and simple games' equipment for the
     slightly older ones;
Making drawing books from scrap paper and newsprint.

Already these ideas are spreading, and in one school in Botswana I even found the time after public examinations being used for this purpose. The top class had stayed on to make infant materials instead of going home as they normally did . . . an inspiring example of co-operation which may well be achieved elsewhere.

---

which are kept high by the spur of competition, with the inevitable result that the books, though attractive, are costly. Colourful books undoubtedly motivate children to learn better, but in the poorer countries what schools need most are simple, cheap, durable books. Hence quality paper and colour printing may just not be justified if more books could be produced for the same cost. It seems very possible that in coming years we may see closer ministry controls on the production of basic texts, possibly through inviting tenders from publishers to produce books to certain minimum specifications, a policy I found used in the production of the Joint English Project in Kano State.[2]

MULTI-PURPOSE MATERIALS

In certain countries, Ghana and Kenya for example, considerable thought is being given to the design of visual materials like charts and book illustrations which can be used across subject boundaries. The Kenya New Primary Approach and the projects which followed it also made some effort to develop and control reading materials linked with other subject content. I also remember one excellent, fully integrated scheme being put on trial in Northern Nigeria in the late 'sixties. Its ideas were never taken up. Perhaps the move was made too early, but nowadays the cause of language-across-the-curriculum is taken very seriously and there is a growing realisation that in the interests of economy as well as those of sound learning, all school materials must be regarded as reading materials and designed as such.

EXPLOITING ALL SOURCES OF MATERIALS FOR TEACHING

Too often, educational administrators and curriculum workers are myopic. They want all materials used in school to come in a box marked 'educational materials only', to be specially manufactured and distributed by a breed of bandits known as 'educational suppliers'.

Two kinds of materials may be underused. The first are those commonly required for other educational purposes such as health education or agricultural extension. The prospect becomes even more feasible once discussion begins to take place on the *design* of such material for dual use, or the production of material with common artwork and different texts for adults and children. The second, and more numerous, are local household and trade materials: pins, glasses, buttons and the like.

Gradually more use is being made of commercial enterprises at national and local level. Plastics factories produce simple containers for Mathematics and Science; furniture makers manufacture flashboards. A match factory in Northern Nigeria was persuaded by the Primary Education Improvement Project to turn out large quantities of matches without heads in boxes for a very reasonable cost; these were then used for counting, construction, decoration in all manner of combinations.

Moreover, I believe that our discussions on the local production and use of school equipment might prove even more fruitful if we changed our attitudes towards curriculum design. Hitherto we have tended to start from a set of syllabus contents and ask ourselves what materials were necessary to teach them properly.

Present economic constraints, however, may force us to ask a different and more challenging set of questions: what concepts and skills do we wish to develop? What educational materials (including natural resources in the environment) do we have at hand? Consequently, how shall we plan and modify content so that we can make use of what we have?

MATERIALS PRODUCED BY TEACHERS AND PUPILS

Finally, it is necessary to consider the extent to which planners should rely on materials locally made by teachers or collected by children. I have already entered a plea that demands made should be reasonable both in respect of the resources available in communities and the zeal of teachers. But, of course, curriculum plans must rely on the skill and ingenuity of teachers who interpret them, particularly if the system supports the teacher in his task.

In this regard, the vital importance of storage space has already been mentioned. Two other initiatives are worth recording: the first from Nigeria where certain mobile teacher trainers have organised collection and storage of waste materials from factories and traders, off-cuts of wood, paper and cloth. Schools can then come to a central point and collect supplies in bulk for their lower primary classes. The second is the Teaching Aids Production Unit based on Francistown Teachers' College, Botswana which offers help and advice to local teachers, provides workshop facilities and designs prototypes for locally based equipment. These services are admirable but by no means unique to Botswana. What is new is the Centre's idea of 'semi-manufactured material'; simple apparatus in kit form which is later assembled by teachers in local workshops. A similar principle has been applied in Uganda and Zambia in the production of big sheets which are later cut out by teachers to provide initial reading apparatus for young children. Both ideas save money, involve the teacher in production of learning materials but at the same time help to ensure that the end product is of a high standard.

THE QUESTION OF RELEVANCE

However efficiently we manage to select materials, their effectiveness will still be in strict proportion to their relevance to the educational context in which they are being used. Issues regarding content have been discussed in an earlier chapter. What is now being discussed in many countries in Africa is whether, alongside materials nationally designed and prescribed, there should not also emerge a body of locally produced material to suit local needs.

There are two good reasons for this: not only do contexts and needs vary but many more people now see the value of getting teachers involved in their own curriculum development, a goal which can certainly never be met by enrolling the odd one or two on a national syllabus committee or writers' panel.

As yet we have more ideas than action in the field of local materials' production though already some initiatives can be seen: local history and geography materials from Kenya and Uganda; Setswana readers produced by students of Serowe Teachers' College and their tutor and subsequently issued for school use; local

Experience from the Caribbean

A common feature of new Reading and Mathematics projects in the Caribbean is the production of supplementary cards and booklets by teachers' groups.

Booklets are usually very short, often no more than two sheets of foolscap paper stapled together and folded to make an eight-page book.

Material is very cheap and there is a wide, wide variety. 'You see,' says the project organiser to me, 'an ordinary teacher is seldom likely to write a whole big book. But if he makes a booklet, one work-card even, and it is used in schools, then he has participated in the operation; he is part of the team. We've won him over.'

writers' workshops for primary teachers in Lesotho. Nevertheless, for this concept to graduate beyond the 'interesting idea' stage, attitudes much change and new policies evolve. The important issues at stake have been recorded already. National curriculum plans need to specify areas where local projects are desirable and necessary. Administrative policies have to accord them the manpower and money to operate effectively. Examination policies must devolve some measure of responsibility to local schools and local areas. Unless these steps are taken, how can we expect sensible men and women to let themselves in for more work and worry?

Table 9 Locally produced curriculum materials: some possibilities

CATEGORY	COMPONENTS
Inventories of learning resources	Physical resources available in the locality; landforms, soils and rocks; lists of plants, insects or animals. Cultural resources: stories and songs, local games and sports, arts, crafts and traditional occupations together with information about the people who know most about them. Modern sector resources: government agencies in communication, health and agriculture and potential sources of information within them; places of production and service agencies. Material resources including what can be bought, made or collected within an area.
Teachers' guides and notes	Booklists of various kinds to help in purchase and selection of texts and supplementary readers (e.g. annotated lists of material available in local language). Supplementary notes to existing national teachers' material including radio material, indicating how they can be modified and enriched to suit local conditions. Separate guides, information sheets and pamphlets in relation to aspects of local language learning, environmental and cultural studies.
Pupils' materials	Relevant reading materials; books, cards and reading games in local languages and related to local interests. Collection of plays and songs. Material dealing with local studies in history, geography, science or agriculture. 'Read and do' pamphlets and cards in science and vocational studies.
Visual aids and teaching equipment	Charts, maps and diagrams of local interest for distribution or replication in workshops. Photographs and slides (for more fortunate areas). Handbooks and information sheets for teachers on the production of aids and equipment from simple materials. Designs and drawings of equipment capable of execution by local craftsmen.

But given that these measures *are* adopted, intermediate technology now exists for local production in the shape of simple, effective offset litho presses, sophisticated duplicators and easy binding systems. With the help of these, a wealth of material can, and should be designed and produced at local level.

Table 9 lists a few of the most obvious categories of local materials.[3]

Materials into schools

The first sections of this chapter have reviewed the communication and co-operation necessary to build schools and to design materials which will reflect the goals of new curricula yet remain within human and financial capabilities to provide.

Although I have, in part, described existing practices, a good deal of the last section on possibilities for local materials, design and production has been hopeful rather than factual. My final section keeps closely to the facts, and hard ones they are. However important it may be to design relevant material and efficient ways of deploying resources, nothing happens to a book unless it gets into the hands of a teacher and a child. Materials distribution systems are essential to curriculum dissemination, yet they are often inefficient and sometimes, at local level, corrupt.

Different patterns operate: sometimes national school supplies companies have been set up, as in Uganda and Kenya, where schools order supplies from a master list and hopefully await their delivery. In Botswana ordering and distribution are handled by local district committees, in parts of Nigeria by local education authorities or state governments through appointed commercial agents. In Sierra Leone certain basic texts are distributed free to schools and parents are expected to supplement them. In many areas, as I have indicated, parents buy materials to lists issued by headmasters.

No system is free of problems. School supplies companies get bogged down in bureaucracy; arrangements with commercial firms are subject to abuse; governments run out of money and transport, parents get cheated by booksellers. The supply position in schools is depressing and the further one gets from the source of distribution the bleaker it appears. Lines of communication are obviously too long; headmasters are given too much responsibility and too little help in deciding what to order, yet too little financial autonomy to make modest local purchases in shops and in the market.

These difficulties are generally realised and there is a surprising degree of consensus in countries visited that new policies should evolve which (i) maintain the advantage of bulk purchase, but decentralise distribution machinery; (ii) give those who order materials more help to make wise purchases; (iii) allow local heads limited financial autonomy to purchase local materials locally.

Some action, born out of this concern, is already being taken. Consultative machinery may be available, as in Botswana, to help heads and local administrators with their choice. Different forms of decentralisation are emerging. In Ghana textbook depots are being set up at district level to facilitate distribution. In Bendel State, Nigeria an interesting library/bookshop scheme operates. Heads are given a certain measure of credit to select materials from the state bookstore. In

Accounting for materials (Nigeria 1971)

The Primary Education Improvement Project was UNICEF aided. UNICEF rules said purchases had to be supported by receipts. Consequently it was only by the intervention of a senior member of their staff who knew how to bully bureaucrats that our lower primary materials list was approved. For very many purchases had to be made in the market: cassava paste, local dyes, empty bottles, ropes, pots. Imagine asking the average market vendor for a receipt!

We were fortunate, but I know many schools in many systems where headmasters can only order through approved educational suppliers and are thus denied access to many of those articles which could save money and make needed links between education in school and out of it.

other countries moves have either taken place or are envisaged to allow heads some increase in freedom of local purchase, though sums in question were usually very limited. Above all, realisation is everywhere apparent that the matter of school supplies is a partnership between an inspectorate, local managers and local headmasters. The 1975 Nigerian guidelines reproduced below represent an attempt, in one system, to make clear the conditions under which such partnership should work.

GUIDELINES ON PURCHASE AND DISTRIBUTION OF TEXTBOOKS AND STATIONERY

1 'LEA's/LSB's should be made responsible for collecting the orders from the schools.'
2 'Each State Ministry should appoint an officer . . . to be solely in charge of this and he is to be designated "SUPPLIES OFFICER". He will be in charge of the Supplies Department and will have a number of junior officers under him.'
3 'The State Ministry should prepare a list of suitable textbooks for use in its state and forward to the LEA's/LSB's for onward transmission to the schools. The Headmaster should be free to choose from this list.'
4 'The State Ministry should select suitable suppliers/contractors through competitive tender and inform the LEA's/LSB's accordingly.'
5 'In January every year, the LEA's/LSB's should send a letter to the schools informing them:

(i) of their approved grants for books etc.
(ii) of the names of the selected suppliers/contractors and their addresses.
(iii) the items for which each contractor has been selected and the tender price.
(iv) contract agreements between the Ministry and the contractor.
(v) four copies each of required invoice forms to be used for orders.
(vi) a dateline for the return of the requisitions to the LEA's/LSB's.'

6 'Each Headmaster should be requested to send his school's requisitions showing full address of the school to the LEA/LSB in quadruplicate. All the four copies will be checked by the LEA/LSB and forwarded to the Ministry Supplies Officer for counter checking to ensure that both the Headmaster and the LEA/LSB are not overspending and are acting in consonance with the Ministry.'
7 'The Ministry should then retain a copy, send one to supplier, one to LEA/LSB and one back to the Headmaster.'
8 'The supplier should be instructed to deliver the goods direct to the schools by a given date.'
9 'The Headmaster should then check the books and stationery delivered to ensure that they are complete. On the advice of the Headmaster, the LEA/LSB will request the Ministry of Education to pay the contractor.'[4]

Yet although these regulations are sound and specific, those of us familiar with Nigerian office procedure still view them with concern. There are many conditions to be satisfied, many in- and out-trays to negotiate before the child actually gets his book. Partnership is essential, but it must be easy to understand and to operate.

A note on local education centres

Middle-aged men can dream dreams – the next few pages contain mine about a strategy which I believe to be foreshadowed in many of the developments described in the last chapters: the emergence of multipurpose professional centres designed mainly, but not entirely, for use by teachers.

Something of this sort has been proposed in Malaysia and Indonesia, but these proposals of mine grow very directly out of African needs and experience. My argument in favour of the establishment of such centres thus consists largely in a summary of the points discussed in Chapters 6 and 7.

Curriculum implementation depends on people, requires local understanding, local organisation and local supervision. Curriculum development and implementation are two sides of the same coin. Once people are involved in discussing and adapting a central curriculum, evaluating it and making it more relevant, they have a sense of involvement, and through it a sense of commitment.

Teacher-training is essential for implementation and new patterns of initial training, as well as in-service training, rely on local supervision and local courses closely related to local needs. Multi-media programmes for teacher education are increasingly common and need local centres from which to operate.

Materials production and distribution programmes may now be seen as closely linked with other aspects of curriculum implementation. Local centres are required not only for distribution, but also as resource and production centres.

As we realise that school education programmes cannot and must not take place in isolation, hence centres where non-formal educators can meet with school-teachers are seen to be necessary.

All these services require a centre which is local and accessible. Yet such centres need to be fully used to justify investment in them. Currently, separate plans exist for non-formal education centres, resource centres, correspondence centres and teachers' centres. Perhaps all these could profitably be merged. Hence the concept of education centres.

Table 10 lists the possible uses of such centres.

CENTRES AND SUB-CENTRES

How and where all the activities in Table 10 should take place, what staff and equipment is needed must necessarily vary according to the context. In some cases, I would see such centres based on a teachers' college, elsewhere independent of it. In urban or semi-urban areas one centre may conveniently offer all services; in rural areas a looser arrangement with sub-centres may prove necessary. But whatever policy were adopted would require not only considerable investment, but also a significant change in attitude towards those ideas of devolution of authority, trust and partnership I have so consistently underscored in this book, backed by all the training implications they carry with them.

I sincerely believe that it is only through the mature and moderate application of these principles that curriculum implementation is likely to succeed.

Table 10 Multiple uses for education centres

FUNCTION	DETAILS
Teacher education	Facilities for *in-service work* such as: (1) professional improvement courses for teachers and headmasters, upgrading and credit earning courses with both academic and professional content; (2) courses of different types linked with distance teaching programmes for teachers, e.g. study groups, listening and viewing groups; (3) discussion groups of various kinds, e.g. on school/community learning, educational policy, objectives and priorities; A centre for supervision of new patterns of initial training (alongside in-service work) and a meeting place for students on extended practical teaching exercises or sandwich courses and different patterns of intenship, also a professional base for their supervisors. Facilities for teachers in non-formal education to meet and where joint training courses and discussions may be held to discuss common and complementary approaches between teachers in formal and non-formal education programmes. A source of informal help and advice to teachers. A meeting place for local professional associations and clubs.
Local curriculum development	Centre from which the following types of *locally based research* projects could be undertaken: (1) situational analysis of conditions in schools, e.g. numbers, equipment, attendance, wastage; (2) action research of various kinds, e.g. reading abilities, home learning; (3) evaluation of current or trial curriculum, e.g. coverage of syllabus topics, familiarity of content to children; Centre from which *curriculum material can be developed and evaluated* where centrally devised trial materials can be tried out in local conditions so that appropriate feedback and subsequent modifications may ensue, where locally applicable curriculum alternatives and related materials can be devised and tried out, and where common and complementary curricular approaches to formal and non-formal education can be discussed and tried out. Centre from which *local approaches to examinations* and assessment can be discussed, tried out and co-ordinated.
Local materials production and resource centre	A resource centre where: (1) small professional reference and lending libraries can be established; (2) simple audiovisual materials, e.g. tapes, slides, charts, can also be borrowed; (3) materials not yet available in schools (e.g. new books, reading schemes) can be displayed and consulted; (4) prototypes of locally produced materials and equipment (e.g. furniture and equipment designable by local carpenters) can be available, especially to local headmasters and managers. Source for making aids and equipment for individuals or groups of teachers where: (1) charts, cards, games, simple equipment, slides, or tapes can be made or copied; (2) material produced centrally in 'kit form' (e.g. compnents for teaching equipment, sheets to cut out and make into individual apparatus) can be assembled. Production centre for locally relevant curriculum materials usable within local areas where: (1) local supplementary materials for formal and non-formal education, e.g. stories, local history and geography materials, can be designed and produced; (2) teachers' guides for the identification and use of local resources can be drawn up. Information and distribution centre where: (1) relevant information concerning curricular and other changes can be made available to teachers; (2) new materials, e.g. teachers' guides and notes issued centrally can be explained and distributed. A local reference library for public use.
Correspondence and distance teaching programmes	A meeting place for: (1) listening, viewing and discussion groups leading towards formal educational qualifications at higher levels, e.g. 'A' level or degree programmes; (2) similar groups at higher level related to non-formal programmes such as agricultural or health programmes.
A social centre for teachers in school on non-formal education	A social centre for teachers in school on non-formal education, where teachers can meet in a relaxed and informal manner, share experience and discuss difficulties.

Notes

1 See Gould, W. T. S., *Planning the Location of Schools*, Ankole District, Uganda, 1973, and others in an excellent series published by the IIEP

2 A lower secondary remedial English text, jointly sponsored by Kano State and the British Council – the books are in black and white on cheaper grade paper but readable and durable.

3 A longer and far more detailed listing is available in H. W. R. Hawes, *Locally based educational research and curriculum development in developing countries – the teacher's role*, IIEP 1976

4 Federal Ministry of Education, Nigeria, *Guidelines on Purchase and Distribution of Textbooks and Stationery*, Lagos 1975.

Chapter 8 Basic education, the community and the school curriculum

Changes in our attitudes

Fifteen or even ten years ago when I talked of Education I meant, almost invariably, schooling. Nowadays I am more careful with my words: when I *mean* schooling I say so; I consciously distinguish between formal and non-formal systems of education, and so do my colleagues in curriculum development work all over Africa.

This change in language reflects a change in attitude – a change for the better. We are, at last, beginning to see school education in perspective as one educational process among many. Parallel to this comes the realisation that education (and this includes school education) is one factor and one factor only contributory to development. We are being cut down to size.

This new attitude stems partly from a new sense of reality. It has become increasingly obvious that current school systems and their curricula can never suffice to give people the knowledge, skills and attitudes needed in a world of change; that current structures and content of formal education create divisions within society which leave behind them a flotsam of disappointed and disillusioned young men and women seeking employment opportunities which do not exist; that even if we should wish to replicate present structures and provide more schooling for more children, it is often impossible to do so in the face of mounting populations and within current levels of financial and material resources.

At the same time, the philosophical basis of our educational policies and curricula are increasingly called to question. We read and begin increasingly to heed statements of marxist and maoist educational policy and philosophy. We note an increasing measure of concern in the writing and policies of bodies such as the World Bank,[1] UNESCO and UNICEF to seek means by which education may, in some way, help to reduce the gaps within societies rather than widen them; we read the literature of 'deschooling', the writings of committed critics of the established order such as Illich, Reimer and Freire and realise that while their suggestions for action may appear impracticable, their analysis of current weaknesses are both powerful and disturbing.

One of the most important single documents to have emerged in the past decade has been the report of the UNESCO sponsored International Commission on Education chaired by Edgar Faure and published in 1972 under the title of *Learning to*

Minimum learning needs – two statements

1 'Minimum needs in developing countries would normally be literacy, numeracy, adequate verbal expression, and some knowledge of citizenship and of the physical and social environment, of health and nutrition learned by methods which rouse curiosity, develop self-reliance, and encourage physical and mental adaptability. In the case of adults, knowledge of family planning, and some conditioning for local employment, or in the subsistence sector for raising productivity, would be included.'

2 'For non-formal education they comprise:

(a) Positive attitudes towards co-operation with one's family and fellow men, towards work and community and national development, and not least of all towards continued learning and the development of ethical values.

(b) Functional literacy and numeracy, sufficient (i) to read with comprehension a national newspaper or magazine, useful agricultural, health and other 'how to do it' bulletins, or manufacturers' instruction sheets; (ii) to write a legible letter to, for example, a friend or to a government bureau requesting information; and (iii) to handle important common computations – such as measurement of land and buildings, calculation of agricultural input costs and revenues, interest charges on credit and rental rates on land.

(c) A scientific outlook and an elementary understanding of the processes of nature in the particular areas, as they pertain, or example, to health and sanitation, to raising crops and animals, to nutrition, food storage and preparation and to the environment and its protection.

(d) Functional knowledge and skills for raising a family and operating a household, including the essential elements of protecting family health, family planning where appropriate, good child care, nutrition and sanitation; cultural activities and recreation; care of the injured and sick; intelligent shopping and use of money; making clothes and other consumer goods, house repairs and environmental improvements; growing and preserving food for family consumption.

(e) Functional knowledge and skills for earning a living, including not only the skills required for a particular local occupation, but also a knowledge of a variety of locally useful common skills for agriculture and nonfarm use.

(f) Functional knowledge and skills for civic participation, including some knowledge of national and local history and ideology, an understanding of one's society; awareness of government structure and functions; taxes and public expenditures; available social services; rights and obligations of individual citizens; principles, aims and functioning of co-operatives and of local voluntary associations.'

Extract (1): From H. M. Phillips *Basic Education – a World Challenge*, John Wiley 1975, p 180.
Extract (2): From P. H. Coombs with R. C. Prosser and Manzoor Ahmed, *New Paths to Learning*, UNICEF International Council for Educational Development 1973, pp 13–14.

Be. The idea of lifelong education which it propounds goes far beyond educational rhetoric, for although the central conception of education as a lifelong activity has been present since mankind started to reflect on the process, the Faure report deepens and strengthens the concept.[2] Its views on the relation of the formal system to the total process are of particular relevance to us. In the simplest analysis the report reminds us:

1 that schooling is just a part of education;
2 that education cannot be conceived of as taking place at certain ages, stages, times and places. It is always unfinished business;
3 that educational opportunities formal and non-formal must relate to each other both horizontally (e.g. school, home, mosque, media, work experience) and vertically throughout the different stages of a learner's life;
4 that there are many paths to learning, no one path being better or worse than another, only more efficient or more appropriate;
5 that methods, materials and delivery systems must also vary to suit purposes and means available.

Basic education, what does it mean?

From such roots, the economic political and educational realities, criticisms of existing educational philosophies, the demands for equity and the influence of educational thinking such as the Faure report, a strong demand has emerged in Africa, in Asia and in Latin America for some form of basic education for the masses as a first phase in a process of lifelong education. Yet as the idea of basic education becomes elaborated and translated into policy in different countries in the world, it becomes increasingly obvious that to different people in different countries it has different meanings.

In official reports, basic education is currently used as follows:

Synonymous with pre-school education (Jamaica)
Synonymous with the whole compulsory school cycle (Zambia)
Synonymous with the first part of the first cycle of schooling and shorter than the conventional primary schooling (say three, four or five years instead of six, seven or eight) (U.S.S.R., Ethiopia, Sierra Leone)
An alternative structure parallel to conventional primary education (Brazil)
An alternative form of schooling for rural peasant societies geared to simple rural transformation (India, where it dates from the time of Ghandi)
The acquisition of basic knowledge, attitudes and skills, by all citizens in school or out (Tanzania)
Mainly in respect of younger learners – excluding adults – (Upper Volta)

This confusion is worrying. I have heard voiced the opinion that the idea of basic education is too imprecise to be of educational worth. However, since I happen to believe in its value, I have attempted to sort out, in my own mind, what I understand the concept to imply.

(i) *Basic education is an idea and not a system.*

It is not conceived as three years, four years or six years, but rather as a set of basic skills, knowledge and attitudes which will enable learners to take charge of their own lives and set them free to learn further. Thus the concept of 'minimum learning needs' is important but such needs will vary according to the educational context.

(ii) *Basic education involves the acceptance of different paths to learning towards its goals.*

Hence different structures, contents and educational materials can be used. To apply this concept to older adults is possible. It is, however, most profitable to consider basic education in relation to (a) children in formal primary schools, (b) children, youth and young adults following alternative paths towards the same general goals. Such paths would include accelerated patterns of formal schooling for older children as well as many varieties of part-time and non-formal education.[3]

(iii) *Basic education is a concept which relates to individual attainment of goals rather than to time spent or ground covered.*

It does not involve a competitive element. The concept of mastery learning by Bloom[4] and others is valuable here, though we must distinguish the ideas themselves from the detailed application of them by American academics which would introduce a sophistication (and a cost) wholly inapplicable in most developing countries.

(iv) *Basic education is very basic.*

It relates to situations as they are, to 'minimum survival needs' of a majority of learners, many of whom are studying in difficult conditions.

(v) *Basic education is not to be considered as terminal in contrast to some other form of education which leads to further study, and not as rural in contrast to urban education.*

On the contrary, it must be thought of as providing the maximum degree of mobility for the learner to meet changing situations and to continue his education to the best of his abilities and opportunity. Provision of basic education should open doors for learners rather than close them.

(vi) *Basic education must be conceived in the context of partnership . . .*

. . . between various educational agencies e.g. the family, the school, non-formal education, the community. It is essential to identify which agencies contribute most effectively towards which educational needs for which groups of learners.

WHAT IS NEW IN THESE IDEAS?

These ideas are not merely rhetorical: they conflict sharply with principles preached with some passion by western educators in developing countries and accepted equally avidly by a growing establishment in the society and by the education industry: the principle that education can be measured in time spent and ground covered; ideas of competition and the normal curve of distribution as a framework for measurement of educational achievement; ideas about the primacy of the school and school teacher in the educational process; concepts of standards, grades, and many more.

Yet although the ideas are new and revolutionary they are headily attractive, particularly to politicians, because they seem to offer a direct and politically acceptable way out of the impasse of attempting to do more with less. Hence the greatest of good sense and maturity are needed, on the one hand to accept the implications of the basic education message, on the other to resist the temptation to give worse schooling to more people and call it basic education.

THE IMPLICATIONS OF THESE IDEAS

Once we look again at the purpose and content of the basic cycle of study[5] it becomes immediately clear that if one accepts the idea of basic education, all manner of new perspectives will open out: for structures, for curriculum planning and development, for the teachers we employ and the training we give them, for the delivery systems we use and for our evaluation of both programmes and their results.

In every category the new perspective would seem to call for changes in approaches and attitudes to be preceded by a great deal of hard work to clarify the ideas and examine their implications for practical action.

CLARIFYING THE IDEAS

This kind of thinking is beginning to emerge even though patchily, much of the initial debate coming from East Africa. In 1974 under the aegis of the UNESCO-UNICEF co-operation programme, a seminar was held in Nairobi on Basic Education in Eastern Africa[6] and followed in 1975 by a workshop in Dar-es-Salaam[7] on teacher education for basic education. In the following year a Basic Education Resource Centre was established in Kenyatta University College as a 'forum for the exchange of ideas and experience on basic education throughout the Eastern African region'. Most recently with assistance and advice from the International Labour Organisation, an Intermediate Technology in Basic Education programme (IBTE) has been launched, based in Nairobi, with the brief to help develop skills and attitudes towards the solving of local problems with local resources.[8] From discussions generated by these initiatives, ideas emerge and debate on these complicated issues is widened.

Experimental projects

The second, probably more significant source of ideas derives from experience gained from four important experimental projects all aimed at helping to bridge the gap between formal and non-formal education in rural areas, all, by implication, committed to throw light on the nature of the contribution of the rural primary school and its curriculum to the wider process of basic education. All four are assisted by UN agencies who help define their goals, monitor their progress, supply expert assistance in varying degrees of permanence, ability and commitment, disseminate optimistic reports about them very widely and very rapidly; who

The one-year itch: a serious disease

Change in personnel constitutes the greatest single threat to effectiveness of curriculum projects in Africa. Indeed I sometimes wonder whether UNESCO experts do more harm than good.

It is nothing to do with their competence (some of my best friends, as they say, are experts) but everything to do with their terms of service. How can a man on a one-year contract do the kind of job which is necessary in a curriculum development and implementation programme? Even if he confidently expects an extension, he is never certain for how long. He is continually looking over his shoulder. Yet the task he is doing is one which above all others requires time, patience and a long view.

provide, in short, that mixture of help and interference which seems inevitable in the aid process.

Two of these projects, the ones at Namutamba and Buea, have already been mentioned. The others are the Bunumbu Community Teachers' College and its pilot schools in Sierra Leone and Kwamsisi Community School Project in Tanzania.

A brief description of the purpose and potential of each of these projects is given below together with some additional comments on the Uganda and Cameroon experience.

THE BUNUMBU COMMUNITY TEACHERS' COLLEGE

The project, which receives support from UNDP and UNESCO, was launched in 1974 based on an existing college in the Eastern Region of Sierra Leone. Its inception is a direct result of the thinking initiated by the Sierra Leone Education Review. The project aims:

1 To train community teachers who will teach children and adults alike as part of their timetable. To this end special training is given, a special timetable and staffing allocations for schools planned, and special remuneration provided to these 'community teachers'. It is envisaged that they might conceivably spend about two-thirds of their time with children, one-third with adults.
2 To launch twenty pilot schools which would, in turn, become community centres or become linked with them and which would mobilise resources not only of the school teachers but of other teachers within the community from the Assistant Agricultural Officer to the craftsmen and the parent. Facilities for adults and youth would normally be built alongside the school. A significant element in the scheme has been the mounting of a full one-year training course for the headmasters in pilot schools.
3 To produce curricular materials relevant to local needs and local areas. In this regard, courses and workshops are arranged to include staff of pilot schools.
4 To enable teachers in training to learn by example as well as by precept through placing emphasis on self-instruction and group learning with the college farm playing an important part in the college life and intended to be run as 'a practical co-operative'; community activities would play a major part in students' practical experience and would extend over a longer time than the conventional teaching practice. Students are also made aware of the use of radio and correspondence material and shown some simple techniques for their design.
5 Thus to develop the teachers' college itself as an education centre and as a community centre for the area.

Significance of the scheme to the Basic Education debate
Obvious messages for co-operation between various elements in the educational community are inherent in this project, but its particular contribution lies in the realisation, central to the scheme, that the contribution of school teachers to Basic Education depends on the nature of their training. It is dangerous to expect conventionally trained teachers to cope satisfactorily with both adults and children and

with a situation which requires different priorities and different approaches from the one for which they were trained.

The approach to partnership between school and community is also significant in the Bunumbu project for we should note that the school and the adult education centre are not one and the same organisation: they are on the same site and share some of the facilities, but each has some space of its own, an arrangement which I see as more workable and psychologically satisfying to both groups of learners.

THE KWAMSISI COMMUNITY SCHOOL PROJECT

This project is a component part of a much wider Primary Education Reform project aided by UNESCO and UNICEF. Its objectives are:

1 'The development of literary and numeracy.
2 'The development of social citizenry with particular emphasis on
   (a) Self-reliance;
   (b) Social and human equality;
   (c) Skills, values and attitudes necessary for good health, hard work and better life in the Ujaama village.'[9]

The Kwamsisi experiment must be seen, like all other education policies in Tanzania, as part of the nation's plans to implement the policies announced by the Arusha declaration and *Education for Self-Reliance* (1967). It represents an attempt to achieve the closest possible integration between school and community education and is based at Kwamsisi village near Korogwe in north-east Tanzania. At the same time a close link is being established with the Korogwe College of National Education whose staff, particularly the itinerant teacher educators, have helped to establish and monitor the project. The ideas and the work in Kwamsisi are significant for a number of reasons:

1 The development of the village is seen as a whole and the school as one part contributing to the process of development. There is a village development committee[10] and five separate committees dealing with particular aspects of village activities including one for education and social welfare. These committees include teachers and even school children.
2 There has been a very serious attempt to determine development needs of the village; to assess the learning requirements which must be satisfied to make development possible; to measure the degree to which different groups, e.g. school children, youth and adults, have different learning needs and therefore require different programmes to satisfy them; finally to translate these needs into specific curriculum plans and learning materials for specific target groups. For instance, one type of *development needs* might relate to the importance of good health; *learning needs* could involve the knowledge, skills and attitudes required from different learners to achieve better community health and *curriculum content*, the separate plans and materials required for adults, youth and school children as part of health teaching.

The problems connected with analysis of learning needs form the basis of a research study on learning needs in rural areas conducted by the International Institute for Educational Planning and based on case study materials from four projects including Kwamsisi and Namutamba.[11]

3 There is, in Kwamsisi, a great effort to achieve what the Faure Report terms horizontal integration. The Tanzanians like to think in terms of national and local 'learning systems' integrating all learning opportunities within communities. At village level in Kwamsisi this means that the dispensary, the carpentry workshop, the day care centre, agricultural experimental projects in poultry keeping and tobacco growing as well as functional literacy programmes are planned alongside the school; their working is seen as complementary to one another. So far as possible, people in these services or outside them having skills to offer, teach them in school while the school teacher contributes his to adults in the community.

4 At the same time, locally devised programmes which involve the use of locally produced material are seen within the wider perspective of a set of national goals for education, the existance of national campaigns (including radio listening groups) such as 'Man is Health' and 'Agriculture is Politics' and the revised school syllabus completed in 1969. In Kwamsisi school, national syllabuses for English, Mathematics, Swahili and political education are unchanged, but local modifications have been made within fields of community studies, self-help and cultural activities.

Significance of the project: As its goals indicate, the Primary Education Reform Project represents an attempt to translate the ideas of basic education into action and the Kwamsisi project was the first in Africa to propose such a great extent of integration. As experience from its initial years is reviewed, it becomes clear that there have been a number of initial disappointments, many the result of over-optimism of the speed at which change can take place.[12] But the concept of integration of the school with the community, together with the idea of local participation in decision-making are both firmly rooted in Tanzania. Thus Kwamsisi is seen as providing valuable lessons from experience towards a direction of change which has already been identified, and the community school, or 'community learning centre' as it is now frequently called, is being rapidly replicated throughout Tanzania.

OTHER PROJECTS AT NAMUTAMBA AND BUEA

The projects in Uganda and Cameroon described in Chapter 3 provide further insights into the practicalities of establishing systems of basic education. In both projects a much greater degree of community involvement is seen as a desirable development but in neither case do we detect that the organisers expect this to come about rapidly or evenly. The unevenness of response is well illustrated by the Uganda project: this has grown and evolved from a fairly modest curriculum scheme concentrating on science teaching in rural areas, towards a much wider and deeper degree of integration both within the curriculum and between school and community learning based on a very clearly articulated set of objectives for basic education.

Fig. E Primary/basic education in Cameroon: suggested reform alternatives according to increased community involvement

ASPECTS OF SCHOOL REFORMS \ REFORM APPROACH	(1) Improvement on the present situation, no specific environmental orientation. Main features: classroom teaching, manual work, French in classes 5–7. Resource persons: only school staff	(2) Environmental emphasis; bilingualism Main features: classroom teaching, manual work. Resource persons: only school staff * French in classes 5–7	(3) Environmental emphasis; bilingualism, Discovery learning. Main features: classroom teaching, manual work. Resource persons: only school staff * French in classes 5–7
Courses/teaching material	New courses and books: English/mathematics/French/rural science/geography/history/civics/natural science	New courses and books: English/mathematics/French/environmental studies	New courses and books as in (2) *additionally:* working material/and record sheets for use in explorations
Specialist teachers	Present system continuing	For senior schools only: agricultural specialists/manual arts	▬▬▬▬▬▬▬
Equipment with tools	Present state of affairs continuing	tools for: farm work/manual arts/observational equipment/safe storage for tools and equipment	▬▬▬▬▬▬▬
Examinations	Reduce scope of objective tests. First School Leaving Certificate set at inter-provincial level (North-West and South-West Province)	*Set* at Divisional Inspectorates, *conducted* by Provincial Delegation or Divisional Inspectorate. Practical skills and work perfomance included	▬▬▬▬▬▬▬
Examinations/Examiners	Present system continuing	School staff, but checked by educational 'extension officers'	▬▬▬▬▬➤
Main administrative support	Present system continuing	Divisional Inspectorate transformed into an 'Educational Consultancy Centre'	▬▬▬▬▬▬▬
Posting	5 Years as a minimum in one place	5 years if 'Educational Consultancy Centres' are created; 5 and more years if such Centres do not exist; posting in home division prefered	▬▬▬▬▬▬▬
Holiday regulations	Reduce holidays and adapt to agricultural calender	▬▬▬▬▬▬▬	
Pre-service training	Change according to new courses and new books	Change according to new courses, new books, need for specialisation in agriculture and manual arts, conduct of environmental studies, work organization	Change according to new courses, new books, need for specialisation in agriculture and manual arts, conduct of environmental studies, work organization, methods of discovery learning (this involves frequent field trips)
In-service training	Topics: new courses, new books, farming methods, methods of discovery learning and explorations	Topics: new courses, new books, work organisation, conduct of environmental studies, manual arts, agriculture, methods of discovery learning and exploration	▬▬▬▬▬➤
Inducements	Present system continuing	Provision for extra work of teacher in-charge of school farm, teacher in-charge of manual arts	▬▬▬▬▬➤
Particular needs for inspection	Proper use of pupils' labour and school funds	integration of classroom teaching and practical work, adaptation of teaching to the environment, proper use of pupils' labour and of school funds	As in (2) and conduct of exploratory activities
Role of parents	Strengthen the Parent-Teacher Association	parents participate in labour control and the use of school income from pupils' labour	Parents supervise children's labour and the use of school income from pupils' labour. Passive sources of information for exploratory activities
School leaver extension	None	None	None

Environmental Studies Section   IPAR – Buea
(Agricultural and Social Aspects)

(4)	(5)	(6)

Environmental emphasis; bilingualism, Discovery learning
Main features:
  classroom teaching
  manual work
Resource persons:
  school staff
  local experts   * French in classes 5–7
	'Community-School'	'Community Learning Centre'

		New courses and books as in (2), but with a wide variety of optional material to be used on different projects. Working material and record sheets for use in explorations
		For senior schools only, specialists for: agriculture/manual arts/adult literacy (on request)/vocational specialists for school leaver programmes
		Tools for a wide range of school-leaver programmes (to be got from Educational Consultancy Centre on request), equipment mentioned in (2), and multi-purpose buildings and workshops
	Set at the local level, supervised by the Divisional Inspectorate, practical skills and work performance included.	
Local committee consisting of school staff and local experts, but checked by educational 'extension officers'		

		As in (2) but extension services of other 'departments' more involved, like:
		  Agricultural Department
		  'Centre d'Assistance aux Petites et Moyennes Entreprises'
		  Health Department
		  Animal Breading, etc.

	Reduce holidays, allow holidays to vary according to local conditions and needs	
As in (3) but in addition learn: how to identify local resource persons and how to cooperate with them in educational matters	As in (4) but get acquainted with approaches to community work	As in (5), but specialist training for teachers responsible for school leaver programmes and adult literacy work

As in (3) and
  identification of local resource persons, learning how to work with them
		As in (4) and learning how to conduct:
		  school leaver programmes
		  adult literacy programmes

Provision for extra work of
  teacher in-charge of school farm
  teacher in-charge of manual arts
  fees for local experts
		Remuneration by community (wholly or partly) to be considered (e.g. out of earnings of practical programmes)

As in (3) and
  ways and means of remuneration of local experts
	As in (4) and
	  keeping teaching in line with the nation-wide applied curriculum
		As in (5) and
		  school leaver projects
		  adult literacy programmes
		School Leaver programmes will be inspected jointly by the education department and the other departments involved (*see* **Main Administration Support**)

Parents supervise labour and the use of school income from pupils' labour; passive and active sources of information·	As in (4) and
	  decision on details of teaching programme
		As in (5) and
		  carry out changes/projects decided upon in post-primary programmes

None	Extension of community/school programmes	Practical and vocational training. centering around community projects: adult literacy; health and hygiene education, etc.

Note—Alternative 4: Existing financial means and existing capacities taken into consideration. seems to be possible for the near future.

Fifteen primary schools are involved in the Namutamba experiment. In each one, what is taught and the degree of community involvement vary. In some schools, community committees have taken over a great deal of control, including financial control of school activities, using the considerable funds available from the profits made by keeping livestock and by agricultural activities; in others the adoption of the project has caused very little change. What I find significant, however, is that project organisers accept this unevenness and are prepared to build on success where it does occur.

In a recent working paper (1977) the staff of the Namutamba project attempted to catalogue some of the activities which their fifteen associated schools were undertaking. I find the list fascinating both for the wealth of activities it reveals and the wide varieties which exist. I have extracted details for six contrasting schools.

The IPAR project in Buea in Cameroon has already been mentioned because of the significant research it has undertaken into the context in which the rural school

Fig. F Different schools – different interests (Uganda 1977)

ORGANISATION AND ACTIVITIES	SCHOOL					
	Namutamba Demonstration	Buyagga Primary	Kawoko Primary	Mityana Church of Uganda	Naama Muslim	Kyankowe
Community participation in planning	x	x	x		x	x
Community members as teachers	x	x			x	x
Self help in building (involving instruction)	x			x		
Nutrition programme	x					
Adult education programme			x		x	
Youth education programme			x	x	x	x
Compound used for teaching e.g. maps laid out	x	x		x		x
Special science room	x	x	x	x		x
Crop husbandry taught and practised	x	x	x	x	x	x
Poultry kept	x				x	x
Cow kept	x	x				x
Piggery		x		x		x
Bee keeping		x				
Rabbits kept	x		x	x	x	x
Wood and metalwork taught		x				
New social studies' programme	x	x		x		
New arts and crafts programme	x	x	x	x	x	x
Experimental maths programme				x		

operates. As the very varied pattern of interaction between the school and its community emerged, and the differences and complexities were revealed, it became more and more apparent to the researchers that, while the ultimate goal of close integration between the school and community learning remained worth attempting, there were a number of possible steps on the paths towards it, whose speed of progress depended on their being understood and accepted by policy makers as well as by the community.

The thoughtful final report of the project contains the valuable table reproduced on pages 170-1.

Implications re-examined

How real are the ideas of basic education and the reactions to them? Do they herald a significant change of attitude towards the whole purpose and function of schooling, or are they merely conference ideas, warm, vague and satisfying because they represent a radicalism which can be safely voiced without the embarrassment of being translated into action?

In the last part of this chapter I should like to examine the implications of the ideas in slightly more detail in an attempt to assess their possible effect on the formal primary school and its curriculum. I examine them under four main headings: the implications for structures, for situational analysis, for curriculum strategy and for curriculum development and evaluation.

(1) IMPLICATIONS FOR STRUCTURES

The idea of basic education implies, on the one hand, a greater integration of school and community learning resources and on the other the acceptance of a variety of alternatives to full-time formal primary schooling. These can range from shortened or accelerated school programmes to a variety of non-formal alternatives often making use of the mass media.

Implicit in the concept of alternatives is the idea that there is a certain basic education 'core curriculum' which may be covered in a number of alternative ways. Alternatives open are shown diagrammatically in Table 11.

(2) IMPLICATIONS FOR THE SITUATIONAL ANALYSIS OF THE CONTEXT

Once the idea of basic education is accepted and once it is realised that minimum learning needs differ and have to be assessed in respect of different contexts, the necessity for making such an analysis becomes more immediate and more compelling.

In relation to data which he collected from three hundred children in the Central and Rift Valley provinces of Kenya, Kenneth King reminds us that,

> 'Before there can be any realistic assessment of the role that primary schools can perhaps play in basic skill formation, it is necessary to construct some sort of inventory of out-of-school work and learning during the primary cycle. This cannot

Table 11 The basic study cycle: alternative patterns and structures

WHERE EDUCATION IS OBTAINED		TIME SPENT	REMARKS
1	School		e.g. short basic cycle followed by continuation cycle.
	Community		
2	School		e.g. short time schooling over longer periods. Further non-formal education in community.
	Community		
	School		e.g. basic cycle taught mostly through non-formal means – e.g. radio – but using the school as a resource.
	Community		
4	School		e.g. longer formal primary cycle with core curriculum and options.
	Community		

Contents of the basic cycle   Further educational experiences: Formal   Non-formal

be generalised across a region or indeed across a country, since there is significant ethnic variation in what is expected of young people.'[13]

Basic skill formation is only one aspect of learning needs and primary school pupils only one of the target groups for basic education. Thus a complicated and continually changing task is revealed which must be attempted yet can only be undertaken once current definitions of and attitudes towards research are widened to include teachers, pupils and other community members in the process of data-gathering and inferring lines of action from it.

One recent initiative in this direction has been the launching in late 1977 of an international programme called CHILD-to-Child initially sponsored by the Institutes of Education and Child Health of London University.

This programme seeks to collect ideas and identify experience from developing countries of how primary school children and their teachers may co-operate in gathering data related to health problems at community level in co-operation with local health workers.[14]

(3) IMPLICATIONS ON CURRICULUM STRATEGY

If we accept, as we must, the necessity of relating formal to non-formal education, activities implicit in the concept of basic education, the tasks of curriculum planning and implementation assume new dimensions. In the first place, one asks what machinery may be devised at central and local level which enables integrated or complementary processes to emerge. This leads towards a re-examination of the nature and functions of our current institutions for curriculum planning which are largely centralised and largely concerned with formal education.

We also become aware that it may be necessary to look yet again at the process of teacher education, to ask ourselves whom we now regard as a teacher and what we now understand by training. We have to consider how far different types of teachers in the community (e.g. school teachers, health teachers, farm teachers, church teachers) should be trained on the job, how far in teacher training institutions and whether such institutions should not encourage such teachers to learn side by side. Once one thinks about these questions, as I have done, it may become necessary to question the present role of conventional teachers' colleges and to wonder whether some alternative institution may not better serve the needs of rural areas.

(4) IMPLICATIONS FOR CURRICULUM DEVELOPMENT AND EVALUATION

It follows that as the clientèle for basic education is more diverse, so processes for curriculum development become of necessity more localised and curriculum plans and materials more varied. At the same time there is need to maintain a national 'standard' particularly in respect of competences in basic skills: hence the balance, as always a delicate one, between central control and local variation, becomes even more crucial. Equally important is the sharing of experience between formal and non-formal approaches. Once one thinks in terms of joint design and in some degree of joint use of programmes and materials for literacy and health, many interesting possibilities are opened up. They range from the production of reading and visual materials based round a common core with different supporting materials for different groups of learners, to the design of projects with common aims but different roles assigned to different groups.

New approaches also imply changes in attitudes to evaluation. The implications of decentralisation on examination policy have been discussed earlier. The concept of basic education adds new perspectives since the idea of identification of learning needs carries with it, as a corollary, the necessity to assess how far and how efficiently they have been met. At the same time, the need for local training in evaluation techniques and the evolution of simple methodologies becomes more pressing.

National responses

Having taken stock of the very considerable policy implications which the ideas of basic education involve, two questions must be asked in an attempt to assess their impact in the countries studied: how far, and at what level are these concepts and implications being discussed, and what action is being taken?

(1) DISCUSSING THE CONCEPTS

Bearing in mind the fact that these ideas have been under review for such a short time, the amount of debate they have provoked is impressive. The United Nations' family of agencies, the World Bank and the international aid agencies are largely responsible for this rapid diffusion since they have put up the funds and provided facilities for meetings and discussions as well as support for experimental projects.

From my attendance at such meetings and my personal contact with professionals in ministries and curriculum development centres I have noted a deep interest in the ideas and, in certain cases, considerable commitment to them.

(2) DISCUSSIONS INTO ACTION

The basic education message calls for greater relevance and efficiency in the provision of the first stage of education, but it is also very much bound up with the concepts of equity, and we who react so favourably to this idea usually do so from the safety of relatively high positions in society, interesting jobs and comfortable incomes. Rural parents and the politicians who listen to their voices are far less secure. When we analyse reactions to the basic education packages proposed for Sierra Leone and Ethiopia, to proposals for shortening sessions in school in Botswana and Uganda, to the idea of alternative period schooling as canvassed in the Zambian Education Review, to the diversification of the curriculum proposed by the IPAR Buea, or even to the community school curriculum at Kwamsisi – we find, in every case the same elements of concern expressed with more or less passion by parents. 'How will these proposals affect the chances of *my* sons and (with slightly less emphasis) *my* daughters to lead a "better" and "fuller" life [with all the cultural and social values implied in these two terms]? My country and my country's children I wish well, but is *my child* being offered more or less?'

Therefore, while it is true that the concepts of basic education are *not* merely conference ideas and that their implications for school curriculum are powerful and will be felt, we must distinguish between those elements in the package which are generally acceptable and those which have deeper social and political connotations.

So far as the philosophies of basic education point towards opening up alternative opportunities for the unschooled, to devolution of decision making, to increased concern for the specification of learning needs and their evaluation, to the exchange of expertise and materials between formal and non-formal educators, to a more flexible content leading towards greater efficiency of instruction – so far they will be accepted and point to action already beginning to emerge.

So far as they constitute a means of reducing inequalities within a society, with the inevitable loss of opportunity and privilege which this entails for some of its members – the ideas will be hotly debated. Thus proposals for shortened sessions, community schools, decentralisation in evaluation, will receive different hearings in different contexts according to the economic and political climate in which they are presented. It is no surprise to me that one notes far more commitment and far more investment, both human and financial, in the policies of basic education among the Tanzanians and Ethiopians than among the Ghanaians, the Swazis or the Nigerians.

Notes

1 E.g. in its Education Sector Review 1974
2 Further useful attempts to isolate and develop the different concepts implied in it have

been undertaken in recent years – e.g. R. H. Dave's *Lifelong Education and School Curriculum*, UNESCO Institute of Education, Hamburg 1973

3 In this chapter I use two terms only: 'formal' and 'non formal'. The distinction made by Coombs between non-formal and informal I find difficult to handle. Rather I see educational opportunities arranged on a continuum from the most formal classroom learning to highly informal situations like those experienced by the girl in the film *Never on Sunday*, who learnt all her languages in bed.

4 E.g. Bloom, B. S., 'Mastery Learning' in Block, J. H. (ed.), *Mastery Learning Theory and Practice*, Holt, Rinehart and Winston 1971, pp 47–63

5 The term 'Basic cycle of study' is used in the report of a UNESCO Committee convened in 1974 under the chairmanship of Dr Prem Kirpal (India). Its report examines aims, structure and curriculum for basic education, is short, wise and well worth reading. It is reproduced in full in Hawes, H. W. R., *Lifelong Education, Schools and Curricula in Developing Countries*, UNESCO Institute of Education, Hamburg 1975

6 UNESCO/UNICEF Co-operation Programme. *Basic Education in Eastern Africa*. Report on a Seminar, Nairobi, Kenya, 19–23 August and 22–26 October 1974

7 *Teacher Education for Basic Education*. Report of a Conference/Workshop held in Tanzania, 24 November–5 December 1975. Nairobi Basic Education Resource Centre for Eastern Africa 1975

8 Very exciting work towards the same end has emerged from the Appropriate Technology Centre – Jos, Plateau State, Nigeria, a project helped and monitored by the Bernard Van Leer Foundation in Holland.

9 Report of the Preparatory Seminar on Case Studies for the Determination of Learning Needs in Rural Areas, 29 November–3 December 1976, UNESCO/ILEP 1977, p 58

10 This structure is now standard throughout Tanzania as a result of the Ujaama Villages Act of 1975. Committees in Kwamsisi predate this act.

11 UNESCO/IIEP Seminar, *op. cit.*

12 UNESCO IIEP Seminar, *op. cit.*, pp 63–64

13 Postlethwaite, T. N., and King, K., *Curriculum Development for Basic Education in Rural Areas*, IIEP Seminar Paper 18, UNESCO Paris 1975, p 27

14 Report published by the Institute of Education and Child Health, London 1978.
 A book for leaders and health workers is also published: Aarons, A., (ed.), *Child to Child*, Macmillian 1616.

Chapter 9 Where do we go from here?

The reader who has come so far with me will appreciate that this is a book about educational planning. It tells the story of our attempts over the last fifteen years to evolve plans and a method of planning by which the most relevant curricula could be selected and transmitted most efficiently to children in primary schools in Africa.

As the process developed it revealed itself on the one hand, as more urgent and necessary, yet on the other as more complex and dynamic. A clear unambiguous methodology for curriculum planning seemed essential. Yet so complex are the interrelated facets involved that no simple plan can meet all our needs.

Herein lies the dilemma of the planner, particularly the planner who works in a centralised system where pressures are great and money short. He needs a framework upon which to base action, the more definite and more prescriptive this is, the easier it is to plan. Such a framework is much valued by those for whom and with whom he works: politicians, the treasury, aid donors, commercial interests, all these appreciate being able to see a course of action stretching far ahead into the future. Their support often confirms us, the planners, in our resolve to make rigid schemes and constitutes an open invitation for us to maintain that arrogant we-know-what's-good-for-you attitude which many of us hold.

But making models is by itself valueless. Planning is for people and the fruits of planning measured in changes in the quality of their lives. People are different, have different values, live in different environments, have different wants and needs for themselves and their children, like to be consulted rather than told what to do, must be respected rather than patronised. Hence there is need for flexibility and understanding in the planning process; consultation and partnership; a certain humility.[1]

Participatory planning

This year's catchword is 'participatory planning'. Like most bits of educational jargon it is public property for anyone to use. Let us therefore annex it and declare that *this book is about the evolution of the concept of participatory planning in the primary school curriculum in African countries.*

Let us also define the term to suit our own purposes. The idea of participatory planning involves on the one hand identifying a policy, priorities and steps for achieving these, while on the other recognising and, as far as possible, managing the conflicts, the unevenness and the divergencies which are inherent in translating these policies into action. It also involves identifying the roles which different agents can and should play in the planning and implementation processes.

In terms of curriculum planning this book has indicated that there *are* certain steps: situational analysis of the educational context in all its varied aspects; the clarification of goals and aims based ultimately on the political and developmental goals of the society; the evolution of a strategy which is based on an assessment of what is possible and not merely what is desirable and which is flexible enough to survive in rapidly changing political, economic and educational climates; the linked processes of curriculum development and implementation involving the refinement of aims and objectives, devising and trying out plans, materials and processes of assessment, training the teachers and other 'implementers', dissemination and diffusion, together with a process of evaluation which must develop alongside the evolving curriculum. At every stage we face the issue of priorities, for in the very tough circumstances which African countries face, where we are continually asked to do more with less, it is never sufficient to ask 'what should we do?', but always necessary to specify what we should do first.

The conflicts and the unevenness we have also recognised. They are more critical within countries than between them, for there is no magic international 'standard' of primary education, no 'modern' or 'old fashioned' curricula, only curricula which prove more or less efficient, more or less appropriate to needs in a society.

Differences have been noted between educational environments and their needs, between the human, administrative and material resources available, and indeed between the relevance of curricula to individual learners. These differences are great and disturbing and must be seen against a tradition of centralised administrative regulations, syllabuses, prescribed texts and nationwide methods of assessment. Just as North American society has traditionally been said to benefit the W.A.S.P. (the White Anglo-Saxon Protestant), primary education in the countries we surveyed in Africa has clearly been weighted heavily in favour of the W.U.M.E. (the Wage Earning, Urban, Middle Class, English Speaker). While from its very origins formal schooling was intended for W.U.M.E.'s, and while it seems inconceivable to me that in the near future an educational revolution will unfold to equalise children's chances, there are many, many ways in which the W.U.M.E.-based curriculum can be modified and its relevance to rural children increased. To this end participatory curriculum planning must strive.

WHO PARTICIPATES AND HOW

Central to the story carried in this book is an examination of the extent and nature of participation. As we review the concepts of curriculum planning, development and implementation, we come to realise, chapter by chapter, how many people are involved in the process and how interdependent they are; from the President with his political philosophy to the carpenter providing cupboards and display space in the rural classroom.

At the very midst of the process are the teachers and those who give them help and support: the headmasters, the inspectors, the local administrators, the teacher trainers, the writers and designers of curriculum materials, the field workers and evaluators. It is upon these that the success and failure of plans depend. The 'higher echelons', the politicians, the professors, the ministry planners, the syllabus makers, the examiners and the overseas experts ignore these people at their peril . . . indeed our story is partly concerned with the sad consequences of ignoring such local expertise, of the follies of overcentralisation in both the design and implementation of curriculum.

But in preaching the virtues of trust and devolution of responsibility one must not ignore two very obvious facts. The first is that education systems are centralised because they reflect political policies and social structures, the second that there is often a great dearth of local expertise, so that even if it were considered desirable to design relevant and efficient curricula to suit learning needs in local areas, there might be no one sufficiently competent to implement them properly.

Two conclusions may, therefore, be drawn. The first, that devolution implies the negotiation of some form of 'contract' between central and local control, an issue which will be examined later in this chapter; the second, that appropriate training in curriculum development and evaluation is necessary for various categories of local workers, if local participation in planning is to be a reality. This, in turn, implies the long overdue emergence of a creed and a methodology of 'commonsense' curriculum development and evaluation, which removes the phoney mystique currently surrounding both processes, and makes them intelligible to the large number of ordinary men and women who need to practise them. The philosophy of the International Centre for Educational Evaluation at Ibadan and the content of the courses it runs tends strongly towards this view.

New directions in curriculum planning

It is appropriate at the end of a book such as this to speculate briefly and tentatively upon possible directions in which policies might develop. However, while interpreting trends from statistical projections is a worthwhile planning exercise, to forecast changes in attitudes is liable to be a very subjective game; readers will readily notice that the likely trends I forecast are strongly influenced by my feelings about the way policies should develop.

Nevertheless reading the future is not entirely a matter of guesswork. We have lessons from the past to build on, some of which are chronicled in this book. We also have the records of other people's successes and failures together with the ideas and the action which have emerged from them. Finally, and most compelling, we have the influences of political, economic and demographic pressures which shape national policies and attitudes to development. Thus we trace a number of deep and important influences on our approaches to what learnings we select for these children of ours who will reach maturity towards the year 2000.

We begin to appreciate further the complexities of development, to redefine it in human as well as economic terms, to add to our measures of growth in gross national product a concern for how it is being distributed, to question very deeply the role of Western aid in the process of development, the norms it sets and the values it inculcates.

We come increasingly to accept that the processes of development are linked and that education's contribution lies as much in the attitudes of adaptability to change it engenders as in the knowledge and skills it teaches.

We begin very seriously to redefine what we mean by 'education' by 'standards' by 'school' and by 'teacher' while at the same time realising that in an interdependent world, a citizen without certain basic knowledge and skills becomes increasingly isolated from the mainstream of society; hence demands for some form of universal primary or basic education in all countries in Africa.

We face a gradual realisation that education planning is a much less mechanistic, more human, more irregular process than economists had originally represented to us and that its qualitative and quantitative aspects are inextricably linked. The parallel lessons we have learned for curriculum planning have already been noted.

Finally we are continually and insistently reminded that all nations in the world are working within a time limit to save themselves from disaster. For African countries to ensure political and economic survival, to safeguard food and water supply, to learn to husband natural resources, to combat disease and malnutrition, to forestall the 'awful arithmetic' of the population explosion before it is too late, requires a mobilisation of all educational resources. Primary education is the largest and possibly most critical area where a new awareness of these 'survival priorities' may be engendered.

Parallel to these influences, one notes a certain modest growth in our knowledge and competencies in methods of choosing, ordering, disseminating and evaluating our curriculum, together with considerable technical advances in the means of production and the delivery of printed and audiovisual materials, which now offer a far wider range of choice as well as new simple and effective facilities for local production.

In the face of these pressures and in the light of current attitudes and initiatives I would detect the following trends emerging in primary curriculum planning in the African countries surveyed:

(i) *A growth of confidence in defining local needs and purposes for primary education; less dependence on models or 'standards' derived from outside.*
In 1975 Julius Nyerere wrote:

> 'We have been too timid – too unliberated – to effect the required radical transformation of the system we inherited. We have made important changes, especially in the curriculum and syllabuses. But we are still mentally committed to "international standards" in education. We still apparently believe that a Tanzanian is not educated unless his education takes a form which is recognisable by, and acceptable to, other countries – and in particular the English-speaking countries. It is from others that we seek our certificates of respectability.'[2]

It will take time for the foreign 'certificates of respectability' to lose their appeal at secondary and tertiary level. At primary level they are already somewhat out of fashion. In Mathematics, and to an increasing degree in Language there is a growing tendency to specify the skills and competencies which a school leaver needs rather than to satisfy any predetermined coverage of content.

Reflected in discussions concerning assessment of primary leavers is the beginning of an awareness that secondary education should seek to build up from where primary school leaves off, instead of setting an entry leval based on its own needs which affects so negatively the whole primary school curriculum. Once this principle is fully accepted the whole purpose and method of the leaving examination comes under review, and once this is changed the whole nature of the actual curriculum in upper primary school alters.

(ii) *An increasing preoccupation with specifying priorities in the primary school curriculum and the relation of these to development needs.*

There is a realisation that the development of communication skills is the first curriculum priority and that in many countries a crisis situation exists in schools, with a large proportion of children unable to comprehend the reading material placed in front of them. Consequently it is necessary to assess the nature and extent of the problem and take action to overcome it through an analysis of what children need language for, through redefining skills to be learnt and the levels at which it is necessary and possible to learn them, through designing appropriate materials which benefit the majority of learners rather than the fortunate few who will achieve secondary entrance. These materials should be flexible enough to serve the range of language competence inevitable in any group of children.

Alongside the priority placed on language and communication, we begin also to detect a concern that curriculum materials in all school subjects should be 'development orientated', should reflect concern over such matters as health, nutrition, food production, conservation of resources and the co-operation and enquiry-mindedness necessary to achieve these. There are no separate 'development education' or 'self-reliance' periods. The knowledge, skills and attitudes necessary for these purposes are woven into the fabric of Language, Mathematics, Social Studies and Science.

(iii) *A greater acceptance of flexibility within the primary school curriculum to suit different abilities and different contexts.*

There are at least three ways in which such flexibility can be seen to be emerging: in the design of *broad national guidelines* and the encouragement of varied ways of interpreting these at regional or local levels; the design of a *national core curriculum* with additional optional and enrichment materials to suit different local contexts; or the design of *plans and materials* at national and local level which permit and encourage flexibility in timetabling and approach, as well as selection and interpretation of content. Each of these three alternatives also involves some degree of regionalisation or localisation of examinations and assessment.

(iv) *Further discussion and elaboration of the 'contract' between local and central control of curricula.*

The 'contract', as I have already indicated, needs to be separately negotiated in each political and social situation but it is necessary everywhere. It relates to centralisation or devolution with regard to statements of objectives, curriculum plans, timetabling, production of materials, implementation strategies, policies of material provision and distribution. In some cases local curriculum committees, panels, resource centres, teachers' colleges, colleges, mobile teachers or headmasters will have greater administrative or financial control than in others. In some systems communities and community education will be more significantly involved than in others but in every case there needs to be a division of responsibility based on discussion. The 'contract', I take to be central to increasing the relevance and efficiency of curriculum planning.

(v) *More concern with designing programmes in the perspective of their implementation.* Two lines of action are here implied: the first involves a very much greater effort made to ascertain the realities of the context in which implementation takes place, hence an increase in research (in its broadest sense) and 'research-mindedness' at all levels; the second, a new pragmatism, a willingness to limit programmes to what is possible in the educational contexts with the learners and the teachers.

(vi) *Greater investment in processes of curriculum implementation and follow up, even if this implies economies elsewhere in the system*
All educational endeavour comes to fruition at one point and one point only – when the learner starts learning something – and we are laboriously realising that all the syllabuses we write, all the books we produce, all the good advice we emit, are effective only in so far as someone understands and uses them; hence the policy implications and the cruel choices – in-services at the expense of pre-service training more and better supervision at the expense of more schools or better class ratios and more teaching time, more materials but less costly ones. Yet not all the choices are painful ones for at numerous points in this book we have encountered instances of how learning to apply new ideas can be woven into every aspect of teacher training, how distinctions between pre-service and in-service training are breaking down and how teachers and children can help each other rather than wait for professional implementers to show them the light.

(vii) *Greater concern with accountability in curriculum planning.*
As the euphoria for modernising curriculum dies down, as costly mistakes are revealed, as resources become ever more strained, so the demands grow, not only for curricula to become more relevant and more efficient, but for means to be found to assess such relevance and efficiency at both central and local level. Hence increased interest and investment in evaluation of programmes, a concern that such evaluation should be purposeful and that there should be a commitment towards acting on the information it uncovers. Once such commitment is made nationally (for the importation of evaluators from outside is yet another example of Nyerere's 'certificates of respectability') there are very clear implications on the setting of objectives and the management of programmes. Indeed I sometimes wonder whether the chief value of an evaluator, like that of a highway policeman, is that he should be large, visible and aggressive, a constant reminder to planners that they are accountable to society for the curricula they produce.

(viii) *An increased and continued commitment to training . . .*
. . . at all levels and for a variety of purposes, for curriculum workers, implementers, administrators, heads and teachers. Such training needs to be very carefully planned so that, like the curriculum, it can be justified in terms of relevance and efficiency.

Our 'commonsense' approach to curriculum development and evaluation must certainly include very practical and immediate elements dealing with such realities as materials design, in-service training and the supply and maintenance of equipment in schools.

ARE THESE POLICY TRENDS OR WISHFUL THINKING?

These are policies which I, personally, believe to be desirable, but my own ideas have been shaped very largely by my friends and colleagues working in ministries, universities and curriculum centres throughout Africa. A closer reading of the text of this book should indicate that though I have deliberately stated these trends in general terms, each one is exemplified to a greater or lesser degree in the thought and action emerging from the countries survey. Sudden radical transformations have not taken place in human attitudes . . . do they ever? . . . but slowly, perceptibly, opinion changes as lessons from experience are absorbed.

The role of overseas aid

I should like to conclude this book by examining one further issue, the future role of overseas aid to curriculum planning in Africa. I have long been impressed and concerned at the disproportionate influence of overseas aid on the things that really matter in African education, for while the ninety per cent contribution which national governments invest in their own systems of education is almost entirely devoted to keeping an overloaded machine running, a significant proportion of overseas aid is invested at the cutting edge of educational development: in making plans, financing innovation, training and retraining those who shape and interpret new policies. It is an awesome responsibility for donors and one, I fancy, which is taken somewhat more lightly than it should be.

Nowhere has overseas influence been more evident or more critical than in curriculum planning. As we survey the new initiatives catalogued in this book, from the 1960's to the present, from the first subject orientated programmes in Mathematics to current community education projects in East and West Africa, we note in every case how influential has been the advice of overseas experts in shaping what African children learn.

The contributions and the shortcomings of the programmes launched and the training provided have been examined in the text. To generalise, with the benefit of hindsight, it would seem that a disproportionate amount of aid has been concentrated on subject based programmes, and very little, comparatively, on achieving that 'whole view' in the setting of objectives, and the devising of strategies and content which has been revealed as essential in curriculum planning for primary schools. Moreover, until very recently, attention towards training personnel in appropriate techniques of curriculum planning, development and implementation has been sadly lacking. But attitudes have changed decisively in recent years. The day of the 'curriculum mongers' is past and future aid is likely to concentrate on giving workers in Africa the means to meet, plan, develop and evaluate new programmes and the skills to do so effectively.

But there is still a good deal of thinking required before this change of heart becomes translated into aid policies and I, therefore, offer my personal interpretation of the new directions of aid I would see emerging side by side with continued assistance in strengthening central machinery for curriculum development and in the improvement of subject curricula, particularly in priority areas such as Language. These processes remain just as important as they ever were but must now be seen alongside others equally essential.

New directions in aid to curriculum development

(i) *Towards clarifying policies and their purpose*
This involves support for national conferences, planning meetings, seminars and discussion groups aimed at promoting a debate on the purposes of education, the broad contents of curricula, the training of teachers and other issues of this magnitude.

While such meetings are entirely national concerns in respect of the decisions they take and the priorities they select, experience from Nigeria and Sierra Leone does suggest that financial support may be valuable in helping to launch them, that increasingly other African countries may have ideas worth adding to the debate and that aid assistance in reporting and publication of proceedings may be welcomed.

There can be no doubt of the need to talk out these issues as preliminary to any reform. The report of an 'expert commission' is never in itself sufficient. People must meet, discuss and make these ideas their own.

(ii) *Towards dissemination of ideas and widening the circle of participation in curriculum planning*
But national meetings only set ideas in motion. The process of curriculum planning involves a great deal of consultation by many people at many levels. For various reasons, national governments invariably find the provision of funding for such meetings difficult to meet. There are few areas where modest investment by aid donors could be more easily and profitably spent than on supporting panel meetings, workshops, discussion groups – all the necessary to-ing and fro-ing which are at the heart of participatory planning.

It might be a sobering thought for some donors to consider how far expenses for certain international conferences, which take big men away from their work, could be redistributed in order to enable small men to do theirs.

(iii) *Towards evolving appropriate methodologies for curriculum planning and development*
Earlier I have stressed the need for new directions in curriculum planning, research and evaluation. The development and refinement of our 'commonsense approach' will be no easy matter, hence the need for working groups and seminars, both internationally and nationally, for writing to emerge and to be modified to suit local needs. There have been welcome initiatives from the IIEP which has sponsored two handbooks on curriculum evaluation and curriculum development,[3] but these

represent only the beginning of a long road. There is little doubt in my mind that most of my colleagues who work in curriculum planning and development share my confusion over what methodologies we should adopt and pass on – and I suspect that some of us are covering up our confusion with long words.

(iv) *Towards establishment and maintenance of local facilities for curriculum planning to operate in accordance and partnership with central bodies*
The evolution of local centres and local committees with responsibilities for curriculum planning and implementation is one of the main preoccupations of this book and their support, especially on a trial basis, would seem an important target for aid. Nevertheless it must be stressed, yet again, that such local initiatives must only be conceived as part of a very carefully thought out policy which assesses and delimits their responsibilities.

(v) *Towards exploration of alternative paths and methodologies through which a basic common-core curriculum can be efficiently transmitted*
(vi) *Towards further clarification of the relationship between school and community in basic education*
As I have indicated in Chapter 8 both these areas are exceptionally sensitive to political and social climates. Yet there is no reason for aid policies to ignore them. Indeed, it is possible that international pressures may be able to exercise important leverage to break down educational conservatism, promote the interests of equity and save resources. If it can be demonstrated, as I believe it *can*, that contact time in school may be significantly reduced, particularly for older children, with no detriment to the quality of the education they receive, that the community has a part to play in partnership with the school, then the dilemma of attempting to provide schooling for more children with less resources becomes, for the first time, soluble. There is, surely, a case here for the mounting of controlled experiments with the help of international aid and the whole-hearted support of national governments.[4]

(vii) *Towards increased investment in research into the context for curriculum planning*
Such research is conducted at various levels, but the greater volume, and that for which the incentive of overseas aid will be particularly needed, is that which is local, immediately relevant to the process of curriculum planning, and undertaken by persons other than full time research workers. For this purpose a new kind of expert needs to emerge, a 'research manager' rather than a research specialist.

(viii) *Towards the development of training schemes, preferably within Africa in a variety of techniques connected with curriculum development and evaluation*
(ix) *Towards the development of skills and facilities to enable African countries to acquire local means of production and distribution of curriculum materials*
These two issues have been listed last, not for any reasons of priority, but because they are the most straightforward, obvious and compelling targets for overseas aid. It will be appreciated that new approaches to the devolution of curriculum planning imply that many more people will need to acquire these skills and that often some sort of two-stage training may be necessary with overseas aid contributing mainly to 'training the trainers'. Yet even here I would have grave doubts about training wholly conducted outside Africa. Problems connected with curriculum are so intimately bound up with 'selection from the culture' that training wholly conducted

in an alien context is bound to suffer in purpose and immediacy. I cannot help wondering why co-operative courses, partly undertaken overseas and partly in a national context, are so often praised but so rarely used.

WILL AID DONORS RESPOND TO THESE APPROACHES?

Readers may detect in these suggestions a somewhat idealistic approach to the aid process. Little of what I am suggesting promotes cultural imperialism or benefits trade. Much of it is intended, rather, to promote what Mao describes as 'walking on two legs'. But I have little doubt that such policies will find favour in the next decade, for experience has educated aid donors as it has curriculum planners, and as experience grows and multilateral aid increases, so stability and self-confidence in nations are revealed as keys to development. Such aid policies I would see as yet another reinforcement of the process of participation which I have identified as the main theme of this book.

Notes

1 Readers will notice that I am interpreting things from a particular political viewpoint. I am assuming that initiative derives from elite groups in society and is developed 'downwards', not from the masses 'upwards'. This I believe to be the situation in African countries surveyed, including Tanzania.
2 Nyerere, J. K., 'Education for Liberation in Africa' in *Prospects*, I, i, 1975, p 10
3 The handbook on evaluation edited by A. Lewy was published in 1977 and is already proving a useful source for planners.
4 For a description of a very significant experiment in Indonesia and the Phillipines (Project Impact), see Sanger, C., *Project Impact*, IDRC, Ottawa 1977.

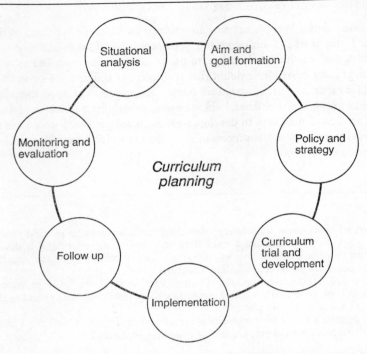

The list that follows has been drawn up as a result of experience gained in the organisation of centralised curriculum projects. It represents a check list of processes involved rather than a guide for sequenced planning. The seven components identified are all important in any rational process of curriculum planning. To some extent thay may be sequential but they are closely integrated and the whole process is dynamic. The collection of basic information never ceases; aim and goal formation are continually being modified. Curriculum planning and development influence and, in turn, are influenced by curriculum implementation. Follow up contributes to situational analysis, while evaluation, in its different forms, affects all the other processes listed.

I   Situational analysis

WHAT KIND OF INFORMATION IS NEEDED?

About the system.
– Basic demographical and statistical information:
  e.g. school numbers and distribution; enrolments and 'flow' through the system.

ages; class sizes; staffing information; financial allocations (projected and actual) with sources.
- Legal and administrative information:
  e.g. current legal provision and requirements; policies and practice in respect of school building, equipment supply, time allocation, progression through grades and stages, assessment and selection. Actual states of buildings and equipment and variation in conditions. The control of primary education; financial and administrative responsibilities accorded to local government, school managers, headmasters and parents.
- Current curricular practice:
  e.g. origins; languages in use; timetables actually followed, programme covered and subjects taught (as distinct from those officially recommended).

About the learners.
- Social and cultural backgrounds:
  e.g. patterns of learning, authority and child rearing within the home and family; norms, values and customs; games, songs and stories; work and duties performed and expected of children.
- Language and perception:
  e.g. languages used, spoken and understood; relationship of mother tongue to language of instruction to content and demands of the curriculum.
- Visual perception of children in relation to materials used.
- Cognitive development:
  e.g. ability to comprehend ideas and processes at various ages and stages and in relationship to the current demands of syllabuses.
- Interests and aspirations of learners.
- Physical and psychomotor development:
  e.g. development in relation to present and possible demands of curriculum; health and nutrition.

About the teachers
- Education and training:
  e.g. length and type of preparation; language understanding and competency; knowledge, skills and understanding, in relation to demands of the curriculum, of national and local needs and goals for development.
- Interests and aspirations:
  e.g. special knowledge, skills and interests; opportunities for them to apply and further these; attitudes towards current curriculum.
- Relations between teachers and between teachers and the community:
  e.g. composition of teaching force; knowledge, understanding and relationships between teachers and community.

About communities
- Resources for learning:
  e.g. physical, cultural and human resources available within communities in relation to present and potential demands of curriculum; parallel learning systems formal to informal.

- Values and attitudes:
  e.g. what is considered important and worthwhile, unacceptable or undesirable; attitudes to present schooling and its curriculum; priorities.
- Needs and goals:
  development and learning needs within wider and narrower communities, relations between these: goals and priorities.

About parallel learning systems, national and international
- Other learning systems parallel to the formal school system:
  e.g. current content and future potential of non-formal programmes, e.g. in Agriculture and Health; of political and religious education; of the mass media. Consideration of how all these can complement and supplement formal programmes.
- Parallel programmes in similar national contexts:
  e.g. research; plans; materials; descriptions of programmes; evaluation of data originating from other African countries and from systems elsewhere with related contexts and problems, e.g. Caribbean, South East Asia.

WHO COLLECTS THE INFORMATION, AND HOW?

The agents
- Consider the role and potential of the following:
  statistical services, administrators, inspectors and advisers, full time research workers, staff of colleges and universities, teachers, students in training, the community (parents, employers).
- In respect of:
  originating information about the educational context; acting as agents for nationally and locally organised research and survey schemes; building up interest and awareness in finding out about the context in order to improve professional competence.

Planning and organisation
- Method:
  Who identifies what information is needed?
  How is it to be collected; validated; collated – and by whom?
- Administration:
  What machinery needs to be set up? How is it to be financed and serviced?
  How is work done by agents to be given appropriate recognition.
- Outcome:
  How are the results to be published; publicised?
  How are they to be incorporated into curriculum planning.

II Aim and goal formation

Having in mind :
1. National political philosophies and policies; economic goals, policies and needs; social values.

2. Differential cultures, needs and aspirations within the local community.
3. The need to safeguard the development of individuals as well as communities.
4. The nature and structure of knowledge.
5. The human and material context of the curriculum and its implementation.

Aims, goals and objectives for :
1. National policy.
2. Different levels and types of education.
3. Different subjects or groups of subjects.
4. Local areas and individual schools.

Have to be discussed, formulated and related to the selection of curriculum content and its evaluation.

The process involves :
1. Diffusion and discussion of ideas; the promotion of a debate at various levels and through different means and degrees of formality.
   Such debate needs to involve a variety of individuals and interests from all parts of the formal education system (organisers, agents and users); from parallel sub-system of non-formal education; from the wider national and local community. Political, economic and social interests must be reflected in the debate.
2. The translation of such discussion into statements of goals, aims and, sometimes, objectives for different levels and purposes. In most cases this must be achieved through an organised structure of meetings, panels and committees.
3. The refinement and classification of such aims goals and objectives bearing in mind the different orders of outcomes expected as well as the nature of the educational context and variations within it.
   e.g. statements of what we might expect a child to know, feel or have the skills to do as a result of a certain period of schooling, together with expected variations in goals between different types and abilities of learners. (Such a statement may well be seen within the framework of some kind of 'core' and 'optional' curricula).
4. Planning implications include:
   - the process of administrative support for such decision making
   - finance for it
   - follow up for it – (e.g. publication and dissemination of results).

These *aims*, *goals* and *objectives* and the *guidelines* for curriculum content they imply must be translated into action in schools through:

III Policy and strategy

Involving decisions about :
1. **Agencies for change and for the co-ordination of change**
   In the ministry.

In educational institutions: universities, colleges, schools.
In special centres.
Through professional institutions.
Among the public.

2. **The pattern and method of change**
   Sources of initiative.
   Changes in pattern structures that relate to curriculum policy.
   Centralisation and decentralisation.
   Primary agents of change, through – syllabus? – materials? – teachers? – exams?
   Degree of flexibility.

3. **The extent of change**   (a) Desirable   (b) Possible
   Alternative possibilities depending on:
   . . . success of trials
   . . . finance available.
   Degree of flexibility

4. **The priorities for change**
   Subjects＼　／political　＼
   Levels　—for—educational—purpose
   Areas　／　＼economic　／

5. **The timing of change**
   When will the process start?
   When will particular outcomes be expected?
   How much flexibility?

6. **Channels of communication**
   Dissemination of information regarding policies to education workers (including teachers) and to the general public.
   Facilities for intercommunication between different agents of change.
   Facilities for efficient feedback and evaluation.

7. **Relationship with other agencies for change**
   With other agents for non-formal education, e.g. adult literacy, agriculture, health.
   With mass media.
   With social and political movements.

And with implications on policies for :
  1. Capital Development
  2. Recruitment of staff
  3. Building and equipment design
  4. Materials development and distribution
  5. Examination policy and design
  6. Teacher recruitment training and retraining
  7. Establishment and training of inspectors and advisers
  8. Recruitment and training of adequate teacher trainers
  9. Structure and management of the system of educational administration
  10. Inter/departmental inter/ministerial co-operation

11. International conservation and policies regarding aid

Such policies have to be refined and modified following more detailed results of:

IV Curriculum trial and development

Depending on :
- the national and local *context* (and variations within it) – (Section I)
- the national and local *aims*, *goals* and *objectives* – (Section II)
- *strategies – policies* – (Section III)
- the human and material resources available for the curriculum development process
- the facilities available for curriculum implementation (human, administrative, financial and material)

Involves the following processes :
1. Planning the detailed organisation of the scheme: responsibilities and deployment of personnel; communication and co-ordination between 'centre' – 'periphery'; timings (with flexibility); administration and finance; pattern of formative and summative elvauation.
2. Diffusion of information about the programme: to headmasters, teachers, parents, educational administrators and supervisors involved in trial programmes; to teachers and other educational personnel in training; through the education service and community as a whole.
3. Planning and conducting a trial programme in schools involving decisions on which schools and teachers are to be involved in the programme; planning the programme of study (syllabus or schemes); planning and producing trial materials; training personnel involved in trials; ensuring adequate dissemination of materials, conducting and monitoring trials; ensuring adequate provision for feedback and evaluation is maintained.
4. Ensuring that *modification* takes place as a result of evaluation and feedback; in the programme; in the materials; in the training; in the monitoring techniques; in timing and flexibility.
5. Planning and conducting parallel trials in *Teachers' Colleges*. Ensuring that understanding and discussion of trial materials is incorporated widely into pre-service and in-service programmes for teachers.
6. Ensuring parallel trials, evaluation and modification in systems is *examination* and *assessment*.

Any large scale centralised scheme must recognise the following to be of crucial importance :
1. Adequate *co-ordination* of subject specialists and *integration* of their work, a process involving:
   (i) prior selection of priorities, themes and areas of integration before panels start detailed subject planning

(ii) provision of facilities for joint planning, meeting and materials production (see Note 1)

(iii) ongoing facilities for monitoring and feedback of the process as a whole

2. Careful selection of trial schools and briefing of their staff.

   Schools must be typical, varied and accessible.

   Staff need to be carefully briefed and staffing stable during the period of trial. Contributions of staff to the scheme's success need to be adequately re-organised and rewarded.

3. Careful *selection, briefing* and *training* of *curriculum development personnel, field supervisors* and *writers* who must:

   (i) fully understand the purpose of the project, its goals, their part in it and how this relates to the task other workers are performing

   (ii) understand the context in which they work and seek further information concerning it; this involves the closest possible contact with trial schools, their teachers and the children who work in them

   (iii) understand the financial and administrative parameters which govern their work, e.g., the time, cost and material limitations within which they must design programmes and materials. Such resources must be shared equally between different parts and stages in the curriculum

   (iv) have adequate and appropriate skills in curriculum development, evaluation and materials production

4. Adequate *time* to enable trial, feedback and modification to take place. In order for a reasonable job to be done a minimum of *two years* must be allowed between start of trial and start of implementation in order to allow for materials to be modified following feedback and evaluation.

   Design of materials for one class (especially in subjects such as English and Mathematics) must depend on information gained from the previous years trial. Thus allowing for a one year initial preparation, *we would expect a six year primary curriculum programme to take nine years before new syllabuses are introduced throughout the cycle.*

5. An *adequate degree of flexibility* to allow unexpected strengths to be explored and unexpected difficulties overcome, also to cater for the inevitable unevenness of the process.

V Curriculum implementation

The process is *gradual* and *uneven*. Variations will occur depending on curriculum strategy and the style of curriculum development adopted.

The following processes are involved:

(a) introducing new plans and materials (books, aids, apparatus) into *schools* and *teacher training* programmes.

(b) consequent changes in building and equipment policies, e.g. new styles of building and furniture; production distribution and storage provision.

(c) changes in organisation, e.g., at school and class level; between school and community; within the education service. Changes may effect staff deployment time-tabling, and school administration.

(d) training and re-training the *education administrators, inspectors, headmasters, tutors* and *teachers* who must know:
- why the changes have been made
- what the changes are
- how to bring them about

Such training will take place – in school
  – in colleges and centres
  – by private study

(e) provision of resource facilities for teachers and other workers in the field
(f) change in patterns of examination and assessment
(g) explanation of changes to parents and community and their involvement

VI Evaluation

Evaluation must take place throughout the programme (not merely at the end); thus it must involve *formative* and *summative* evaluation. The following process is involved:

(a) deciding the policy for evaluation; nature, purpose, extent, degree of investment.
1. It is necessary for: the *reason* for evaluation to be made clear; the *scope* of evaluation to be decided; the *means* to be provided; the *outcomes* to influence future action.
2. Both *product* and *process* must be evaluated in order, primarily, to discover whether the curriculum meets the needs for which it was designed and whether the process of curriculum change is being carried out efficiently.

(b) selection of evaluator(s) and their briefing. It will be appreciated that most evaluation is done by project workers and teachers. An evaluator only co-ordinates their work.

(c) ensuring adequate channels of communication:
1. so that the process of evaluation is closely connected at every stage with the development and trial of materials.
2. so that feedback results in action.

(d) designing the system of evaluation and carrying it out: tasks will include:
1. evaluation of objectives and the links between objectives, materials and what learners learn.
2. evaluation of the process in respect of:
    (i) its efficiency: e.g. timetable, writing and production techniques, communication, organisation of trials and feedback
    (ii) its correlation with the means available for implementation and permanent adoption: e.g., in relation to commitment, abilities and means of those charged with implementation (especially teachers in the field and under training).
    (iii) its links with systems of public assessment and selection.

3. evaluation of outcomes:
  - in learners, teachers and curriculum workers
  - in respect of immediate and longer term effects of new curricula
(e) modifying the curriculum and the processes of curriculum development and evaluation as a result of information received.

VII Follow up

1. By definition curriculum development is a continuing process. The following are therefore required:
  (a) continued induction of teachers and other educational personnel – pre-service – in-service
  (b) continued support from headmasters, administrators and inspectors
  (c) continued collection of information
  (d) continued review of objectives in relation to changing needs of individuals and society
  (e) continued modification of materials
  (f) continued evaluation
  (g) continued review of assessment procedures

Note

Suggestions for joint panel meetings
Lesotho 1978

The following suggestions, made in 1977, are in connection with the large scale primary curriculum change planned in Lesotho. The joint panel meetings are regarded as an important first step in the process of change.

'COMPOSITION OF GROUPS AND SUB-GROUPS

1. *The panels*
It is important that panels contain a good proportion of teachers and that all discussions take place in the perspective of what *is* in Lesotho schools and not of what *ought to be*.

Each panel needs to contain at least one member who specialises in the needs of young children and one who is aware of language capabilities of children and teachers.

2. *The co-ordinating committee*
should contain one representative from each panel as well as some others. The project director should lead the co-ordinating committee.

The co-ordinating committee is a purely professional and advisory body. Direction of the project remains under the control of the Project Director and (if appointed) the project steering committee.

3. *The programme*
The programme for 3 weeks would involve:

(i) Initial plenary sessions for all panel members.
(ii) Panel meetings including some joint meetings of related panels and meetings of the lower primary panel.
(iii) Co-ordinating committee meetings to co-ordinate panel work.

Initial plenary sessions are necessary
(i) to explain the programme.
(ii) to review work already undertaken by panels.
(iii) to review the implications of
(a) the decisions of the national seminar.
(b) general policy decisions affecting the curriculum as a whole.
(c) the results of situational analyses of schools.
(iv) to present and discuss a more detailed analysis of aims of education and to examine the implications on the whole curriculum.
(v) to present and discuss the concept of "national themes" which form a background to syllabus content.

The co-ordinating committee would
(i) discuss and suggest balance of time between various subjects.
(ii) examine financial and material limits and apportion "ceilings" between subjects.
   Certain hard decisions would result, e.g. which subjects could or could not recommend pupils books to be bought; amount of apparatus which can be recommended.
   The final cost of materials *must* be within the amount recommended nationally as a book fee to parents.
(iii) examine national priorities and suggest concrete ways in which they could be brought into the curriculum and into curriculum materials at various levels.
(iv) subsequently examine, criticise and collate draft syllabuses submitted by panels.
(v) examine and recommend what advice may be given to schools in relation to co-curricular activities and community service.

The panels should
(i) review current syllabuses and materials.
(ii) review any situational analysis already made – e.g. reviews of materials and literacy surveys.
(iii) review work already undertaken by the panel.
(iv) review relevant material available from other African countries.
(v) discuss detailed objectives related to what children in Lesotho can be expected to achieve in specific subjects and specific levels.
(vi) produce *outline* syllabuses indicating
(a) core
(b) enrichment material
(c) options
(vii) make specific suggestions concerning testing and examination policies both in respect of internal and external examinations.

(viii) suggest basic material to be produced and indicate who will be entrusted with it.
 (ix) suggest writing plans for the next year with tasks and deadlines.
  (x) make specific suggestions on the kind of additional teacher-made material which could emerge from local workshops.
 (xi) indicate how material is to be tried out and how evaluated.
(xii) plan future programmes for panel activities.

Cross membership between panels
  (i) A lower primary group should have already been formed drawing on member-ship of all panels.
 (ii) Joint meetings of panels should occur for specific tasks as suggested by the co-ordinating committee.
(iii) Certain panels must keep in very close step, e.g.
English/Sesotho
Maths/Science
Social/Cultural Studies
Science/Practical Activities
 (iv) The language panel must keep a close watching brief on all written materials.

CONCLUSION

The above agenda represents three weeks very hard work and sets the scene for a task which will continue over many years. No panel member should be appointed or accept the commitment unless he or she is satisfied that this investment of time is necessary and possible. Panels *must* be working panels.[1]

---

1 *Primary school curriculum change in Lesotho*. Op cit. (1977), pp 62–64

Appendix 2 Official time allocations in schools in ten countries

COUNTRY (first group)

SUBJECT	Lesotho CLASS 2 (h m)	Lesotho TERMINAL CLASS (h m)	Swaziland CLASS 2 (h m)	Swaziland TERMINAL CLASS (h m)	Botswana CLASS 2 (h m)	Botswana TERMINAL CLASS (h m)	Zambia CLASS 2 (h m)	Zambia TERMINAL CLASS (h m)	Tanzania (1) CLASS 2 (h m)	Tanzania (1) TERMINAL CLASS (h m)	Tanzania (2) CLASS 2 (h m)	Tanzania (2) TERMINAL CLASS (h m)
1 Languages (a) English	6 00	6 40	4 00	7 00	2 00	5 30	3 00	6 00	3 20	4 00	1 00	1 20
(b) Local language	4 00	3 20	6 00	3 30	3 00	3 00	6 30	3 30	6 00	3 20	2 20	2 00
2 Mathematics	3 30	4 00	2 30	4 00	3 45	4 00	2 30	4 00	3 20	5 20	1 40	2 00
3 General science	2 00	3 30	0 30	1 00	2 30	2 00	—	2 00	1 20	2 40	0 40	1 20
4 Social studies	—	3 20	—	2 00	2 30	3 00	—	2 40	—	4 40	0 40	3 00
5 Religious education	2 00	1 20	1 30	1 00	—	1 00	1 30	2 00	0 40	0 40	0 40	0 40
6 Physical education	1 40	1 20	—	0 30	2 30	1 00	0 30	1 20	1 20	0 40	1 00	1 20
7 Cultural and practical activities	4 00	3 40	3 00	4 00	—	8 30	1 30	6 00	4 00	5 20	2 00	6 00
TOTAL (hours and minutes)	23 10	27 10	17 30	23 00	16 15	28 00	15 30	27 30	26 40	20 00	10 00	18 00

COUNTRY (second group)

SUBJECT	Kenya CLASS 2 (h m)	Kenya TERMINAL CLASS (h m)	Uganda CLASS 2 (h m)	Uganda TERMINAL CLASS (h m)	Nigeria (1) CLASS 2 (h m)	Nigeria (1) TERMINAL CLASS (h m)	Nigeria (2) CLASS 2 (h m)	Nigeria (2) TERMINAL CLASS (h m)	Ghana CLASS 2 (h m)	Ghana TERMINAL CLASS (h m)	Sierra Leone CLASS 2 (h m)	Sierra Leone TERMINAL CLASS (h m)
1 Languages (a) English	2 00	5 50	3 20	4 00	6 25	5 50	3 35	5 00	4 00	4 00	6 50	8 10
(b) Local language	4 30	2 20	5 40	2 00	2 20	2 20	2 50	1 00	4 00	3 00	—	—
2 Mathematics	3 00	4 40	2 30	4 40	4 05	4 40	3 55	3 00	3 30	3 30	4 10	3 20
3 General science	1 30	3 30	2 00	4 00	2 20	2 20	0 50	2 00	2 00	2 00	1 10	3 30
4 Social studies	—	3 30	—	4 00	2 55	2 55	—	1 00	—	2 00	1 40	2 30
5 Religious education	1 30	1 45	2 30	2 40	1 45	2 55	2 10	2 30	1 30	1 30	1 15	1 30
6 Physical education	2 30	1 45	2 30	2 00	1 45	1 45	0 45	1 30	2 00	2 00	1 15	1 30
7 Cultural and practical activities	2 30	2 55	1 30	3 20	1 45	3 30	2 35	4 00	3 30	4 30	4 10	3 40
TOTAL (hours and minutes)	17 30	26 15	20 00	26 40	23 20	25 40	17 20	20 00	22 30	22 30	20 30	24 10

Appendix 3   Time allocations in three countries in the last three official syllabuses

Lesotho

1957 (hours and minutes)

SUBJECT	1	2	3	4	5	6	7
1 Languages (a) English	3 00	4 00	4 00	4 00	4 00	5 20	5 20
(b) Local language	5 30	4 00	5 00	5 00	2 30	3 20	3 20
2 Mathematics	3 30	3 30	3 30	3 30	3 30	2 40	2 40
3 General science	—	1 00	1 00	1 00	1 00	2 20	3 20
4 Social studies	—	2 00	2 00	2 00	2 00	3 20	3 20
5 Religious education	2 00	2 00	2 00	2 00	3 30	3 20	3 20
6 Physical education	2 00	2 30	2 30	1 30	1 30	1 40	1 20
7 Cultural and practical activities	4 00	6 00	6 00	6 00	6 00	6 40	6 40
TOTAL	20 00	25 00	25 00	25 00	25 00	27 40	27 40

1963

SUBJECT	1	2	3	4	5	6	7
1 Languages (a) English	3 00	4 00	4 00	4 00	4 00	5 20	5 20
(b) Local language	5 30	5 00	5 00	5 00	2 30	3 20	3 20
2 Mathematics	3 30	3 30	3 30	3 30	3 30	3 20	3 20
3 General science	—	1 00	1 00	1 00	1 00	2 20	3 20
4 Social studies	—	2 00	2 00	2 00	2 00	3 20	3 20
5 Religious education	2 00	2 00	2 00	2 00	1 00	1 20	1 20
6 Physical education	2 00	2 30	2 30	1 30	1 00	1 40	1 40
7 Cultural and practical activities	4 00	6 00	6 00	6 00	6 00	6 40	6 40
TOTAL	20 00	25 00	25 00	25 00	25 00	25 00	25 00

1967

SUBJECT	1	2	3	4	5	6	7
1 Languages (a) English	3 30	6 00	6 00	6 30	6 30	6 40	6 40
(b) Local language	—	4 00	4 00	4 00	4 00	3 20	3 20
2 Mathematics	3 30	3 30	3 30	4 00	4 00	4 00	4 00
3 General science	—	—	—	2 00	2 00	3 20	3 20
4 Social studies	—	—	2 00	2 00	2 00	3 20	3 20
5 Religious education	1 40	2 00	1 40	1 40	1 40	1 20	1 20
6 Physical education	1 40	1 40	1 40	1 40	1 45	1 45	1 20
7 Cultural and practical activities	4 00	4 00	4 00	4 40	4 40	5 00	5 00
TOTAL	18 20	23 10	23 10	24 50	24 50	27 10	27 10

Kenya

1953

SUBJECT	1	2	3	4	5	6	7
1 Languages (a) English	—	—	3 00	2 30	6 40	6 40	5 20
(b) Local language	5 00	5 00	4 30	4 00	2 40	2 40	3 20
2 Mathematics	2 30	1 00	2 30	2 30	4 40	4 40	4 40
3 General science	1 00	1 00	1 00	1 00	2 00	2 00	2 00
4 Social studies	—	—	1 00	1 00	3 20	2 00	2 00
5 Religious education	2 30	2 30	2 30	2 30	3 20	3 20	3 20
6 Physical education	2 30	2 30	2 30	2 30	3 20	3 20	3 20
7 Cultural and practical activities	1 30	1 30	1 40	2 30	4 00	4 00	5 20
TOTAL	15 00	15 00	20 00	20 00	30 00	30 00	30 00

1967

SUBJECT	1	2	3	4	5	6	7
1 Languages (a) English	2 00	2 00	4 00	4 00	4 00	5 20	5 20
(b) Local language	5 00	4 30	5 00	5 00	2 30	3 20	3 20
2 Mathematics	3 00	3 00	3 30	3 30	3 30	3 20	3 20
3 General science	0 30	1 30	1 00	2 00	2 00	2 20	3 20
4 Social studies	—	—	2 00	2 00	2 00	3 20	3 20
5 Religious education	2 00	1 30	2 00	2 00	1 00	1 20	1 20
6 Physical education	2 30	2 30	2 00	1 30	1 00	1 40	1 40
7 Cultural and practical activities	2 30	2 00	2 00	6 00	6 00	6 40	6 40
TOTAL	17 30	17 30	20 00	25 00	25 00	25 00	25 00

1976

SUBJECT	1	2	3	4	5	6	7
1 Languages (a) English	4 00	4 00	3 30				
(b) Local language	5 00	5 00	4 30		5 50	5 50	5 50
2 Mathematics	2 30	3 00	3 00		2 20	2 20	2 20
3 General science	—	—	2 30		4 40	4 40	4 40
4 Social studies	2 30	2 30	2 30		6 15	6 15	6 15
5 Religious education	1 30	1 30	1 30		1 45	1 45	1 45
6 Physical education	1 15	1 15	1 40		1 45	1 45	1 45
7 Cultural and practical activities	1 15	1 15	1 30		2 25	2 55	2 25
TOTAL	19 45	19 45	20 25		26 15	26 15	26 15

Sierra Leone

1956

SUBJECT	1	2	3	4	5	6	7
1 Languages (a) English	10 05	11 10	8 00	8 00	7 35	7 35	—
(b) Local language	—	—	—	—	—	—	—
2 Mathematics	3 10	2 50	3 45	3 45	3 45	1 15	—
3 General science	0 20	0 20	1 15	1 15	1 15	1 15	—
4 Social studies	—	—	0 50	0 50	0 50	0 50	—
5 Religious education	1 40	1 40	2 35	2 35	2 30	2 30	—
6 Physical education	1 15	1 15	1 35	1 35	1 45	1 45	—
7 Cultural and practical activities	3 05	2 20	3 40	3 40	3 40	3 40	—
TOTAL	19 35	19 35	21 35	21 35	21 35	21 35	—

1964

SUBJECT	1	2	3	4	5	6	7
1 Languages (a) English	8 15	8 15	9 50	9 20	9 20	9 20	—
(b) Local language	—	—	—	—	—	—	—
2 Mathematics	4 10	4 10	1 00	3 20	3 20	3 20	—
3 General science	1 15	1 15	1 00	1 00	1 00	1 00	—
4 Social studies	2 00	2 00	1 50	2 50	2 50	2 50	—
5 Religious education	1 15	1 15	1 40	0 40	0 40	0 40	—
6 Physical education	1 15	1 15	1 40	2 10	2 10	0 10	—
7 Cultural and practical activities	5 15	5 15	3 50	3 20	3 20	3 20	—
TOTAL	23 10	23 10	25 00	25 00	25 00	25 00	—

1976

SUBJECT	1	2	3	4	5	6	7
1 Languages (a) English	6 50	6 50	9 00	9 00	9 00	8 10	8 10
(b) Local language	—	—	—	—	—	—	—
2 Mathematics	4 10	4 10	3 20	3 20	3 20	3 20	3 20
3 General science	1 30	1 30	1 40	2 30	1 30	3 30	3 30
4 Social studies	1 40	1 40	1 30	1 30	1 30	1 30	1 30
5 Religious education	1 15	1 15	1 10	1 30	1 30	1 30	1 30
6 Physical education	1 15	1 15	1 10	1 45	1 30	1 30	1 30
7 Cultural and practical activities	4 10	4 10	3 20	1 45	1 40	3 40	3 40
TOTAL	20 30	20 30	21 40	22 20	22 20	24 10	24 10

Select Reading List and Bibliography

Selected reading list on curriculum planning

The following twenty titles have been selected from the large and growing body of literature concerned with curriculum planning and development in Europe and the United States of America. They represent useful basic reference material for curriculum planners.

BLOOM, BENJAMIN S. (ed.), *Taxonomy of Educational Objectives: the Classification of Education Goals: Handbook 1 The Cognitive Domain*, Longman, London, 1956.

BRUNER, JEROME S., *The Process of Education*, Oxford University Press, 1960.

BRUNER, JEROME S., *Towards a Theory of Instruction*, Oxford University Press, 1966.

BRUNER, JEROME S., *The Relevance of Education*, Allen and Unwin, London, 1972.

DAVIES, IVOR K., *Objectives in Curriculum Design*, McGraw-Hill, Maidenhead, 1976.

GOLBY, M., GREENWALD, J. and WEST, R., *Curriculum Design*, Croom Helm, London, 1975.

GROBMAN, HULDA, *Evaluation Activities of Curriculum Projects*, Rand McNally, Chicago, 1968.

HAMILTON, D., *Curriculum Evaluation*, Open Books, London, 1976.

HARRIS, A., LAWN, M. and PRESCOTT, W., *Curriculum Innovation*, Croom Helm, London, 1975.

HOOPER, D. (ed.), *The Curriculum – Context, Design and Development*, Oliver and Boyd, London, 1971.

LAWTON, DENIS, *Social Change, Education Theory and Curriculum Planning*, University of London Press, 1973.

LEWY, A., *Planning the School Curriculum*, UNESCO/IIEP, Paris, 1977.

OECD, *New Patterns of Teacher Education and Tasks: Teachers as Innovators*, OECD, Paris, 1976.

OECD/CERI, *The Nature of the Curriculum for the Eighties Onwards*, OECD, Paris, 1972.

OECD/CERI, *Handbook on Curriculum Development*, OECD, Paris, 1975.

THE OPEN UNIVERSITY, *Educational studies: A second level course, Curriculum Design and Development*, 32 Units (13 titles), The Open University Press, Milton Keynes, 1976–7.

OWEN, J. G., *The Management of Curriculum Development*, Cambridge University Press, 1973.

TABA, HILDA, *Curriculum Development, Theory and Practice*, Harcourt Brace and World, New York, 1975.

TYLER, RALPH, GAGNÉ, ROBERT and SCRIVEN, MICHAEL, *Perspectives of Curriculum Evaluation*, Rand McNally, Chicago, 1967.

TYLER, RALPH, *Basic Principles of Curriculum and Instruction*, University of Chicago Press, 1949.

Bibliography

This is a specialist bibliography of works related to curriculum development for primary schools in English Speaking Africa. It is divided into four parts.

Part 1 contains a selected list of works relevant to developing countries generally.

Part 2 lists titles related to Africa.

Part 3 comprises references to specific countries.

Part 4 contains selected works relating to the African Education Programme and the international curriculum projects which derived from it and followed it: AMP; APSP; ASSP; SEPA; EARMP; WARMP.

PART I: WORKS RELATED TO PRIMARY SCHOOL CURRICULUM AND CURRICULUM DEVELOPMENT IN DEVELOPING COUNTRIES

ALLES, JINAPALA, *Learning in Childhood – What are the Basics?* UNESCO, Unit for Co-operation with UNICEF, Paris, January 1976.

ANDERSON, C. A., 'The sorcerer's apprentice: education in developing nations', *Comparative Education*, vi, 1, Oxford, 1970, pp 5–18.

ANKRAH-DOVE, L. (ed.), *Teachers Groups and Centres in Developing Countries*, London University Institute of Education (Department of Education in Developing Countries), 1978.

ASIAN PROGRAMME OF EDUCATIONAL INNOVATION FOR DEVELOPMENT, *Implementing Curriculum Change – A Symposium of Experiences from the Asian Region*, UNESCO Regional Office for Education in Asia, Bangkok, 6–18 September 1976.

BEEBY, C. E., *The Quality of Education in Developing Countries*, Harvard University Press, 1966.

BEEBY, C. E., *Curriculum Planning, Report of the Fourth Commonwealth Education Conference, 1968*, Her Majesty's Stationery Office, London, 1968.

BEEBY, C. E. (ed.), *Qualitative Aspects of Educational Planning*, UNESCO/IIEP, Paris, 1969.

BERRY, J. W. and DASEN, P. R. (eds), *Culture and Cognition: Readings in Cross-Cultural Psychology*, Methuen, London, 1974.

BRIMER, M. A. and PAULI, L., *Wastage in Education! A World Problem*, UNESCO, Paris, 1971.

DAVE, R. H., *Lifelong Education and School Curriculum*, UNESCO Institute for Education, Hamburg, 1973.

DAVE, R. H. (ed.), *Asian Study in Curriculum Development: Research Design and Questionnaires*, National Institute for Educational Research, Tokyo, 1969.

DORE, RONALD, *The Diploma Disease: Education, Qualifications and Development*, Unwin Educational Books, London, 1976.

DOTTRENS, ROBERT, *The Primary School Curriculum*, UNESCO, Paris, 1962.

FOSTER, P. and SHEFFIELD, J. (eds), *Education and Rural Developments*, World Year Book of Education 1974, Evans, London, 1973.

GRIFFITHS, V. L., *The Problems of Rural Education*, UNESCO/IIEP, Paris, 1968.

HAVELOCK, R. G. and HUBERMAN, A. M., *Solving Educational Problems*, The theory and reality of innovation in developing countries, UNESCO/IBE, Paris, 1977.

HAWES, H. W. R., *Lifelong Education Schools and Curricula in Developing Countries*, UNESCO Institute for Education, Hamburg, 1975.

HAWES, H. W. R., 'Locally based educational research and curriculum development in developing countries: the teacher's role', *IIEP Occasional Paper* 40, UNESCO, Paris, 1976.

HAWES, H. W. R., *Planning the primary school curriculum in developing countries*, UNESCO/IIEP, Paris, 1972.

HOWSON, A. G., 'The international transfer of teaching materials', *Educational Development International*, Stevenage, (for the British Council), October 1973, pp 143–147.

KERR, J. F., *Curriculum change in emergent countries*, University of Leicester School of Education, 1969.

KING, K. (ed.), *Education and community in Africa: proceedings of a seminar*, Centre for African Studies, University of Edinburgh, 1976.

KING, K., 'Minimum learning needs for the third world: new panacea or new problems?' *Prospects*, vi, 1, UNESCO, Paris, 1976, pp 39–56.

LEWY, A. (ed.), *Handbook of Curriculum Evaluation*, UNESCO/Longman, New York, 1977.

PHILLIPS, H. M., *Basic Education: A World Challenge: Measures and Innovations for Children and Youth in Developing Countries*, Wiley, London, 1975.

PRITCHARD, MERVYN W. and LYONS, RAYMOND F., *Primary School Inspection: A Supporting Service for Education*, UNESCO/IIEP, Paris, 1972.

RAZIK, TAHER, *Systems Approach to Teacher Training and Curriculum Development: the Case of the Developing Countries*, UNESCO/IIEP, Paris, 1972.

SEAMO, Regional Centre for Educational Innovation and Technology, *Life-skills and Objectives for Primary Education: A preliminary tryout*, INNOTECH, Saigon, December 1973.

UNESCO/UNICEF Cooperative Programme, *Basic Services for children: a continuing search for learning priorities*, UNESCO/IBE, Paris, 1978, Parts I and II.

UNESCO, *Learning to be: The World of Education Today and Tomorrow*, The International Commission on the Development of Education, UNESCO, Paris, 1972.

UNIVERSITY OF LONDON INSTITUTE OF EDUCATION, (Department of Education in Developing Countries). Report of a Workshop 28 March to 1 April 1977, *Teaching Mother-Tongue Reading in Multi-lingual Environments*, London, 1977.

VIVIAN, S., *A Handbook on In-Service Training in Developing Countries of the Commonwealth*, Commonwealth Secretariat, London, 1977.

PART 2: RELEVANT WORKS ON PRIMARY EDUCATION AND CURRICULUM DEVELOPMENT FOR PRIMARY SCHOOLS IN ENGLISH SPEAKING AFRICA

AFRICAN CURRICULUM ORGANIZATION, Report of the planning meeting held from 11–17 January 1976 at the Conference Centre, University of Ibadan, Nigeria, 1976.

AFRICAN CURRICULUM ORGANIZATION, Report of the training course on the techniques of data collection and analysis in educational research, First Representative Council Meeting, ICEE and DSE, Ibadan, 6–18 September 1976.

AFRICAN EDUCATION COMMISSION, *Education in Africa: a study of West, South and Equatorial Africa*, New York: Phelps-Stokes Fund, abridged, with an introduction by L. J. Lewis (from the reports of the African Education Commission and the second African Education Commission), Oxford University Press, 1962.

AFRICAN REGIONAL SEMINAR FOR ADVANCED TRAINING IN SYSTEMATIC CURRICULUM DEVELOPMENT AND EVALUATION, Achimota, Ghana, 1975, *Report*, IIEP, Paris, 1975.

AFRICAN REGIONAL SEMINAR ON EDUCATIONAL EVALUATION, Dar es Salaam, 1975, *Report*, IIEP, Paris, 1975.

BAMGBOSE, AYO (ed.), *Mother Tongue Education: the West African Experience*, Hodder & Stoughton, London, 1976.

BAUR, MICHAEL, *Curriculumzentren in Afrika*, DSE, Bonn, June 1977.

BIGALA, J. C. B., 'Need for curriculum innovation', *Education in Eastern Africa*, v, 1, 1975, Nairobi, pp 71–77.

CASTLE, E. B., *Growing up in East Africa*, Oxford University Press, 1966.

DYSAI, HUBERT M., 'Integrated Science Education in African Primary Schools', *Prospects*, iv, 1, UNESCO, Paris, 1974, pp 63–71.

EDEM, D. A., 'Education for employment: the role of the primary schools', *West African Journal of Education* 17, Ibadan, February 1973, pp 143–150.

ELSTGEEST, J., 'Integrated science education', *Education in Botswana, Lesotho and Swaziland* 10, Roma, June 1965, pp 27–36.

FAFUNWA, A. B., 'Some guiding principles of education in Africa', *West African Journal of Education* 15, Ibadan, February 1971, pp 5–7.

FAKUADE, R. A., 'The case for modern mathematics', *West African Journal of Education* 17, Ibadan, June 1973, pp 285–289.

GAY, JOHN and COLE, MICHAEL, *The New Mathematics and an Old Culture: a study of learning among the Kpelle of Liberia*, Holt, Reinhart and Winston, New York, 1967.

GODFREDSON, E., 'An Institute of Education and the improvement of primary education', Report of the AAA Conference, April 1968, *Teacher Education in New Countries* 9, London, February 1969, pp 203–225.

GRIFFITHS, V. L., *Teacher Centred: quality in Sudan primary education 1930 to 1970*, Longman, London, 1975.

GRAY COWAN, L., O'CONNELL, JAMES and SCANLON, DAVID G., *Education and Nation-Building in Africa*, Praeger, New York, Washington, London, 1965.

HAWES, H. W. R., 'Primary school curriculum development in Africa: hopes and facts', *Journal of Curriculum Studies* 2, Glasgow, November 1970, pp 108–117.

HISKETT, M., 'Traditional Islamic and modern western education in tropical Africa: the problems of integration', *World Development* 2, Oxford, February 1974, pp 41–43.

INTERNATIONAL INSTITUTE FOR EDUCATIONAL PLANNING, Report of the preparatory seminar on case studies for the determination of learning needs for rural areas, Nairobi, 29 November to 3 December 1976, organized by the IIEP in co-operation with the German Foundation for International Development, IIEP, Paris, 1977.

MANONE, CARL J. (ed.), *University of East Africa Conference on Teacher Education*, Makerere University College, Kampala, 1967.

MENKA, A. F., 'Curriculum Development Trends in African Countries', *Prospects*, vi, 3, UNESCO, Paris, 1976, pp 451–458.

MOUMOUNI, ABDOU, 'Elements for a dossier: education in the least developed countries (3) – the return to native languages and cultures', *Prospects*, v, 1., UNESCO, Paris, 1975, pp 63–70.

NUFFIELD FOUNDATION REPORT, *African Education: a study of educational policy and practice in British Tropical Africa*, (produced on behalf of the Nuffield Foundation and the Colonial Office), Crown Agent for the Colonies, London, 1953.

OKUNROTIFA, P. O., 'Curriculum improvement through action research', *Teacher Education in New Countries* 12, London, November 1971, pp 153–163.

PONSIOEN, J. A. (ed.), *Educational Innovations in Africa: Policies and Administration*, (based on a symposium held in Addis Ababa, September 1971, sponsored by ISS, CESO and the UN Economic Commission for Africa), Institute of Social Studies, The Hague, 1972.

POSTLETHWAITE, T. N. and KING, K., 'Curriculum Development for Basic Education in Rural Areas', *IIEP Seminar Paper* 18, UNESCO/IIEP, Paris, 1975.

PRABASI, S. C., 'Aspects of innovation in education: a preliminary analysis of African case studies'. In PONSIOEN, J. A., *Educational innovations in Africa – policies and administration*, Institute of Social Studies, The Hague, 1972, pp 73–82.

SUPPLITT, G. and BUDE, U. (eds), *Work Orientated Education in Africa: report of a conference 15–21 October 1972, Berlin*, German Foundation for International Development, Bonn, 1972.

TEACHER EDUCATION FOR BASIC EDUCATION, Report of a Conference-Workshop held in Tanzania, 24 November to 5 December 1975, Basic Education Resource Centre for Eastern Africa, Kenyatta University College, Nairobi, 1976.

UNESCO, Conference of African States on the Development of Education in Africa, Addis Ababa, 1961, UNESCO/UN Economic Commission for Africa, Paris, 1961.

OAU/UNESCO Conference of African Ministers of Education, 'Education and Scientific and Technical Training in Africa', Nairobi, July 1968, *UNESCO Chronicle*, xiv, 6, Paris, 1968, pp 225–232.

OAU/UNESCO, Conference of Ministers of Education of African Member States, *Innovations in African Education*, Lagos, 27 January to 4 February 1976, UNESCO, Paris, 1976.

UNESCO Conference of African Ministers of Education, Abidjan, 17–24 March 1964, *Final Report*, UNESCO, Paris, 1964.

UNESCO, Report of the UNESCO seminar on the reform of primary school curriculum in Africa, Dakar, Senegal, 25–30 November 1974, UNESCO Regional Office for Education in Africa, Dakar, 1974.

UNESCO, *Practical guide to in-service teacher training in Africa*, UNESCO, Paris, 1970.

UNESCO, *Interactions Between Linguistic and Mathematics Education*, Report of symposium sponsored by UNESCO, CEDO and ICMI, Nairobi, 1–11 September 1974, UNESCO, Paris, 1974.

UNESCO/UNICEF, 'Basic education in Eastern Africa', Report on a seminar, Nairobi, 19–23 August, 22–26 October 1974, UNESCO Africa Regional Office, Nairobi, 1974.
UNICEF, 'Seminar on the Development of Science and Mathematics Concepts in Young Children in African Countries', Seminar organised by UNESCO and UNICEF in association with the Science Programme for Africa, UNESCO, Nairobi, 1974.
WILLIAMS, G. A. A., 'The development of a modern mathematics curriculum in Africa', Arithmetic Teacher, 4, Washington, April 1976, pp 254–261.
YOUNG, B. L., 'Primary science in Africa', School Science Review 55, London, September 1973, pp 16–25.

PART 3: REFERENCES TO INDIVIDUAL COUNTRIES

Each set of references is listed to include (a) statements of policy which have influence on curriculum planning (including printed syllabuses) and (b) other works relevant to the quality of primary school education.

Botswana
Statements of policy
HUSEN, TORSTEN (Chairman), Kagisano ka Thuto: Education for Kagisano, Report of the National Commission on Education, Gaborone, April 1977.
MINISTRY OF EDUCATION, The aims and objectives of education in Botswana, Address by the Minister of Education to a conference of teachers' college tutors and education officers at the Teacher Training College, Lobatse, 1971, Government Printer, Gaborone, 1971.
MINISTRY OF EDUCATION, Education in Botswana: its aims and objectives, Review and forecast statement to Parliament by the Minister of Education, Government Printer, Gaborone, 1971.
MINISTRY OF EDUCATION, Interim report on the in-service project working in primary education, May 1973 to February 1975, Government Printer, Gaborone, 1975.
MINISTRY OF EDUCATION, Second interim report on the in-service project working in primary education, March 1975 to October 1975, Government Printer, Gaborone, 1975.
MINISTRY OF EDUCATION, Primary education, in-service training project – The role of the teacher, in the classroom, in the staff-room, in the community. Teachers and Administrators, Government Printer, Gaborone, 1975.
MINISTRY OF EDUCATION, Primary school syllabus, 1969, Government Printer, Gaborone, 1969.
MINISTRY OF FINANCE AND PLANNING, Third Five-Year Development Plan, 1970–75, Government Printer, Gaborone, 1970.
MINISTRY OF FINANCE AND DEVELOPMENT PLANNING, National Development Plan, 1973–1978, Government Printer, Gaborone, 1973.
Other references
HAWES, H. W. R., 'An African Primary Curriculum Survey: country profile, Botswana', Research report, University of London, Institute of Education (Department of Education in Developing Countries), 1976.
NICHOLS, D., 'Science in Primary Schools', Education in Botswana, Lesotho and Swaziland 9, Roma, January 1975, pp 36–39.
PRESTIDGE, J., 'Some aspects of mathematics in the primary school', Education in Botswana, Lesotho and Swaziland 9, Roma, January 1975, pp 40–43.
SWALLOW, A., 'The changing face of primary education,' Education in Botswana, Lesotho and Swaziland 9, Roma, January 1975, pp 24–28.
VAN RENSBURG, P., Education and development in an emerging country, Scandinavian Institute of African Studies, Uppsala, 1967.
WHITE, C. J. B., 'Training of unqualified teachers through correspondence education in

Botswana', in PONSIOEN, J. A. (ed.), *Education Innovation in Africa. Policies and administration*, Institute of Social Studies, The Hague, 1972, pp 184–191.

Cameroon
Statements of policy

CAMEROON, UNITED REPUBLIC OF, *Third Five Year Economic and Social Development Plan 1971–76*, Ministry of Planning and Territorial Development, Yaoundé, 1971.

CAMEROON, UNITED REPUBLIC OF, *Fourth Five Year Economic and Social Development Plan 1976–81*, Ministry of Planning and Territorial Development, Yaoundé, 1976.

IPAR-BUEA, Institute for the Reform of Primary Education, *Report on the Reform of Primary Education*, Buea, April 1977.

MINISTRY OF NATIONAL EDUCATION, 'The reform of primary education in Cameroon', Report of a seminar for administrative and political cadres held at Yaoundé, 26–29 March 1973, IPAR, Yaounde, 1973.

Other references

BARAH, J. K., 'Bridging the gap between school and community', *Prospects*, i, 2, UNESCO, Paris, 1970, pp 19–24.

BERGMAN, H. and BUDE, U., 'A survey of primary schools and their communities for general education policy-making: The case of two provinces in Cameroon', *International Review of Education*, xxiii, 1, Hamburg, 1977, pp 3–34.

BUDE, U., 'Work and environment oriented curricula within the framework of African primary school reform', IPAR *Working Paper* 3, Buea, August 1973.

MINISTRY OF NATIONAL EDUCATION, Country report of the United Republic to the UNESCO seminar on the reform of the primary school curriculum in Africa, Dakar, Senegal, 25–30 November 1974, UNESCO Regional Office for Education in Africa, Dakar, 1974.

CONSTABLE, D., 'Bilingualism in the United Republic of Cameroon: proficiency and distribution', *Comparative Education*, x, 3, Oxford, October 1974, pp 233–246.

GREENOUGH, RICHARD, 'Rural Schools and Economic Development in Cameroon', *UNESCO Chronicle*, Paris, April 1968, pp 149–151.

LALLEZ, R., 'An experiment in the ruralization of education: IPAR and the Cameroon Reform', UNESCO/IBE, Paris, 1974.

ROBINSON, L., *Innovation in Primary Education: Some Proposals based on experience in West Cameroon 1968–72*, IPAR, Buea, 1972.

Ghana
Statements of policy

MINISTRY OF EDUCATION, *The new structure and content of education for Ghana*, Ministry of Education, Accra, 1974.

MINISTRY OF EDUCATION, 'Development of education in Ghana, 1973–1975', Report to the 35th session of the international conference on education, IBE, Geneva, September 1975.

Other references

BOADI, L., 'Mother Tongue Education in Ghana', In BAMGBOSE A. (ed.), *Mother Tongue Education in Africa*, Hodder and Stoughton, London, 1976, pp 83–112.

BASSA-QUANSAH, 'The double shift system in Ghanaian primary schools', *Teacher Education in New Countries*, xi, 2, London, November 1970, pp 134–142.

BORTEI DOKU, S. O., 'Innovations in elementary science teaching and teacher training in Ghana', In PONSIOEN, J. A. (ed.), *Educational innovations in Africa: policies and administration*, Institute of Social Studies, The Hague, 1972, pp 226–231.

DZOBO, N. K., 'The modern education system of Ghana: its role in national development', *Ghana Journal of Education*, ii, 1, Accra, January 1971, pp 10–20.

DZOBO, N. K., *Innovations in teacher education and the problem of the unemployed school leavers in Ghana*, Faculty of Education, University of Cape Coast, 1972.

FOSTER, P., *Education and social change in Ghana*, Routledge and Kegan Paul, London, 1966.

MINISTRY OF EDUCATION, 'The new primary education in Ghana', *The New Era* 56, Cambridge, March 1975, pp 51–52.

MINISTRY OF EDUCATION AND THE GHANA NATIONAL FAMILY PLANNING PROGRAMME, Report on population and family life education survey in schools and colleges, Ghana Teaching Service, Curriculum and Development Division, Accra, 1975.

HAWES, H. W. R. and AARONS, A., 'An African Primary Curriculum Survey: country profile: Ghana', Research report, University of London Institute of Education (Department of Education in Developing Countries), 1976.

HAWKES, NICOLAS, 'The Medium of Instruction in Primary Schools in Ghana', *West African Journal of Modern Languages* 1, 1975, pp 56–65.

WILLIAMS, P., 'Ghana's teaching service', *West Africa*, 2985, 2 September 1974.

Kenya
Statements of policy

GOVERNMENT OF KENYA, *Education Commission Report*, (The Ominde Commission), The English Press, Nairobi, 1964.

GOVERNMENT OF KENYA, *African Socialism and its Application to Planning in Kenya*, Government Printer, Nairobi, 1965.

GOVERNMENT OF KENYA, Kenya Curriculum Mission, *A study of curriculum development in Kenya*, (the Bessy Report), Government Printer, Nairobi, 1972.

GOVERNMENT OF KENYA, *Report of the National Commission on Educational Objectives and Priorities*, (The Gachathi Committee), Government Printer, Nairobi, 1977.

KENYA INSTITUTE OF EDUCATION, *Annual Reports 1969–77*, Nairobi.

MINISTRY OF EDUCATION, *Primary School Syllabuses*, Nairobi, 1967.

MINISTRY OF EDUCATION, *Kenya Syllabus of Primary Schools*, Issued in separate booklets 1973–77. Includes Geography ('73), History ('73), Home Science ('75), Kiswahili ('75), Methodology ('75), Mother Tongue ('75), Music ('75), Mathematics ('76), Science ('76), English ('76). Jomo Kenyatta Foundation, Nairobi.

Other references

BENNETT, N., 'Primary education in rural communities: an investment in ignorance?' *Journal of Development Studies* 6, London, July 1970, pp 92–103.

BROWNSTEIN, L., *Education and development in rural Kenya: a study of primary school graduates*, Praeger, New York, London, 1972.

CHEGE, F. and ERAGAS, Z., 'Primary school education in Kenya – an attempt at evaluation', *Journal of East Africa Research and Development*, iii, 2, Nairobi, 1973, pp 95–109.

COURT, DAVID and GHAI, DARAM (eds), *Education, Society and Development: New Perspectives from Kenya*, Oxford University Press, Nairobi, 1974.

GAKURU, O. N., *Pre-primary education and access to primary school*, Institute of Development Studies, Nairobi, 1977.

GORMAN, T. P., 'The development of language policy in Kenya with particular reference to the education system', in WHITELY, W. H. (ed.), *Language in Kenya*, Nairobi, 1974, pp 397–453.

HAKEMULDER, J. R., 'UNESCO–UNICEF Project on Primary Teacher Training in Kenya', in PONSIOEN, J. A. (ed.), *Educational Innovations in Africa: Policies and Administration*, Institute of Social Studies, The Hague, 1972, pp 152–173.

HAWES, H. W. R. and AARONS, A., 'An African Primary Curriculum Survey: country profile: Kenya', Research report, University of London, Institute of Education, Department of Education in Developing Countries, 1976.

HEMPHILL, R. J., 'Language use and language teaching in the primary schools of Kenya', in WHITELY, W. H. (ed.), *Language in Kenya*, Nairobi, pp 455–479.

HUTASOIT, M. and PRATOR, C., Study of the 'New Primary Approach' in the schools of Kenya: carried out February–March 1965 at request of the Ministry of Education, with support of the Ford Foundation, Ministry of Education, Nairobi, 1965 (mimeo).

JONES, T. P., 'Activity, creativity and the new primary approach', *Kenya Education Review* 1, Nairobi, 3 December 1974, pp 10–16.

KAY, S., 'Curriculum innovations and traditional culture: a case study of Kenya', *Comparative Education*, 11, Oxford, 3 October 1975, pp 183–191.

KING, K., 'Development and Education in the Narok District of Kenya', *African Affairs* 285, 1972, pp 389–407.

KING, KENNETH, 'Primary schools in Kenya: some critical constraints on their effectiveness', in COURT, DAVID and GHAI, DARAM (eds), *Education, Society and Development: New Perspectives from Kenya*, Oxford University Press, Nairobi, 1974, pp 123–148.

MOOCK, J. L., 'Pragmatism and the Primary School: the case of the non-rural village', in COURT, DAVID and GHAI, DARAM (eds), *Education, Society and Development: New Perspectives from Kenya*, Oxford University Press, Nairobi, 1974, pp 105–122.

OLUOCH, C. P., 'Kenya Primary Education Curriculum and Rural Development', in SUPPLITT, G. and BUDE, J. (eds), *Work Orientated Education in Africa*, German Foundation for International Development, Bonn, 1972, pp 127–142.

SAVAGE, M., 'Kenya's curriculum development centre', *Times Educational Supplement* 2746, London, 5 January 1968.

SHEFFIELD, J. R. (ed.), *Education, Employment and Rural Development*, (Kericho Conference), East African Publishing House, Nairobi, 1967.

SHEFFIELD, J. R., *Education in the Republic of Kenya: an historical study*, Teachers College Press, New York, 1973.

SIFUNA, D. N., *Revolution in primary education: the new approach in Kenya*, East Africa Literature Bureau, Nairobi, 1975.

SOMERSET, H. C. A., 'Who goes to Secondary School? Relevance, Reliability and Equity in Secondary School Selection', in COURT, DAVID and GHAI, DARAM (eds), *Education, Society and Development: New Perspectives from Kenya*, Oxford University Press, Nairobi, 1974, pp 149–186.

SOMERSET, H. C. A., *Aptitude Tasks, Socio-economic Status and Secondary School Selection: the possibilities and limits of change*, Institute of Development Studies, Nairobi, 1978.

STABLER, E., *Education since Uhuru: the schools of Kenya*, Wesleyan University Press, Middleton, 1969.

Lesotho

Statements of policy

GOVERNMENT OF LESOTHO, *First Five Year Development Plan 1970/71–1974/75*, Government Printer, Roma, 1971.

GOVERNMENT OF LESOTHO, *Second Five Year Development Plan 1975/76–1979–80*, Government Printer, Maseru, 1975.

HAWES, H. W. R., 'Primary School Curriculum Change in Lesotho: UNICEF's commitment in context', consultant's report, April 1977, Institute of Education, London, 1977.

MINISTRY OF EDUCATION, *Report of the Education Study Commission*, Maseru, 1976.

LESOTHO NATIONAL TEACHERS' TRAINING COLLEGE, *Director's Annual Reports*, Maseru, 1976, 1977.

UNESCO, UNESCO/Danish mission to Lesotho: a report, UNESCO, Paris, April 1971, (2 parts).

UNESCO, *Alternative strategies for education in Lesotho*, Report by UNESCO, ILO policy mission, UNESCO, Paris, September 1973.

MINISTRY OF EDUCATION, *Syllabus for primary schools*, Government printer, Roma, 1967.

Other references

CLINES, P., 'A child from Botswana, Lesotho or Swaziland: Bilingualism and 1990', *Education in Botswana, Lesotho and Swaziland* 3, Roma, November 1970, pp 24–35.

HAWES, H. W. R., 'An African Primary Curriculum Survey: country profile, Lesotho', Research report, University of London, Institute of Education (Department of Education in Developing Countries), 1976.

MAES, Y., 'Formal education and its relevance to self help community development', *Education in Botswana, Lesotho and Swaziland* 7, Roma, March 1974, pp 1–3.

MOHAPELOA, J. M., 'Education for frustration', *West African Journal of Education* 17, Ibadan, February 1973, pp 127–142.

THELEJANE, T. S., 'Primary education in a developing country', *Education in Botswana, Lesotho and Swaziland* 8, Roma, August 1974, pp 24–27.

VIVIAN, S., 'Education in the context of an action programme for rural development', *Education in Botswana, Lesotho and Swaziland* 4, Roma, April 1971, pp 3–8.

VIVIAN, S., 'Social studies in primary schools and training colleges', *Education in Botswana, Lesotho and Swaziland* 3, Roma, November 1970, pp 3–6.

WARD, M., 'Primary school enrolment in Lesotho', *Education in Botswana, Lesotho and Swaziland* 9, Roma, January 1975, pp 44–50.

WILLIAMS, J. C., *Lesotho: three manpower problems: education, health, population growth*, Africa Institute, Pretoria, 1971.

Nigeria
Statements of policy

ADARALEGBE, A. (ed.), *Philosophy for Nigerian Education: proceedings of the National Conference on Curriculum Development, Lagos, 1969*, Heinemann, London, 1972.

FEDERAL REPUBLIC OF NIGERIA, *Second National Development Plan 1970–74*, Federal Ministry of Information, Printing Division, Lagos, 1970.

FEDERAL REPUBLIC OF NIGERIA, *Third National Development Plan 1975–80*, Central Planning Office, Lagos, 1975.

FEDERAL REPUBLIC OF NIGERIA, *National Policy on Education 1977*, Federal Ministry of Education Printing Division, Lagos, 1977.

NIGERIA EDUCATION RESEARCH COUNCIL, 'Guidelines on Primary School Curriculum', *Report of the National Workshop on Primary Education*, 26 April to 8 May 1971, – NERC, Lagos, 1973.

NIGERIA – STATE GOVERNMENTS, State governments issue primary school syllabuses either as separate subject syllabuses, e.g. Benue-Plateau State (1975–76) or, more commonly, as one volume. Recent issues include Lagos State (1971), East Central State: now Iwo, Imo and Anambra (1975) and Western State: now Oyo, Ondo and Ogun (1976).

Other references

ADESINA, SEGUN, 'Conditions for Success in planning universal primary education in Nigeria', *West African Journal of Education*, xviii, 3, Ibadan, October 1974, pp 293–308.

AFOLAYAN, A., 'The Six-Year Primary Project in Nigeria', in BAMGBOSE, A. (ed.), *Mother Tongue Education: the West African Experience*, Hodder and Stoughton, London, 1976, pp 113–134.

BALOGUN, T. A., 'The national curriculum conference in Nigeria, 8–12 September 1969', *West African Journal of Education*, xiv, 1, Ibadan, February 1970, pp 5–8.

FAFUNWA, A. B., 'Education in the mother tongue: A Nigerian experiment', *West African Journal of Education*, xix, 2, Ibadan, June 1975, pp 213–228.

FAFUNWA, A. B., *History of Nigerian Education*, Allen and Unwin, London, 1974.

GARDNER, R. and ONYABE, V., *Challenges of Universal Primary Education for Nigeria*, Institute of Education, Ahmadu Bello University, Zaria, 1975.

HAWES, H. W. R. and AARONS, A., 'An African Primary Curriculum Survey: country profile: Nigeria', Research report, University of London Institute of Education (Department of Education in Developing Countries), 1976.

HAWES, H. W. R., 'The administrative implications of curriculum change: a case study from Nigeria', *West African Journal of Education*, xvi, 1, 16 February 1972, pp 69–76.

KOLAWOLE, D. O., 'Primary Education Improvement Project in Northern Nigeria' in UNESCO/UNICEF *Basic Services for Children*, UNESCO/IBE, Paris, 1978, pp. 36–48.

MAXWELL, W., 'Curriculum development in Nigeria', *Prospects*, i, 4, UNESCO, Paris, 1970, pp 35–39.

NORTHERN STATES OF NIGERIA, *Inspectors' Handbook: a Guide for Primary School Inspection*, Evans Bros (Nigeria) Ltd, on behalf of the Institute of Education, Ahmadu Bello University, 1973.

OGUNYEMI, E., 'Science curriculum design in a developing country', *West African Journal of Education*, xiii, 3, October 1969, pp 140–144.

OGUNYEMI, M., *Primary School Curriculum Reform in the Western State of Nigeria*, UNESCO, IIEP, Paris, 1974.

PRITCHARD, MERVYN W., 'Primary School Inspection in Nigeria', *International Institute of Educational Planning Research Report* 12, UNESCO/IIEP, Paris, 1976.

ROTIMI, B. O., 'School inspectors as innovators in curriculum renewal', *West African Journal of Education*, xvi, 3, Ibadan, October 1972, pp 375–381.

WILLIAMS, G. A., 'Dynamics of curriculum change in mathematics: Lagos State mathematics project', *West African Journal of Education*, xviii, 18, Ibadan, June 1974, pp 241–235.

FAHRMEIER, EDWARD D., 'The effect of school attendance on intellectual development in Northern Nigeria', *Child Development*, xlvi, 1, Chicago, March 1975, pp 281–285.

TAIWO, C. O., 'Nigeria: Language problems and solutions', *Prospects*, vi, 3, UNESCO, Paris, 1976, pp 406–416.

WILLIAMSON, K., 'The Rivers Readers Project in Nigeria', in BAMGBOSE, A. (ed.), *Mother Tongue Education in Africa*, Hodder and Stoughton, London, 1976, pp 135–153.

Sierra Leone

Statements of Policy

CURRICULUM REVISION UNIT, Institute of Education, *Report of the First National Curriculum Conference*, June 1976, Institute of Education, Freetown, 1976.

MINISTRY OF DEVELOPMENT AND ECONOMIC PLANNING, Central Planning Unit, *National Development Plan 1974–75 – 1978–79*, Government Printing Department, Freetown, August, 1974.

MINISTRY OF DEVELOPMENT AND ECONOMIC PLANNING, Central Planning Unit, *National Development Plan 1974–75 – 1978–79*, (condensed version), Freetown, December 1975.

MINISTRY OF EDUCATION AND INSTITUTE OF EDUCATION, *Report of the National Seminar on Teacher Education*, Institute of Education, Freetown, 1977.

MINISTRY OF EDUCATION, *Revised primary school syllabus*, Government Printer, Freetown, 1964.

UNIVERSITY OF SIERRA LEONE, '*All our future*', *Report of the Education Review 1973–74*, Government Printer, Freetown, 1976.

Other references

FYLE, C., 'The Use of Mother Tongue in Education in Sierra Leone', in BAMGBOSE A. (ed.), *Mother Tongue Education in Africa*, Hodder and Stoughton, London, 1976, pp 42–62.

GOMES, INNOCENT D., 'Primary Science in Sierra Leone', *Science and Children*, xi, 8, Washington D.C., May 1974, pp 17–18.

HAWES, H. W. R., 'An African Primary Curriculum Survey: country profile: Sierra Leone', Research report, University of London, Institute of Education, Department of Education in Developing Countries, 1976.

MINISTRY OF EDUCATION, *Handbook of suggestions for teachers in primary schools*, Government Printer, Freetown, 1965.

NGEGBA, F. B. S., 'The Bunumbu experience in Sierra Leone' in UNESCO/UNICEF, *Basic Services for Children*, UNESCO/IBE, Paris, 1978, pp. 16–36.

RAVEN, RONALD J., 'The Training of Science Teachers in Sierra Leone', *Science Education*, lix, 1, New York, 1975, pp 51–58.

Swaziland

Statements of policy

EDUCATION DEPARTMENT, *Syllabuses for African Primary Schools: Grade 1 to Standard VI inclusive*, Government Printers, Mbabane, January 1952.

GOVERNMENT OF SWAZILAND, *Second National Development Plan, 1973–77*, Swaziland Printing and Publishing Co., Mbabane, 1972.

MAKHOSINI, RT HON. PRINCE, *The Philosophy, Policies and Objectives of the Imbokodvo National Movement*, Swaziland Government Printer, Mbabane, 1972.

MINISTRY OF EDUCATION, *Report of the National Commission in Education*, Government Printer, Mbabane, 1975.

MINISTER OF EDUCATION, Speech to seminar on curriculum development for basic primary education, *Swaziland Teachers Journal*, Mbabane, November 1975.

MINISTRY OF EDUCATION, *The National Primary School Curriculum Plan*, Ministry of Education, Mbabane, 1974.

Other references

ARNOLD, L. M., 'An experiment in second language teaching in Swaziland', *Teacher Education in New Countries*, x, 2, London, November 1969, pp 156–164.

COOK, P., 'A summary national primary school curriculum plan', *Swaziland Teachers' Journal*, Mbabane, November 1975, pp 21–26.

GOODAY, D. M., 'The primary school leaver problem', *Education in Botswana, Lesotho and Swaziland*, iv, Roma, April 1972, pp 27–36.

GOODAY, D. M., 'The schools' agriculture pilot project in Swaziland', *Educational Development International*, ii, 2, Stevenage, (for the British Council), April 1974, pp 94–98.

GREEN, C., 'The In-Service Primary Teacher Training Project in Swaziland', *Innovation*, 10, newsletter of the International Educational Reporting Service, UNESCO/IBE, Geneva, December 1976, pp 4–6.

GREEN, C., 'In-service training', *Swaziland Teachers' Journal*, Mbabane, November 1975.

HAWES, H. W. R. and AARONS, A., 'An African Primary Curriculum Survey: country profile: Swaziland', Research report, University of London, Institute of Education, Department of Education in Developing Countries, 1976.

ROE, P. J., 'English Through Activity: the Swaziland English Scheme', *Education Development International* 1, Stevenage, for the British Council, October 1973, pp 139–142.

ROE, B. (ed.), *Education in Southern Africa*, Collier-McMillan, London, 1970.

Tanzania

Statements of policy

MINISTRY OF NATIONAL EDUCATION, *Community School Syllabus*, Dar es Salaam, 1977.

MINISTRY OF NATIONAL EDUCATION, *Syllabuses for Primary Schools* (subject syllabuses – issued separately), Dar es Salaam, 1969.

NYERERE, J. K., *Education for Self-Reliance*, Government Printer, Dar es Salaam, 1967.

NYERERE, J. K., *Freedom and development: a selection from writings and speeches, 1968–73*, Oxford University Press, Dar es Salaam, 1973.

NYERERE, J. K., 'Education for liberation in Africa', *Prospects*, v, 1, UNESCO, Paris, 1975, pp 3–11.

NYERERE, J. K., *The Arusha Declaration – Ten Years After*, Government Printer, Dar es Salaam, 1977.

TANU, *Musoma Declaration*, Proceedings of the National Executive Committee Meeting held at Musoma in November 1974: Directive on the Implementation of 'Education for Self-Reliance'. Party H.Q., P.O. Box 9151, Dar es Salaam, 1974.

Other references

AUGUR, G. A., *Tanzanian education since Uruhu*, a bibliography 1961–71 incorporating a study of Tanzania today and yesterday and a guide to further sources of information on education in Tanzania, Institute of Education, Dar es Salaam, 1971.

CAMERON, J. and DODD, W., *Society, Schools and Progress in Tanzania*, Pergamon Press, London, 1970.

COURT, DAVID, 'The social function of formal schooling: the views of Foster and the experience of Tanzania', Institute of Development Studies, *Discussion Paper 128*, University of Nairobi, January 1973.

CENTRE FOR THE STUDY OF EDUCATION IN CHANGING SOCIETIES, *Primary education in Sukumaland (Tanzania)*, summary report of a study, Wolters-Noordhoffff, Groningen, 1969.

DODD, WILLIAM A., 'Education for Self-Reliance' in Tanzania: a study of its vocational aspects, Teachers' College Press, New York, 1969.

DUBBELDAM, L. F. B., The Primary School and the Community in Mwanza District, Tanzania, Centre for study of education in changing societies, Wolters-Noordhoff, Groningen, 1970.

ELSTGEEST, J., 'Reform: ritual and reality', Education in Botswana, Lesotho and Swaziland 8, Roma, August 1974, pp 1–11.

GASESE, E. S., 'Struggle over the school in a Tanzanian village', Papers in Education and Development 2, Department of Education, University of Dar es Salaam, May 1976, pp 77–97.

HINZEN, H. and HUNSDÖRFER, V. H. (ed.), Education for Liberation and Development – The Tanzanian Experience, Evans, London, 1979.

KINUNDA, MICHAEL J., 'The Place of Evaluation in the Tanzanian System of Education', International Institute of Educational Planning, Seminar 4, 1975, UNESCO/IIEP, Paris, 1975.

MHINA, J. E. F., 'The Kibaha education centre in Tanzania', PONSIOEN, J. A., Educational Innovation in Africa: policies and administration, Institute of Social Studies, The Hague, 1972, pp 98–106.

MWOBAHE, B. L. and MBILINYI, M. S., Challenge of Education for Self Reliance, Report of a workshop, Institute of Education, University of Dar es Salaam, 1975.

MUGANYIZI, L., 'Implementation and usefulness of self reliance in schools', Findings of research carried out in Bukoba District 1975. Papers in Education and Development 2, Department of Education, University of Dar es Salaam, May 1976, pp 97–121.

NDUNGURU, S., 'Education for self-reliance and the curriculum', East Africa Journal, Nairobi, February 1971, pp 31–36.

OMARI, ISSA M., 'Development order of spatial concepts among school children in Tanzania', Journal of Cross-Cultural Psychology, vi, 4, Bellingham, Washington, December 1975, pp 444–456.

OPEN UNIVERSITY (U.K.), 'Curriculum Materials and Teacher Education (Tanzania)', special unit produced for course Curriculum Design and Development. Includes also copies of the Arusha Declaration and 'Education for Self Reliance'. The Open University, Milton Keynes, 1976.

RESNICK, I. N. (ed.), Tanzania: revolution by education, Longman, Dar es Salaam, London, 1968.

SHENGENA, J. J., 'The teaching of political education in Tanzanian schools', Taamuli, iii, 2, Dar es Salaam, July 1973, pp 27–35.

TANZANIA/UNESCO/UNICEF, Primary education reform project: evaluation report 1, Institute of Education, University of Dar es Salaam, December 1973.

TOSH, A., Primary education reform project report, 1 November 1970 to 31 December 1972, UNESCO, Paris, 1972.

TOSH, A., Education and the development of rural areas: a case study, UNESCO/UNICEF joint programme of education assistance, Paris, December 1974.

VARKESSIER, C. M., Socialisation in a changing society: Sukuma childhood in rural and urban Mwanza, Tanzania, Centre for Study of Education in Changing Societies, The Hague, 1973.

WOBER, M., 'Is Illich for Africa?: relevance of formal education in Tanzania', Transition, ix, 44, Accra, 1974, pp 37–44.

WHITE, H. J., The development of primary education, Tanzania, 1961–71, University of Dar es Salaam, Department of Education, 1971.

Uganda

Statements of policy

NATIONAL CURRICULUM DEVELOPMENT CENTRE, Inaugural national Curriculum Conference Report 1973, Sapoba Press, Kampala, 1974.

UGANDA GOVERNMENT, 'Education in Uganda', Report of the Uganda Education Commission 1963, Government Printer, Entebbe, 1973.
UGANDA GOVERNMENT, Ministry of Economic Development and Planning, *Work for Progress: Uganda's Second Five-Year Plan 1966–71*, Government Printer, Entebbe, 1967.
UGANDA GOVERNMENT, Ministry of Economic Development and Planning, *Third Five-Year Development Plan 1971–76*, Government Printer, Entebbe, 1971.
MINISTRY OF EDUCATION, *Primary School Syllabus*, Uganda Bookshop Press, Kampala, 1965.
Other references
GOULD, W. T. S., *Planning the location of schools: Ankole District, Uganda*, UNESCO/IIEP, Paris, 1973.
HAWES, H. W. R., 'The primary school curriculum in Uganda', *Uganda Journal*, xxxiv, 2, Kampala, 1970, pp 179–193.
HARTWELL, A. S., Primary schooling and employment: the case of Uganda, *West African Journal of Education*, xvii, 1, Ibadan, February 1973, pp 99–104.
HEYNEMAN, S. P., 'Influences on academic achievement: A comparison of results from Uganda and more industrialised societies', *Sociology of Education*, xlix, 3, Washington DC, 1976, pp 200–211.
KIYIMBA, D. S., 'Education for Rural Development: The Namutamba Pilot Project', National Curriculum Development Centre's *Inaugural National Curriculum Conference Report 1973*, Sapoba Press, Kampala, 1974, pp 26–32.
OCITTI, J. P., *African indigenous education as practiced by the Acholi of Uganda*, East African Literature Bureau, Nairobi, 1973.
OTAALA, B., *The development of operational thinking in primary school children*, an examination of some aspects of Piaget's theory among the Iteso children of Uganda, Teachers' College Press, New York, 1973.
PRATT, C., 'The development of local audio-visual production centres', *Educational Development International*, Stevenage, (for the British Council), May 1973, pp 32–38.
UNDP/UNESCO, *Experimental pilot project on the role of education in rural environment*, Uganda, 1970–73, *The Namutamba Project*, a report, UNESCO, Paris, 1973.
VIVIAN, S., 'In-service education for primary teachers in Uganda', *Teacher Education in New Countries*, ix, 1, London, May 1968, pp 40–49.

Zambia

Statements of policy
GOVERNMENT OF ZAMBIA, *Second National Development Plan 1972–76*, Ministry of Development Planning and Guidance, Lusaka, 1971.
KAUNDA, K., *Humanism, A Guide to the Nation*, Government Printer, Lusaka, 1967.
KAUNDA, K., *Zambia's Economic Revolution: The Mulungushi Declaration*, Government Printer, Lusaka, 1968.
MINISTRY OF EDUCATION, *Approved Syllabus for Primary Schools*, Government Printer, Lusaka, 1971.
MINISTRY OF EDUCATION, *Curriculum Development in Zambia*, Government Printer, Lusaka, 1974.
MINISTRY OF EDUCATION, *Draft statement on Educational Reform*, Government Printer, Lusaka, 1976.
MINISTRY OF EDUCATION, *Education Reform Proposals and Recommendations*, Government Printer, Lusaka, 1977.
Other references
KAUNDA, K., *A Humanist in Africa*, Letters to Colin M. Morris, Longman, London, 1966.
LEACOCK, ELEANOR BURKE, *Primary Schooling in Zambia*, National Center for Educational Research and Development, Washington, March 1972.
MCADAM, B., 'English medium in the Zambian primary system', *Teacher Education in New Countries* 11, London, February 1971, pp 221–228.

MCADAM, B., 'The development of the Zambia primary course', *Education Development International* 1, Stevenage, (for the British Council), July 1973, pp 58–60.

PARKER, F., 'Zambia, Education and National Development', in THOMAS, R. MURRAY, SANDS, LESTER B. and BRUBACKER, DALE (eds), *Strategies for Curriculum Change; cases from thirteen nations*, International Textbook Co., Scranton, Penn., 1968, pp 228–250.

PRITCHARD, MERVYN W., 'Primary School Inspection in Zambia', International Institute of Educational Planning, *Research Report* 16, UNESCO/IIEP, Paris, 1976.

PART 4: SELECT LIST OF REFERENCES RELEVANT TO AFRICAN EDUCATION PROGRAMME

ADDY, L., 'The Entebbe maths', *Ghana Teachers Journal*, lii, 4, Accra, October 1966, pp 1–12.

AFRICAN MATHEMATICS PROGRAMME, Final report to USAID on the African Mathematics Programme of 16 June to 31 May 1975, by Education Development Center, Newton, Mass, 1975.

AFRICAN PRIMARY SCIENCE PROGRAMME, *Source Book for Evaluation*, Nigeria, University of Ibadan, March 1970.

AFRICAN SOCIAL STUDIES PROGRAMME, Reports of Executive Secretary, African Social Studies Programme, ASSP Secretariat, Nairobi. 1st report 1969, 2nd report 1970, 3rd report 1970–72, 4th report October 1972–October 1974.

AFRICAN SOCIAL STUDIES PROGRAMME, Report on the social studies workshops held in August 1970 at Addis Ababa, Nairobi and Gaborone, ASSP Secretariat, Nairobi, 1970.

AFRICAN SOCIAL STUDIES PROGRAMME, Report of the social studies seminar held in Nairobi, Kenya, 27–29 January 1971, ASSP Secretariat, Nairobi, 1971.

AFRICAN SOCIAL STUDIES PROGRAMME, Report of the social studies workshop held at the National Institute of Education, Makerere University, Kampala, 17–25 April 1972, under joint sponsorship of ASSP and the NIE, ASSP Secretariat, Nairobi, 1972.

AFRICAN SOCIAL STUDIES PROGRAMME, Report of writing workshop held at the Education Centre of the University of Nairobi, 3–31 August 1972, ASSP Secretariat, Nairobi, 1972.

AFRICAN SOCIAL STUDIES PROGRAMME, Report of a conference of ASSP held at Nairobi, 12–18 January 1975, ASSP Secretariat, Nairobi, 1975.

AFRICAN SOCIAL STUDIES PROGRAMME, Report of the ASSP writing workshop, Nairobi, August 1975, ASSP Secretariat, Nairobi, 1975.

ALDRICH, J. L., 'Thoughts on a cross-national programme: African education programme', *Educational Leadership* 27, Washington, November 1969, pp 131–136.

BULLEY, H. C. A., *Evaluation of a Social Studies Programme*, ASSP Secretariat, Nairobi, 1971.

CARLISLE, R., *In-service training of teachers*, a working paper, APSP monograph series, EDC, Newton, Mass, December 1971.

CARLISLE, R., *Making a start for teachers*, APSP monograph series, EDC, Newton, Mass, October 1970.

COPE, G., 'African elementary science conference at Kano', *ESI Quarterly Report*, Watertown, Mass, summer/fall, 1965, pp 113–116.

DONDO, J. M. C., KRYSTALL, A. and THOMAS, D., Report of an evaluation of the African Social Studies Programme to the Ford Foundation, The Ford Foundation, May 1974 (mimeo).

DUCKWORTH, E., *A comparison study for evaluating primary school science in Africa*, APSP/ EDC, Newton, Mass, October 1971.

DUCKWORTH, E., *Evaluation of the African Primary Science Programme*, APSP monograph series, EDC, Newton, Mass, 1970.

DYASI, HUBERT M., 'The teaching-learning strategy of the Primary Science Project for Africa', International Institute for Educational Planning, *Seminar Paper 30*, UNESCO/ IIEP, Paris, 1975.

DYASI, H. M., 'The Science Education Programme in Africa', in PONSIOEN, J. A. (ed.), *Educational innovations in Africa: policies and administration*, Institute of Social Studies, The Hague, 1972.

EDUCATION DEVELOPMENT CENTER, Final report to the Ford Foundation on grant 66–432 for the establishment of an African Institute for Educational Research and Development/ African Social Studies Programme, EDC, Newton, Mass, 30 June 1972.

EDUCATION DEVELOPMENT CENTER, Final report to USAID on African Mathematics Programme contract no. USAID afr–711, 26 June 1970 – 31 May 1975. EDC, Newton, Mass, June 1975.

EDUCATION DEVELOPMENT CENTER, Report of an African Education Programme, EDC, Newton, Mass, 1967.

EDUCATION DEVELOPMENT CENTER AND CENTRE FOR CURRICULUM RENEWAL AND EDUCATIONAL DEVELOPMENT OVERSEAS, Report of a conference of African educators, EDC and CREDO at Queen's College, Oxford, 10–16 September 1967. Part I: The conference and its findings, Part II: The background papers, CREDO, London, 1967.

EDUCATION DEVELOPMENT CENTER AND CENTRE FOR CURRICULUM RENEWAL AND EDUCATIONAL DEVELOPMENT OVERSEAS, Report of a conference of African educators, EDC and CREDO on social studies, held at Mombasa, Kenya, 19–30 August 1968. EDC, Newton, Mass, and CREDO, London, 1968.

EDUCATION DEVELOPMENT CENTER, Final report to USAID on contract for research and development in beginning science curriculum for English speaking Tropical Africa (APSP), EDC, Newton, Mass, 1972.

EDUCATION DEVELOPMENT CENTER, Programme statement African Primary Science Programme and Science Education Programme for Africa, EDC, Newton, Mass, 1973.

EDUCATIONAL SERVICES INCORPORATED, Report of an African Education Programme: a preliminary programme review, ESI, Watertown, Mass, February 1965.

EDUCATIONAL SERVICES INCORPORATED, Report of an American summer study, Endicott House, 19 June – 29 July 1961, ESI, Watertown, Mass, September 1961.

GREENAUGH, R., 'African curriculum development centre for primary science: Domasi Science Centre', Times Educational Supplement 147, London, 2759, 5 April 1968.

HAAG, V. H., 'An African mathematics programme', Ghana Teachers Journal 53, Accra, January 1967, pp 55–60.

IGBOKO, P. M., 'Improving school mathematics', West African Journal of Education, xi, 2, Ibadan, June 1967, pp 85–88.

MARTIN, W. T. and ALDRICH, J. L., 'The African Education Programme', ESI Quarterly Report, Watertown, Mass, summer-fall 1965, pp 107–112.

MARTIN, W. T. and PINCK, D. C., Curriculum improvement and innovation: a partnership of students, school teachers and research scholars, Robert Bentley Inc., Cambridge, Mass, 1966.

OGUNYEMI, E. L., 'Science curriculum design in a developing country', West African Journal of Education, xiii, 3, Ibadan, October 1969, pp 140–144.

OHUCHE, O., 'SEPA science and learning theory', Science Teachers Education monograph series 1, SEPA, Accra, December 1974.

OSIYALE, AKINDELE O., 'Primary School Science in Africa', ESI Quarterly Report, Watertown, Mass, spring/summer 1966, pp 74–76.

OWIREDU, D. U., 'The African Social Studies Programme', in PONSIOEN, J. A. (ed.), Educational Innovations in Africa: policies and administration, Institute of Social Studies, The Hague, 1972.

OYELESE, J. O., 'The second Entebbe mathematics workshop, summer 1963', ESI Quarterly Report, Watertown, Mass, winter/spring 1964, pp 93–101.

ROBINS, R., Programming for change in science education, APSP monograph series, EDC, Newton, Mass, 1970.

SCIENCE EDUCATION PROGRAMME FOR AFRICA, Report of the SEPA teacher training materials workshop, 9 August to 3 September 1971, Nairobi, Kenya, SEPA Secretariat, Accra, 1971.

SCIENCE EDUCATION PROGRAMME FOR AFRICA, Report of the six months course, April–October 1972, SEPA Secretariat, Accra, 1972.

SCIENCE EDUCATION PROGRAMME FOR AFRICA, Report on a workshop for science lecturers of teacher training colleges at the Science Curriculum Development Centre, Njala University College, Sierra Leone, 14 August–10 September 1972, SEPA Secretariat, Accra, 1972.

SCIENCE EDUCATION PROGRAMME FOR AFRICA, *SEPA Handbook for Teachers*, SEPA Secretariat, Accra, September 1974.

UNIVERSITY OF SIERRA LEONE, Institute of Education, Report of the social studies workshop held at Freetown, Sierra Leone, 16 July to 3 August 1973, Social Studies Division, Curriculum Revision Unit, Freetown, 1973.

UKEJE, O., 'The Entebbe Mathematics', *West African Journal of Education*, ix, 1, Ibadan, February 1965, pp 15–18.

WILLIAMS, G. A., 'Dynamics of curriculum change in mathematics. Lagos State Mathematics Project', *West African Journal of Education*, xviii, 2, Ibadan, June 1974, pp 241–253.

WILLIAMS, G. A., 'The Entebbe Mathematics Project', *International Review of Education* 17, UNESCO Institute for Education, Hamburg, 1971, pp 210–214.

YOLOYE, E. A., 'Trends in elementary science curricula', *West African Journal of Education*, x, 1, Ibadan, February 1966, pp 18–21.

Index

The Index is in two parts:

Index A : country index
References to curriculum projects and related issues in English Speaking African countries

Index B : general index
Only references having bearing on the primary school curriculum are listed; for names of authors or titles of works quoted see Bibliography

Index A

Occupational education, 94
Peak Course, 55–6
Promotional recognition for local contributions of teachers
– in research, 32 (note)
– in raising local quality of education, 140
Religious Knowledge – new approaches to Christian teaching, 92
Research on home learning of children (King), 173–4
Research section established at K.I.E., 30
Research Seminar on Growth of Scientific and Mathematical Concepts in African Children (Nairobi), 30
School supplies companies, 155
Social Studies – conference at Mombasa (1968), 42
– headquarters of A.S.S.P. at Nairobi, 42
Syllabus – new Primary syllabuses published and available, 106
Teachers' Centres, 63–4, 128–30
– at Siriba and Machakos, 128, 130
Teacher in-service programmes involving distance teaching, 134

LESOTHO

Building and equipment in schools, 20
Consultants' report on Primary school curriculum change (Hawes 1977), 115–17, 196–8
Core curriculum and options, 106
Curriculum Research Unit, 30
Financial allocations for primary schools, 20
Integrated curriculum unit on transport, 89
Language medium, 77–9
Mathematics – re-emphasis on basic skills in numeracy, 91–2
National Debate and Seminar on Primary Education (1978), 115
Panel structure – new, 89
Research into reading abilities – Lesotho Distance Teaching Centre, 95, 106 (note)
Research unit – primary curriculum, 30
School garden as a basis in curriculum investigation, 90
Shortened sessions for lower classes, 75–6
Teacher Education – alternative patterns operated by National Teachers' College, 135, 137
Writers' workshops, 152, 154

LIBERIA

Mathematics – curriculum in relation to cultural environment, 69 (note)
– participation in regional mathematics programme, 38
Science – curriculum centre, 41

MALAWI

Examinations – development of techniques at Regional Testing Centre, 103
Party goals and the curriculum, 35
Presidential stand against 'modern methods', 53
Science Curriculum Centre, Domasi, 41

NIGERIA

Appropriate Technology Centre, Plateau State, 177 (note)
Basic cycle – lengthening period for general education, 75
Cultural and Creative Art Syllabus, 89

Curriculum units in Bendel and Oyo State Ministries, 47
English series – Kano State Joint English Project, 151, 160 (note)
Evaluation – International Centre and Evaluation of P.E.I.P. and Science Programme, 67
'Hidden Library Scheme', Benue State, 149
Infant Methods Diploma, Ahmadu Bello University, 127
Initial teaching alphabet, 32 (note)
Islamic Religious Knowledge – new approaches, 92
Institutes of Education, Ahmadu Bello, Nsukka, Ife, Lagos, Ibadan, 44–5
Institute of Education, Ahmadu Bello, Boards of Studies, 45
International Centre for Educational Evaluation, Ibadan, 30, 67
Language – medium, 77–80
– skills required by learners listed, 91
Library/bookshop scheme, Bendel State, 155
Mathematics – opposition to 'New Maths', 92
Mobile Teacher Trainers, 63, 127
National Curriculum Conference, 53–4
National Workshop on Primary Education, 52, 54
National Seminar on Policy of Education, 53
National Teachers Institute, Kaduna, 134
Nigerian Education Research Council, 47, 70 (note)
Primary Education Improvement Project (P.E.I.P.), 57, 63, 88, 127
School equipment – using local industries, 151
School supplies policies, 157
Science – Curriculum Centre, Nsukka, 41
– preliminary conference A.P.S.P. (Kano, 1965), 41
– project (UNESCO sponsored) Midwest/Bendel States, 54
– series, 'Primary Science', 94
– syllabus, criteria for selecting and evaluating content, 94
Science Teachers' Association of Nigeria, 129
Social Studies – new approaches, 88, 94
Teacher training – variations in policy, 16, 17
Universal Primary Education, 11
Universal Primary Education, Eastern Region (1957) and Western Region (1955), 69 (note)
Yoruba Medium Project, Ife, 61–3

SIERRA LEONE

Aims for Primary education, 73
Basic education – concept and proposals for shortened cycle, 75, 163
– reactions to proposals, 176
Community Teachers' College, Bunumbu, 134, 167–8
Double shifts in schools, 76
Education Review, 31–2, 32 (note), 53, 73
English texts and language skills in young children, 95
Institute of Education, 45, 47
– research section, 30
Raising entry age in schools, 75
School supplies policy, 155
Science – Curriculum Centre, Njala, 41–2
– Discovery Science Club, 129
– Primary Science Teachers Group (Freetown), 126, 129
– training for teacher educators, Njala, 42
Social Studies syllabus – innovations, 89, 94
Teachers' Colleges – preparation of community teachers, 134, 167–8
Teacher Education – National Seminar (1976), 132–4

Social Studies – African Social Studies Programme, 42
Teacher Education – Workshop on Teacher Education for Basic Education UNESCO/UNICEF 1975, 165

West African Examinations Council: Test, Development and Research Unit and Examination Reform, 103

Index B